The Mother of the Reformation

THE MOTHER OF THE REFORMATION

The Amazing Life and Story of Katharine Luther

by Ernst Kroker

Translated by Mark E. DeGarmeaux

Peer Reviewed

CONCORDIA PUBLISHING HOUSE • SAINT LOUIS

Published 2013 Concordia Publishing House
3558 S. Jefferson Ave., St. Louis, MO 63118-3968
1-800-325-3040 www.cph.org

Original edition *Katharina von Bora*, by Verlag Johannes Herrmann Zwickau 1906, translated with permission of the Concordia-Verlag Zwickaw 2011.l

English translation © 2013 Mark E. DeGarmeaux

Cover photo: Katharine Luther (nee von Bora), 1528 (oil on panel), Cranach, Lucas, the Elder (1472–1553) (attr. to) / Lutherhalle, Wittenberg, Germany / The Bridgeman Art Library XPH 308471

Back cover photo © GeorgiosArt/iStockphoto.com

Manufactured in the United States of America

Library of Congress Cataloging-in-Publication Data

Kroker, Ernst, 1859-1927.

[Katharina von Bora, Martin Luthers Frau. English]

The Mother of the Reformation : The Amazing Life and Story of Katharine Luther / by Ernst Kroker ; translated by Mark E. DeGarmeaux.

pages cm

ISBN 978-0-7586-3526-6

1. Luther, Katharina von Bora, 1499-1552. 2. Luther, Martin, 1483-1546--Family. 3. Reformation--Germany--Biography. I. DeGarmeaux, Mark E., translator. II. Kroker, Ernst, 1859-1927. Katharina von Bora, Martin Luthers Frau. Translation of: III. Title.

BR328.K713 2013

284.1092--dc23

[B]   2012037624

2   3   4   5   6   7   8   9   10   22   21   20   19   18   17   16   15

Table of Contents

TRANSLATOR'S DEDICATION AND PREFACE

For Rebecca

Luther had his "chain" (German: Kette, Katie).
I have my "noose" (Hebrew: rivqah, Rebecca).

When my wife Rebecca was in college, she was assigned to write a paper about Katie von Bora Luther. She found very few sources, and for various reasons the assignment was cancelled and the paper never written. In 1992 we were touring in Germany along with the choir of Bethany Lutheran College. On a free day we visited Altenburg, and in a used bookstore we found this treasured and hard-to-find book, Ernst Kroker's classic biography of Katie Luther. For birthday and Christmas presents for my wife, I would translate some pages each year. It has been an enjoyable experience, and very interesting to get this perspective on Katie Luther.

I can never list all the people who deserve thanks for this project. First, I will simply say thank you to my wife for her loving patience and support through our many years together so far. I sincerely thank our dear friends in the Evangelical Lutheran Free Church in Germany for granting permission to publish this translation. I must give particular thanks to Dr. James A. Booker and Dr. Jon S. Bruss for help with checking the translation. My fellow pastors in the Evangelical Lutheran Synod and my colleagues at Bethany Lutheran College have been wonderfully supportive of my efforts in various fields of study. And Professor Arnold Koelpin deserves thanks for assigning that college paper and awakening our interest in the fascinating figure whom Kroker calls Martin Luther's Frau.

INTRODUCTION

On the four hundredth anniversary of her birth [thus in 1899], Katharine von Bora, Luther's "Katie," found a noted biographer in Albrecht Thoma. With equal diligence and love, Thoma gathered together all the little passages that had come down to us about her life and her character and tried to compile them into a unified presentation. He called his work a historical biography.

With the nature of what has been passed down to us, it is not really possible to write a life history of Katie. We will have to content ourselves with a depiction of her life and character. The individual pieces do not make up a complete colorful painting, but, put together, they are like a mosaic. A mosaic cannot compete with an oil painting either in splendor of color or in the richness of details or the refinement of the transitions. Yet even with its limitations it has its own artistic rules, and these apply also to our picture of Katie's life. Here, too, the most important task is to insert the countless little pieces in the right place and to emphasize the outlines of the picture clearly, but certainly also to keep the whole thing tightly together.

The presentation that Thoma has given us—apart from individual mistakes—suffers from a certain unevenness of treatment. The author tries again and again to take up the biographic thread, which is thin from the very outset, and with Katie's marriage is cut off for a period of twenty years. Other people's engagements and weddings, visits and travels, diseases and deaths give no picture of her life. Through what has come down to us, we are led, rather, to a three-part arrangement of the rich material. The first parts, which discuss her youth, are essentially biographical; the next parts, which describe her as homemaker, wife, and mother, gives us the foundation of her character; and the last parts, which tell of the hard times of her widowhood, are again biographical. Finally, in a summary and closing section, the picture of her character is brought out as precisely and as true to life as possible.

I think I can be confident that my portrayal is based on the best witnesses. However, the scholarly proofs are lacking, which—I hope—most readers will not really miss; for the wider audience, an abundance of notes is useless. For the narrow circle of scholars, I have followed one of the important sources about Luther and Katie's life, so I don't particularly need to justify that here. For this I may refer to the introduction to my publication of Luther's *Table Talk* in the Mathesi collection. My essay "Katharine von Bora, Her Birthplace and Her Youth" in the *New Archive for Saxon History and Archaeology*, Volume 26 (Dresden 1905), pages 251–73, forms the scholarly basis for the first section of this book. Those are the introductory words, which I gave by way of the first edition of my book in the year 1906, also. Since then, with the celebration of the Reformation anniversary in 1917, several new biographies of Katie have appeared. How these books are related to my book, their authors probably know best. As the publishing house of Johannes Herrmann in Zwickau, Saxony, publishes a second edition of my book at the forthcoming commemoration of Luther and Katie's marriage, on June 13, 1925, it is with the desire of bringing the book to a wider audience. The text did not need to go through thorough changes; one will notice some additions and correction in details, however, in numerous places.

Leipzig, Easter 1925
Ernst Kroker

MAPS

North Sea

DENMARK

Baltic Sea

ENGLAND

HOLSTEIN

Hamburg

POMERANIA

HOLLAND

Amsterdam

ZEELAND

Wittenburg

BRANENBURG

Rhine

Leipzig

SILESIA

BRABANT

PALATINATE

SAXONY

GERMANY

HAINAUT

LUXEMBURG

Nuremberg

BOHEMIA

MORAVIA

Prague

POLAND

LORRAINE

FRANCE

BAVARIA

Danube

AUSTRIA

SWISS CONFEDERATION

TYROL

CARINTHIA

Vienna

STYRIA

SAVOY

Milan

Venice

CARNIOLA

HUNGARY

Genoa

Florence

PAPAL STATES

OTTOMON EMPIRE

Rome

© CPH

Mediterranean Sea

The Holy Roman Empire c.a. 1530

Germany

1.

LIPPENDORF, BREHNA, NIMBSCHEN

Katie's Birthplace

"Doctor Martin Luther gave a coin to his Katharina—born January 29, 1499." That's the inscription, in Latin, on a coin that Katie herself supposedly wore around her neck as a gift from her husband. If we can accept this account as reliable, then this first date of Katie's life, her birthdate, is also the last we hear about her youth for a long time. Just ten years later, in 1509, she began her stay in the Cistercian convent at Nimbschen, according to contemporaneous documents. And only two accounts from later times, a letter and a chronicle, tell us that before she entered Nimbschen she had already been at the Benedictine convent school at Brehna for a while, since 1504 or the beginning of 1505. Everything between her birth and her stay in Brehna is still unknown to us. And we are confronted with many questions we would like to have answered. What were her parents' names? No one has passed their names on to us. Where was she born? Seven or eight places contend for that honor. And why was she brought to the convent at such a tender age? Why didn't her parents have her grow up at home?

Research has been most eagerly concerned with the question of her birthplace, because if this were proven, then we might also expect to learn from those documents which branch of the noble von Bora family our Katie comes from and who her parents were. But no account from that period tells us her birthplace, and so almost every Saxon village and hamlet where some von Bora lived and worked sometime in the fifteenth or sixteenth century has some scholar who, with greater or lesser astuteness and with stronger or weaker reasons, tried to prove: "Katie was born here."

For a long time Steinlausig, a few hours north of Bitterfeld on the Mulde, was considered Katie's birthplace. As a matter of fact, in the fifteenth century a branch of von Boras lived in the vicinity of Bitterfeld in the province of Saxony. Even at Katie's time there was a Hans von Bora at Steinlausig. But this Hans von Bora from Steinlausig cannot have been Katie's father, because he died without leaving a son, while we know from Katie that she had several brothers. And much less could Katie, as a very young girl, have been in the cloister at Steinlausig for a while before she entered Nimbschen, because Steinlausig was a cloister for monks; perhaps this account is confused with Brehna, where she really stayed at the convent school. We can also rule out Dohna near Dresden and Simselwitz near Döbeln, Moderwitz near Neustadt on the Orla, and Motterwitz near Leisnig as Katie's birthplace. And if one reaches out to what was then Silesia, or even Hungary, while searching for her home, the leads have proved to be very unreliable there.

We do not need to follow every lead. Most of the paths one might take in searching for her birthplace are easily seen as wild goose chases. All the places that lie in Thuringia or in what was Electoral Saxony, like Steinlausig, or those that are in the former Silesia or in Hungary, are ruled out from the start. A lead that points us in the right direction, but doesn't take us all the way to the goal, is found in the university notice, in which Philipp Melanchthon and Paul Eber report Katie's death on December 21, 1552 to the community of Wittenberg University. She had fled to Torgau at that time because of the plague. They say she was "born of a noble family of knightly rank in Meissen." This does not mean the city, but the region, the March of Meissen.

The unholy Leipzig treaty, which had been settled on August 26, 1485, between Elector Ernst and Duke Albrecht of Saxony, had torn the rich inheritance of the Wettins into two pieces for all time. Klaus Narr compared the carved-up regions of that time to a torn garment that didn't fit either of the two princes. And the division resulted in distrust, and then open hostility, between the two lines of the princely house. At the beginning of the age of the Reformation, Fredrick the Wise ruled in Electoral Saxony, in loyal union with his brother Duke John the Steadfast. Duke George the Bearded ruled in Ducal Saxony. The Electorate covered Electoral Saxony and most of southern Thuringia with the cities of Gotha, Weimar, Eisenach, and Coburg. The March of Meissen, along with the cities of Freiberg, Dresden, and Leipzig, formed the core of the Ducal Saxony.

Electoral Saxony, the county of Thuringia, the March of Meissen—these were areas with definitive boundaries at that time. Every Saxon, every Thuringian, every Meissner, was clear about his territory, and if men such as Melanchthon and Eber, the most faithful friends of Luther and his house, tell us in a public document that Katie was born in Meissen, then we have to look for her birthplace, not in Electoral Saxony or in Thuringia, but in the March of Meissen. Here, however, von Boras are reported in two localities around the turn of the fifteenth century, and both villages now lay claim to being Katie's birthplace: Lippendorf, three miles south of Leipzig, and Hirschfeld, one hour east of Nossen.

Not far from Nossen and Hirschfeld are the old ancestral residences of the family to which Katherine von Bora belongs, the villages of Wendischbora and Deutschenbora. They get their name from the pine trees that were there in ancient times, of course in even larger and thicker woodlands than now, where the hills are covered by individual wooded areas only east of Nossen. At one time the Hermunduri[1] lived here, but not in villages, because the Germanic peoples did not like living close together. They lived as free men in the forest, and their farms were often quite far apart. Then, when the Germanic tribes poured into the richer west and south in the great migration, the Slavs from the east followed and settled the country from the Oder to the Saale. They customarily settled in villages and then along the fruitful valleys near the rivers and streams. For half a millennium they were the rulers of the

---

[1] A Germanic tribe.

country. Only in the ninth and tenth centuries were the Germans again strong enough for the difficult battle to reconquer the area east of the Saale that they had lost. At that time the Slavic villages were filled with German knights and farmers. And gradually even the rougher forestland, which the Slavs had avoided, was cleared by the Germans and converted into fertile farmland.

Wendischbora, as the name already indicates, is a Wendish or Slavic settlement. The Slavic *Bor* corresponds to the German *Föhre*; it means pine tree. *Bor* also occurs as a separate name. Already in the second half of the eleventh century a Slavic nobleman named Bora is mentioned; he was very wealthy in the March of Meissen. The knightly von Bora clan, however, probably did not descend from this old Slavic chieftain Bora.

The von Bora's, rather, were of German blood, like the Minckwitz's, Staupitz's, Haugwitz's, and Haubitz's, like the von Lochau and von Mochau and von Ponickau and all the others with names ending in –itz and –au, who, since the eleventh and twelfth centuries, fought against the Wends in the armies of the counts of the March of Meissen or the electors of Saxony. They were German knights: Franks, Swabians, Bavarians, Thuringians, and Lower Saxons. The counts had called them into the conquered Eastern March[2] and gave them land and people. In return the knights provided an army for the princes. Each knight was named after the village where his prince had given him a fiefdom, and since the Slavs founded most Saxon villages, most of the Saxon aristocratic families bear Slavic names.

The knights who inhabited Wendischbora or Deutschenbora since the twelfth century were also designated this way in deeds: von Bor, von Bora, or von Borau. On their coats of arms they had a red lion on a golden field, and on their helmet the tail of a peacock. They were closely connected to the rich Cistercian cloister Altzelle near Nosse. Their family estates were located there. Other branches of the family moved to Electoral Saxony into the area of Bitterfeld and into Osterland south of Leipzig, such as the wealthy Friedricus vom Bor between Pegau and Borna, already around 1350, in the

---

[2] Ostmark, the region in Saxony east of the Elbe.

eastern Thuringia into the vicinity of Weissenfels. When they lost the ancestral residences of Wendischbora and Deutschenbora, they still held on to the property near Hirschfeld for a while.

Around the year 1500, a Hans von Bora lived here. According to the timing he could be Katie's father. But the accounts we have about Katie and her brothers otherwise lead us, not to Hirschfeld, but to the area south of Leipzig, where likewise, at that time, a Hans von Bora resided in Lippendorf between Pegau and Borna, and where even today there are two memorials that commemorate Katie for us.

If we get off the train that takes us south along the Pleissenau, at the Kieritzsch train-station, halfway between Leipzig and Altenburg, and if we go from that station to the village of Kieritzsch, then we soon see a signpost on the left: "To the Luther monument." The dirt road that branches off the main road leads us west for twenty minutes to a granite obelisk that rises in the middle of an iron lattice. Under bronze medallions of Luther and his Katie, the base bears the inscription: "In memory of Dr. M. Luther and Kath. Luther 1883."

Since the tricentennial of the Reformation in 1817, a simple memorial stone has stood here, whose weathered ruins are now some distance from the monument. The monument, a work of the Stuttgart master Adolf Donndorf, was completed on August 10, 1884. It defines the place where the small property Zölsdorf once stood, which Luther bought from his brother-in-law Hans von Bora for 610 *Gulden* the week before Pentecost 1540. Luther himself called it an inheritance from the von Boras. He bequeathed it to Katie in his will in 1542. There is no longer one brick on top of another at the small property. Katie often liked to stay there, and she directed her heart's desire and gave attention to this place, which had also caused her and her husband much concern.

The monument stands alone in the middle of the fields, rarely visited by strangers. The path that leads to it from Kieritzsch is probably still the same one from Katie's time. But at least the most valuable remnant is preserved, the manorhouse, which was already dilapidated and sunk to ruin before the mid-eighteenth century. At one time colorfully painted and amazingly realistic reliefs of Luther

5

and his wife hung there. They can now be seen in the church of the nearby village Kieritzsch, though they are still too often overlooked. We have no better portrait of Katie. Of course, it shows her at an older age. It bears the date 1540, so it was made in the year in which Luther bought the property. And it doesn't flatter Katie, but even in its current state it faithfully portrays with a distinct liveliness the industrious and energetic "Lady of Zölsdorf," as Luther jokingly calls her in his letters.

From the Donndorf monument, where we are on sacred ground, if we look across the field far to the north, there behind the houses of the nearby village of Kieritzsch we see the two connected villages of Medewitzsch and Lippendorf: Medewitzsch with its manorial estate, Lippendorf with a stately court property or free property, on whose manorhouse an inscription now reads: "Birthplace of Katherine Luther, born von Bora, January 29, 1499–1899."

In fact, a Hans von Bora lived here on the property at Lippendorf at the time Katie was born. His ancestors had already been property owners for over one hundred years in the area between Pegau and Borna, and he was still living in Lippendorf when he was invested with the manor at Saale in 1482 near Schkortleben north of Weissenfels. Since the manorial estate at Saale was named after the noble Saale family, when Count Philipp the Magnanimous of Hesse married Lady Margarethe von der Saale on March 4, 1540, in fatal bigamy, he wrote a letter to Luther on April 5, 1540 and addressed him as his brother-in-law, because Luther's Lady Katie was related to his own Lady Margarethe von der Saale.

Hans von Bora of Lippendorf thus seems to have had a claim to the Saale manor through his relationship to the Saale family. Two documents and a *Kopialbuch* in the Saxon main public records at Dresden have retained for us the following data from his life: On December 11, 1482 at Wiessenfels, Elector Ernst and Duke Albrecht of Saxony invest this Hans von Bora of Lippendorf with the village, farmstead, and residence at the Saale under the care of Weissenfels. The Saxon councilman Caspar von Schönberg and Heinrich von Miltitz are listed as witnesses. In the second document, which was executed on the same day in Weissenfels, the same princes gave their consent that Hans von Bora of Lippendorf designated this fiefdom of his at Saale as a bequest to the honorable Katharine, his wedded wife. The two Saxon councilmen von Miltitz and von Schönberg are again named as guardians of the young woman, and Michel Krawinkel as a third besides them.

Such designations of bequests were made necessary by the Saxon law of succession, which was hard on widows. These designations were to assure the woman a certain income from parts of the hereditary property if her husband preceded her in death. Therefore they were customarily issued soon after the wedding. Thus we may conclude from this document that Hans von Bora of Lippendorf, who also owned the residence at the Saale, was married to Katharine shortly before December 11, 1482. The document does not indicate from which family his wife originated.

Twenty-three years later, on May 15, 1505, Hans von Bora of Lippendorf had a new designation of bequests, endorsed by Duke George the Bearded. So his first wife, Katharine, must have died. His second wife was called Margarete, and he designated as a bequest to her all his goods at Lippendorf. He probably reserved the manor von der Saale, which he does not mention in this document, as the inheritance for the children of his first marriage, who were still minors.

Katie's Parents: Hans and Katharine von Bora of Lippendorf

We may name this Hans or Jan von Bora of Lippendorf as Katie's father and his first wife, Katharine, as Katie's mother. The strongest proofs for this are: 1) the family connections that existed between Katie and Margarethe von der Saale according to what Philipp of Hesse had said, because according to the testimony of the documents, the residence at the Saale was invested, not to the Hans von Bora from Hirschfield, but the one from Lippendorf; furthermore, 2) that Katie was transferred to the convent at exactly the time when the Hans von Bora of Lippendorf lost his first wife Katharine and brought his second wife Margarete home to Brehna;

and finally, 3) the fact that, later on, Katie's brothers also lived in the very region where Lippendorf is located and were related to and married into other aristocratic families of the region of Leipzig.

Katie's Brothers and Sister

Katie had at least three brothers, perhaps a sister as well. Before we turn to her own life, we shall first take yet another look at the family circle from which she was taken when she entered the convent at such a young age.

The oldest brother, **Hans von Bora**, shared their father's first name, just as Katie shared their mother's. He later went to the court of Duke Albrecht of Prussia, probably at Luther's request, and received employment from the prince at Memel in East Prussia where he stayed in the early 1530s. Beginning in 1534, he was in his homeland again, as indicated by a letter of Luther from May 6, 1538. He had to return from Prussia in order to take over the small property of Zölsdorf a half hour south of Lippendorf and in order to retain it for his children as an inherited home. Perhaps he didn't even actually buy it, but he had to *claim* it as his and his brothers' property—as Luther expressly states, obviously from the inheritance of their mother, who had now died (1534). He himself was also married to a widow from Seydewitz, who came from a family with political position. She brought along one or more children from her first marriage as well. But the dowry she brought to him probably was hardly enough to pay the brothers for their share of Zölsdorf. Hans couldn't make a living on the small property. He had to sell it again in 1540.

However, Katie might not have wanted to let the last remnant of their father's inheritance pass into other hands, and she persuaded her husband to buy Zölsdorf. The purchase price amounted to 610 *Gulden*. To us this amount seems ridiculously low, but money was worth more at that time than now—exactly how much higher even the scholars cannot tell us with certainty; some consider it double, others reckon it almost eight times the current value.

Luther also took care of his brother-in-law Hans. In good conscience he was able to recommend him as a loyal and pious man, whose skill and diligence he would dare to praise. It was to Luther's recommendation that Hans owed his office as a manager at the convent of the nuns of St. George in Leipzig, where the Reformation had been introduced in 1539. And when this position had to be given up in 1541, Luther again stood ready to intercede. For a while there was talk about how Hans should be transferred to the convent at Brehna or the convent at Nimbschen—thus one of the two convents his sister had been in—but nothing came of this. After he had again been manager at the Cloister of St. Mary at Cronschwitz near Weida in Vogtland for a short time, the Elector finally invested him with Kartause, an old monastic property near Crimmitschau.

Another brother of Katie's, **Klemens von Bora**, likewise was brought to the court of Duke Albrecht of Prussia at Königsberg, but by his bad behavior he lost the prince's favor, and Luther could do nothing further for him but to ask his patron, the duke, to provide the young apprentice with a horse and the necessary travel money to send him home with a kind recommendation to the Elector of Saxony. In 1549 he was invested with the free property at Dohna. He was still living in 1573.

The first name of Katie's **third brother** is not known. He was married and with his wife Christina had a son Florian von Bora, who, as a boy in 1542, was raised in Luther's house in Wittenberg; perhaps his father had already died at that time. Even after her husband's death, Katie provided for this nephew Florian. Heinrich von Einsiedel at the Castle Gnandstein, which is a few hours southeast of Lippendorf and Zölsdorf in the region of Leipzig, was also a benefactor of the family.

Finally, we have a report, from even more recent time, that a **Maria von Bora** from Zölsdorf was married to Wolf Siegenmund of Niemeck around 1525. If this report has been passed on to us correctly, then Maria von Bora may have been a sister of Katie's.

Katie in the Convent

The only other relative mentioned is an Aunt Magdalena von Bora, probably a sister of Katie's father. When Katie was born, this aunt had already lived as a nun in Nimbschen for a long time. The

Nimbschen convent recruited for itself—if one may speak this way—from the noble families of a relatively small area, whose boundaries are marked by Pegau in the west, Leipzig and Wurzen in the north, and Leisnig in the east. Lippendorf is also within this region. Hirschfeld, on the other hand, is far away. That is also why the von Bora's from Hirschfeld brought their daughters, not to Nimbschen, but to convents that were closer for them, such as Döbeln and Riesa.

So all the information we have about Katie and her relatives takes us to the area south of Leipzig, to Zölsdorf and Lippendorf. Katie was probably born on the estate at Lippendorf on January 29, 1499. Her father was Hans von Bora. Her mother Katharine's maiden name was probably von Haubitz, based on an account that is from a later time but is reliable on this point. Her mother died young, and either in 1504 or the beginning of the next year her father brought the motherless girl to the cloister school of the Benedictine nuns at Brehna near Bitterfeld in the province of Saxony. For eighteen years Katie was enclosed within convent walls, first in Brehna, and then in Nimbschen.

Family connections might also have been a deciding factor in her father's choice of the Brehna convent. A branch of his family lived in the area of Bitterfeld. He probably didn't intend at that time to have his daughter educated for the religious life, but simply wanted her to receive a good education. The *Rule of Saint Benedict* urged the Benedictines to promote academics. The schools connected with their cloisters were famous, and they admitted and instructed even famous children, who were not intended for the religious life. Katie certainly received a better education with the Benedictine nuns in Brehna than she could have received otherwise as a young girl of the nobility anywhere else in the country at that time.

At the same time there was also a young girl from Leipzig with her at the convent school in Brehna: Klara Preusser, a daughter of the Leipzig magistrate, Doctor Johann Preusser. She came from an old, wealthy family. Even now Preusser Street in Leipzig still bears their name. She had probably lost both parents already as a young girl, and so she, too, had been brought to the Benedictines in

Brehna for her education. Here she got to know and became friends with Katie. Many years later, when Katie was already married to Luther and Klara was married to the Magdeburg chancellor Doktor Lorenz Zoch in Halle, Klara wrote a letter on October 30, 1531 reminding her school friend Katie of how they spent their youth together. She promised to visit her in Wittenberg and to renew their old friendship from the convent at Brehna. This letter, unfortunately, is the only information we have about Katie's stay in Brehna.

In 1505 Katie's father, already at an older age, married for the second time and this, his second marriage, had a major impact on Katie's future. Her father left her at the cloister school in Brehna for a few more years, but in 1508 or the beginning of the next year he intended for her to enter religious life and brought her to the Nimbschen Convent. It is possible, and even probable, that her stepmother Margarete affected this decision. But the family's bad financial situation also influenced this decision. For, in any case, Katie's education at the convent school always had to be paid for in supplies to the Benedictines in Brehna every year, and the Lippendorf branch of the family was not rich. The free property at Lippendorf was quite a grand estate, but neither the manor at the Saale, nor the property at Lippendorf, were among the larger properties in the country. It seems Hans von Bora got into debt, either by bad business dealings or by hard luck, so that finally he had to give up the family property at Lippendorf and the estate at the Saale. His sons' inheritance, as we already heard, consisted of only the little property at Zölsdorf, which their father probably had bought around 1520 with what was left of his fortune. His bad financial position may also have determined that he give in to the requests of his second wife and turn Katie's temporary stay in the convent into a permanent one, in order to provide for her support and to ward off poverty.

But why didn't he leave her in Brehna? The reason for this decision was probably some pressing situation in the family. In Nimbschen the nuns' accommodations were free; whoever wanted to give something was allowed to do so, but it was not mandatory. On the other hand, the consecration of nuns was rather expensive in other monasteries. This may have been the case also with the Benedictines in Brehna and that's why Hans von Bora brought his daughter to the Cistercians at Nimbschen. A relative on her mother's side, Margarete of Haubitz, was also chosen to be the abbess there at the end of 1508 or the beginning of 1509, and furthermore, Katie's aunt, Magdalena von Bora, had already lived there as a nun for a long time.

Coincidentally, shortly after Katie entered Nimbschen cloister records were begun, which also give the names. The oldest record book covers May 1, 1509 to April 27, 1510. The content of these records is not consistent. Nevertheless for most years a precise listing of the convent residents is recorded, so that we know the names of all of the young women of nobility who were with Katie in Nimbschen. At the head of the list was the Abbess Margarete von Haubitz, and the Prioress. Then follow the names of the nuns, apparently without distinguishing the young girls who were not yet old enough to be consecrated as nuns but who were already being educated in the convent as well. And at the end, the lay sisters and the servants are listed. In these directories the nuns and novices appear in the order in which they entered the convent, from oldest to youngest. Katharine von Bora is thirty-fourth in the record book of 1509 at age ten, the second to the last. She had been accepted just shortly before this time. Only Ave von Schönfeld follows after her. Also in the record books of 1510 at age eleven, of 1511 at age twelve, and of 1512 at age thirteen, Katharine von Bora remains the second last, and Ave von Schönfeld is the last on the list. Only in the records for 1513 is Margarete (Martha) von Schönfeld added at age fourteen, in 1516 Barbara von Plausig at age seventeen, in 1517 Katharine von Kertzsch and Katharine Scherl at age eighteen.

According to these records, the convent Throne of Mary, or Throne of God, in Nimbschen was neither a small nor a poor convent. It wasn't, however, first established at Nimbschen. Count Heinrich the Illustrious had founded it first in the city of Torgau. Ever since that time, the Cistercians of Nimbschen had a rich income from the region of Torgau. But already around 1250 the princely founder had moved the convent from Torgau to his favorite city, Grimma. Even in this city, the girls of the nobility do not seem to have fared well. In 1258 they bought the property at Nimbschen from the knight Hartung von Rideburg and built a new cloister on the south side next to the court, which they had erected in 1291. At least it seems that the cloister church was consecrated that year, and with it a rich indulgence was announced to the faithful.

The Cloister's Setting

Religious orders liked to establish themselves in fertile areas that have a beautiful landscape, somewhat away from the cities. Forest and water, field and garden, had to supply food for the convent's residents, and the business of the world had to go on outside its walls so that they could dedicate themselves, undisturbed, to pious works. Nimbschen, too, is situated in the midst of a quiet, lovely landscape. The road that leads from Grimma to the south leads over the steep-sloping height, which here takes the Mulde north, then back down into a fertile valley. In a wide arc, wooded hills border the west, and to the east the calmly flowing river borders the meadows and fruitful fields. The road passes through the middle of this. A large pond on the right, bordered by a marsh, once supplied food for Lent, and where the road slowly rises again to the convent woods in the south, on the left between the shady forest and the sunny fields with the orchard, are the large convent grounds and the ruins of the Throne of Mary Convent. Only the high-rising gables and the huge walls of a main building with large, open windows are still standing today. The church, the close, and the provost's residence have vanished, and only by excavation could the foundation walls be exposed.

Relics

The cloister church was once rich with relics. A long list from September 4, 1508 enumerates the holy objects before which Katie also knelt in devotion and where she joined with her companions in singing the prescribed Latin hymns at all twelve altars: crucifixes, larger and smaller monstrances, boxes or shrines, and tables, most made of precious metal and covered with gold. Even more precious than the containers were their contents. There were pieces of the manger and the cross of Christ, as well as pieces from the cross of the thief who had hung at the Lord's right hand, pieces of the crown of thorns that had been pressed onto the Lord's head, and pieces from the whipping post to which they had bound him, even a sliver from the table of the Last Supper, and a piece of the Lord's burial shroud. Besides this there was soil from the most sacred places in the Holy Land: from Christ's tomb and the tomb of the Virgin Mary, from the Mount of Olives where the Lord had wept over Jerusalem, from the garden of Gethsemane, from Mount Calvary, and from the place where Christ's feet had stood before He ascended into heaven. There were hairs from the holy Virgin Mary and remnants of her veil, her robe, her tunic, likewise from the dress of the beautiful and repentant sinner Mary Magdalene, from the dress of Saint Elisabeth of Thuringia, and from the cowl of Saint Bernard, the great Renewer of the Cistercian Order. Some of the Apostle Paul's blood could be seen in two displays. The convent was directed to ask for intercession from an almost infinite list of saints, with a larger or smaller piece of their bones, teeth, or arm bones. No fewer than 367 individual pieces were counted.

Pilgrimage and Indulgence

Making pilgrimage to Nimbschen at the high church festivals of Christmas, Easter, or Pentecost, or at the four holidays of the Virgin Mary, and participating there on certain days by praying and kneeling or saying the prayers at the cloister and in the churchyard, or donating pious gifts could bring an indulgence of forty days for more grievous sins, and indulgence of one year for lesser sins. The highest holiday of the monastic church was the anniversary of its own church dedication. It was even called "*aplas*" by the people because of the indulgence [*Ablaß*] that was announced on that day. As in other places of pilgrimage, a type of annual fair was also connected with the church dedication in Nimbschen, and in order to maintain order among the booths, the villages nearby the convent, Grossbardau and Kleinbardau, each had to station three men to keep watch day and night, until they were finally released from the burdensome night duty, at least. With the introduction of the

Reformation these celebrations, which were well attended and lucrative for the convent, came to an end. The remaining nuns—in 1536 there were only nine left—still used the cloister church for some time for Divine Service. Then it gradually fell into disuse and was finally torn down. The stones were probably used in the barns and stables of nearby farmsteads.

Convent Buildings, Workers, and Finances

Nothing more is left of the close either, which encircled the cloister toward the church and which at one time contained the nuns' cells, the dormitory, and the dining hall (refectory). This part of the convent was called the "back cloister," which was farthest away from and closed off to the outside world. A small gate here let the nuns into their gardens.

The large building, whose ruins are now the last remnants of Nimbschen, probably belonged to the provost's residence, which formed the front part of the convent. The smaller buildings here have also disappeared, for example: the gatehouse, in which the gate watchman, Thalheim, monitored those coming in and going out; the brewery, in which the light convent beer, the so-called *Kofent*, was brewed; the bakery and the slaughterhouse; the smithy and the mill. The only thing that can still be seen here and there is the run of the old millrace.[3]

The most beautiful rooms of the provost's residence were certainly reserved for the Lady Domina, the abbess. She lived here with the servants who were particularly assigned to serve her: one young girl and two boys. The guest cell or guest chamber was also here. In addition, the manager lived here. He kept record of the convent's income and administered it under the abbess; a guard and a secretary assisted him. The two religious lords of Pforte who served as father confessors in the convent—Nimbschen was under the supervision of the Cistercian cloister at Pforte near Kösen—likewise had their residence in the front court until the year 1526. They received free food and 1 *Schock*, 17 *Groschen*, and 3 *Pfennig* each as annual salary, and an errand-boy was kept to serve them.

---

[3] Millrace: a channel that carries water to and from a mill wheel.

Also, the cellar master, the baker, the miller, and the smith, whose wages are recorded in the annual accounts, as well as the wood-cutter who cut the firewood in the oak forests at the convent, and the furnacemen, who had to heat the "hells," that is, the furnaces—these would have lived in the "front coister." In the records, six farm workers are also listed: two men who tended the horses, a cattle herdsman, a swineherd, a goose girl, and a cheese woman, as well as three milkmaids and a second cheese woman in the cattle yard, and several milkmaids on the farmstead and in the small estate on the other side of the Mulde. The entire domestic staff, which numbered almost forty, was fed out of the convent kitchen, where one cook and two cook's maids were busy.

For the most part, what the convent needed was built into the convent economy. The income began to be recorded accurately in the 1530s. In the convent cattle yard—unseen from the front area—there were 57 head of beef cattle and 30 horses, i.e. one stallion, 17 field horses, 8 foals, and 4 carriage horses. The carriage horses were probably harnessed each year at St. Martin's Day [November 11], when the abbess drove to Torgau with a nun in order to collect the convent dues there, or if the Elector was in the area and ordered that a wagon be waiting. In addition there were 674 sheep and 44 pigs; there had been a massive death among the pigs, earlier there had been close to 80. The fields were planted with wheat and rye, barley and oats, peas and carrots, but the soil was not really favorable for wheat. Also hemp, flax, and hops supported the convent. The meadows and forests, the ponds and the natural fishing holes in the Mulde, were well maintained. Capons, chickens, and eggs were brought in large quantities by the villages that were duty-bound to support the convent.

The real estate, which the convent had owned from its beginning in the district of Torgau, had been greatly expanded through the centuries by pious donations or their own purchases. The farmsteads, the properties, and villages that belonged to the religious young women, or the individual farms which annually had to pay them a certain amount of dues in grain or in cash, encircled the convent like a wreath. They were not without quarrels with other monasteries in this regard, and particularly in the villages close to the convent the farmers felt oppressed by the frequent compulsory labor. The people from Grossbardau and Kleinbardau had to plow the convent fields, spread manure on them, had to mow and cut them, bring in the grain and thresh it. They had to harvest hops, reap and ret hemp and flax, store and chop cabbage, cut wood, keep the millrace free of mud and ice, and shear the sheep; on the farmsteads at Grossbothen and Kleinbothen there were 1,800 sheep!

If they had to work for the convent the whole day, they received meals and drinks, and even cash for shearing the sheep. But the convent tried to get rid of such compensation, and beginning in the sixteenth century the wages, which had been set much earlier, were either not paid at all, or else they were no longer commensurate to the work. On the other hand, the remuneration was relatively high if the farmers had to participate as drivers in the hunts in the convent woods or the meadows; 3–4 *Groschen* were paid for a wild pig, 2 *Groschen* for a deer, and 1 *Groschen* for a hare. Nevertheless, the farmers felt burdened by this service as well. Services, which had originally been given voluntarily, and which were to be rewarded by God, had gradually been turned into hard compulsory labor by virtue of custom and under pressure from the convent.

Many things, of course, could not be supplied by the convent properties, since they were to be found only in the cities: cloth, all kinds of tools, salted and dried fish from the sea. To purchase these things the Nimbschen convent normally did not turn to nearby Grimma or to Leipzig, the trade center, which was a ducal city, but to Torgau, the city where the Elector resided. Here in Torgau, at the time when Katharine von Bora was in Nimbschen, lived Leonhard Koppe, the councilman and tax collector, an honest man with whom we will become better acquainted later. He supplied the nuns at Nimbschen with herring, dried cod and eels, beer (the good, strong beer brewed in Torgau was famous), iron, and iron tools. And when the abbess was in Torgau on St. Martin's Day, accounts were also settled with Koppe.

Order in the Convent

"The abbess and the assembly of the Nimbschen cloister"—numerous documents from Nimbschen begin with these words. The abbess was elected from the number of the nuns or conventuals, but she was nevertheless like a ruler at the head of the convent, and the only ones above her were the Elector of Saxony as secular protector and the Abbott of Torgau as religious leader. In accordance with her special position she had a special residence and a special staff of servants. The running of the convent was in her hands, and in all matters the decision was hers, although she was obligated to seek the advice of her older colleagues, the so-called seniors. The physical and spiritual welfare of the sisters was entrusted to her. She was to be equally fair and kindhearted to all; she should favor none over others with regard to food or clothing. She had to provide for the feeding and caring of the sick, and encourage the sisters' pious way of life. Therefore, in order to maintain chastity and order, she had full power of discipline. She could have disobedient or inexcusably lazy nuns locked up, withhold food and drink from them except bread and water, even subject them to corporal punishment.

Margarete von Haubtiz, who was abbess in Nimbschen at Katie's time, is described as "an honorable, pious, sensible picture of a woman." Since she was related to Katie, she was more affectionately disposed toward the young girl. Severity and harshness do not seem to have been in her character at all. When Abbott Balthasar of Torgau visited the Nimbschen convent on April 29, 1509, shortly after her selection as abbess, he wrote a long complaint and instruction because of various abuses and offenses against the rule of Saint Bernard. It had so little effect on her that at another inspection on January 7, 1512, the abbot had to repeat the old complaints almost word for word. Also, we do not hear a single time that she adopted strict measures against the dissemination of Lutheran teachings, as happened in other monasteries. Even after Katie and her eight companions successfully escaped, the abbess did not think of keeping the other nuns by force. She, along with Abbott Peter of Pforte, contented herself with lodging a complaint to Elector Fredrick the Wise, and in the end she, along with the sisters who had remained with her, accepted the new teaching. She died in Nimbschen in 1536.

As ministers and counselors stand alongside a ruler, alongside the abbess stood the prioress and subprioress and the seniors, who held a well-defined office in the convent. In Nimbschen there is mention of a cellar-mistress, a bursar (which was the treasurer), a verger, a singer, a head of the infirmary (for a long time this was Katie's aunt Magdalena von Bora), and a hostess for guests. The gate girl had supervision over the entrance into the close.

The sisters lived in the close according to the *Rule of Saint Bernard of Clairvaux*, the second father and founder of the widespread Cistercian order, which bears its name after Citeaux (Cistercium), the monastery south of Dijon in Burgundy. In Germany, too, the Cistercians had rendered great service by cultivating wilderness regions, but the original simplicity of the Order was gradually suffocated in its wealth. The habit of the Order of the Cistercians or that of Saint Bernard was a white cowl with black cincture and black veil. The *Rule*, which obligated them to poverty and chastity, humility and absolute obedience, was strict to the letter. The day was filled with prayers, singing, and reading devotional texts from Matins to Compline, the last devotion before nighttime. Only after the noon meal, were the nuns at Nimbschen permitted an hour of midday rest.

It was keenly observed that the cloister's silence should not be broken. In the choir, which was separated from the front part of the church by barriers, no one was allowed to speak. Likewise, silence should prevail in the refectory and in the dormitory. But the Nimbschen nuns may also have had a type of gesture-language or sign language, with which they could hold their tongues and still communicate with each other, or sometimes they would even disobey if the obligation of silence became too burdensome.

Abbott Balthasar of Pforte repeatedly complained that the strict rules were not observed carefully enough. He reprimanded the irregular singing that was against the *Rule* and insisted that the sisters should sing only the regular and harmonious songs, which were accepted by the Cistercians in their missal. He praised monastic silence as the key to religion and warned against breaking it, because disobedience would someday require an accounting of every idle word. He laid on the conscience of the abbess and prioress their great responsibility. He laid on the heart of the older sisters their obligations toward the younger. He admonished them all to die completely to the world and to live only for their heavenly Bridegroom. The inner convent was to remain locked to laymen and clergymen, and the latticework in the parlor should be made narrower so that it would be impossible for a hand or a gift to pass through. Even the two father confessors should enter the convent only if a nun was ill, and they should certainly guard against giving offense to another sister. Among themselves, however, with the permission of the abbess, the sisters might also occasionally have their pastimes in a spirit of love and harmony.

According to the abbot's wishes, this long Latin instruction[4] from the year 1509, which deals with some individual points in even greater detail, was to be read four times a year and explained to the nuns point by point by the abbess or the prioress. Katie, too, was among the more or less attentive listeners, but she surely understood very little of what was read, for she had been brought to Nimbschen just before this, at age ten. She was not the only one who had entered the convent at such a young age. On February 18, 1495, Elector Fredrick the Wise had forbidden the nuns at Nimbschen from accepting new young girls or children without his prior knowledge. But it seems this instruction was only on paper or else the Elector himself must have revoked it when the abuses that had shown up at that time, with the resulting crowding of the convent, had been eliminated again. Among those who shared Katie's fate were several who likewise had lived in the convent from childhood on.

No schoolmistress or superintendent of novices is mentioned in Nimbschen at the time, but that is probably just an unintentional gap in the information passed on to us, because these young girls, who were to be consecrated after just a few years, certainly could

---

[4] It was repeated three years later, but this is extant only in a German translation from that time.

not continue without instruction. Abbot Balthasar emphatically urges that the older and more intelligent sisters be obliged to instruct and teach those who were younger and as yet uneducated. In addition there was a small convent school in Nimbschen (now we would call it a boarding school), where young girls received lodging, meals, and instruction. In the convent records they are listed by name for the first time in the fiscal year of 1516–17, nine in number, all from the nobility. In the older records of 1509–15, they were not yet specifically listed, but it would be wrong to conclude that there were no schoolgirls in Nimbschen during these years, because again in the records of 1517–18 they are not mentioned. On the other hand, they are listed by name again in the records of 1518–19, five in number, among them four who had already been in the school two years earlier, and the same five again the next year.

Education in the Nimbschen Convent

What did they learn in Nimbschen? It wouldn't have been very much. But they certainly would have been taught to read and write, and the basics of Latin, at least enough so that they vaguely understood the Latin texts they later had to read or sing in church. When Luther once asked Katie's aunt Magdalena von Bora whether she wanted to go back to the convent, she quickly answered: *"Non, non!"* Katie didn't learn just individual Latin words at Nimbschen. And it is expressly said that later, as Luther's wife, Katie occasionally joined in with Latin words in the Latin conversation carried on by the lodgers.[5] It may well be that later on she learned, from Luther's habit, to speak German and Latin mixed together, but she probably had already laid the foundation in the monasteries at Brehna and Nimbschen.

However, the main object of monastic education was introducing and familiarizing the girls with monastic life. The young girls who were prepared for consecration in the convent

---

[5] *Tischgenossen.* There was a group of people who often ate with Luther. I have translated this as "lodgers" because it includes regular diners, not just occasional guests.

were already to learn to treasure strict chastity and modesty as the most precious pearl of virginity. Their words, conduct, and habits should be pure and chaste, as well as their hearts. They should bow their head in modesty. They should also avoid all worldly adornment in what they wore. Chatting and wandering around were forbidden to them, just like school children. To distinguish them from the boarding school girls and the nuns, they were called "the adolescent virgins." Katie belonged in this group for the first five or six years, from the time she entered the convent up to the beginning of her novitiate in 1514. At the end of her year of probation, she was consecrated on October 8, 1515.

Shortly before her consecration, two of her young friends had already become nuns, the two sisters, Ave and Margarete von Schönfeld. Together they had donated 3 *Schock* and 20 *Groschen* to the convent on May 7, 1515. Ilse von Kitzscher, who became a nun some time after Katie's consecration, donated 40 *Groschen*. Katie could only offer 30 *Groschen* on the day of her consecration.

The year of probation, or trial period that preceded her consecration, the so-called "profession" was to offer the young novice the opportunity to get used to the *Rule* of the Order and to become completely clear about whether she could really take the vows. Therefore, in some convents the abbess was obligated to ask the novices each time after reading the *Rule* of the Order whether they could keep it or not, and before their consecration she should again present the *Rule* to them and examine them as to whether they were determined to remain steadfast. With Katie the answer to these questions could hardly be in doubt. Even though it hadn't been her internal impulse, nor even her voluntary resolve to enter the convent, still from her earliest youth she knew nothing other than that she was intended for Holy Orders. And before Luther's teachings reached her convent, she didn't seem at all reluctant to bear or feel burdened by the fetters she had not taken on herself. Not even once do we hear her complain later about her monastic obligation. On the contrary, even twenty years later, Pentecost 1540, she extolled the fervent zeal with which she and her colleagues had prayed in the convent, and it seemed to her as though now she prayed less often and less fervently.

If God's grace were truly compelled by the number of prayers, by the fervor of singing and by fasting, monks and nuns would have been on the right path to salvation. And yet even the most sincere and most pious among them was filled with doubts and driven by a yearning that no longer found satisfaction in the practices of monastic piety that strove for what is higher and nobler. It was Luther who clearly and plainly expressed for the first time what many thousands unwittingly and yet painfully felt rising in their souls. He guided them away from the legends of the saints, the teachings of the church fathers, and the laws of the papacy, back to Holy Scripture as the clearest source of salvation, and his words rumbled over the German nation like a springtime storm.

2.

FROM NIMBSCHEN TO WITTENBERG

Luther in the Monastery

In 1505, a short time after her father brought Katie to the convent school at Brehna, Pope Julius II made the momentous decision to replace the old venerable Basilica of Saint Peter in Rome with a splendid new building according to the plans of Bramante.[1] About the same time, on July 17, 1505, in the university city of Erfurt a young law student, Martin Luther, stood at the gate of the Augustinian monastery, seeking admission. The foundation stone for Saint Peter's was laid on April 16, 1506 in the presence of the Pope and numerous church princes. The reconstruction was to set the power and the glory of the papacy before the eyes of the whole Christian world. In the quiet Augustinian monastery, however, a young monk, who almost despaired from pangs of conscience, and after years of struggling in his soul, would come to the realization that this papacy in all its power and glory was of no help to the desperate soul. His stay in the monastery, where he had hoped to find peace, became for him only the preparation for a whole life full of struggles, but also full of victories and rich in blessings.

Doctor Johann von Staupitz cast the first light into Luther's clouded mind. This distinguished, pious, well-educated man, for whom Luther retained the most heartfelt gratitude his whole lifetime, had been the Vicar General of the Augustinian Order since

---

[1] Donato Bramante, Italian architect and painter, born about 1444; died in Rome, March 11, 1514.

1503. For Luther he became a second father, a spiritual father. Staupitz tore Luther from his self-tormenting brooding over sins that were not sins, and comforted him by referring him to God's all-merciful kindness that does not reject the penitent. He filled him with faith in the Redeemer through whom we become partakers of divine grace. His astute and expert insight detected at the same time, however, that a fiery spirit such as this ought not to be smothered in the oppressive silence and narrowness of the monastery. At his instigation Luther stepped out of his monastic cell and into university professorship. Soon afterward, he was appointed as a professor at the new University of Wittenberg. Luther moved from Erfurt to Wittenberg at the same time Katie went from Brehna to Nimbschen, at the end of 1508.

Luther in Wittenberg

Even in Wittenberg, Luther lived as a brother of the Order in the monastery of the Augustinians, the Black Friars, as they were called due to their black cowls. A return to Erfurt, a pilgrimage to Rome, the return to Wittenberg, his promotion to Doctor of Theology, and his quiet activity as a teacher at the University and a preacher in the parish church and in the monastery filled the next year of his life. Luther's brothers and superiors had confidence in him and selected him as subprior in 1512 and made him district vicar in 1515 over the ten Augustinian monasteries of Saxony. Several like-minded friends already saw him as their leader: friends like George Spalatin, the influential court chaplain of Elector Fredrick the Wise; Wenceslaus Link, the prior of the Augustinian monastery at Wittenberg; and Johann Lang, who likewise moved from Erfurt to Wittenberg, but returned to Erfurt in 1516 as prior of the Augustinian monastery there.

Luther's name was still rarely mentioned in wider circles. From the second decade of the sixteenth century, we have several handwritten lists of scholars who were considered the most important in Germany at that time. Henning Göde and Christoph Scheurl were named among the lawyers in Wittenberg, and among the theologians, Andreas Karlstadt; but Luther's name is absent.

An external cause pushed him onto the battleground where his powerful figure soon towered above them all. The new building of Saint Peter's, the beginning of which had coincided with his entrance into the monastery, continued to exert a most crucial influence on his future life. The amounts of money, which the foundations had already devoured, were enormous. It was said that the building was just as deep below ground as it would rise later above ground. In order to bring in funds, a new indulgence was announced to Christendom. This business was brought to Germany by Archbishop Albrecht, the Hohenzollern, who in an unprecedented move, and against church law, gained control of the two archdioceses of Magdeburg and Mainz and the bishopric of Halberstadt. On his behalf, Johann Tetzel traveled throughout central Germany with the indulgence coffer, and the shameless way in which this Dominican monk ran the ugly business forced Luther to emerge from his seclusion. On October 31, 1517, Luther nailed his Ninety-five Theses to the door of the Castle Church in Wittenberg.

The Reformation Begins

That trumpet blast was the call to battle, and Luther did not shrink from the decision, even though at the beginning only a handful gathered around him when he so boldly sounded the rallying cry. One of the greatest scenes in the drama of world history is when this simple monk in the little city of Wittenberg with only Holy Scripture in his hand stepped onto the field against the Bishop of Rome, who called himself Pope and his church's princes! Was it any wonder that Luther was at first willing to have things better explained to him?

But in their blindness the papists did not want understanding; they required absolute submission. The rather light skirmishes with cardinal legate Cajetan in Augsburg and with the papal chamberlain Karl von Miltitz in Altenburg were quickly followed by the Great Disputation with Eck at the Pleissenburg in Leipzig in 1519. The next year, 1520, brought the three powerful polemical writings of Luther: *To the Christian Nobility of the German Nation*, *The Babylonian Captivity of the Church*, *The Freedom of the*

Christian—each writing, a new campaign; each attack, a new victory.

Luther Excommunicated

The excommunication launched by the Pope, bounced off without effect. But the brainstorms of the German monk flashed brilliantly, blow by blow, against the Roman papacy and its self-made dominion. With his head held high, Luther stood before the Emperor in Worms on that fateful day of April 18, 1521. Restless in the Wartburg, he began the greatest work of his life, the translation of the Bible into the German language. On March 5, 1522, when he returned from the Thuringian mountains to Wittenberg, which was shaken with unrest, he was ready for the task that was waiting for him: to lay the groundwork for a renewed church, amidst general tumult. Holy Scripture was to be the foundation stone, and the church was not to become a showy building like Saint Peter's. He and his co-workers simply and faithfully added stone upon stone. Resolutely he deterred the storms and agitators; he opposed revolution with all his might. His life's work would be the Reformation.

From Monk to Reformer

Outside in the fresh air of the mountain forests of Thuringia, Luther had become a different person as well. He was no longer the emaciated monk (someone in Leipzig had thought one could count all his bones). His body had become fuller, his attitude self-confident. This is how the young Swiss Johann Kessler, who studied in Wittenberg 1522–23, describes him:

> When I saw Martin in 1522 when he was forty-one, he had a natural, rather strong, upright bearing, so that he leaned more backwards than forwards, with head held high toward heaven, with deep dark eyes and eyebrows, blinking and twinkling like a star that can't be ignored.

One phrase in Kessler's description could easily be misunderstood and actually was. At that time the words, "a natural, rather strong person" [*ainer natürlich zimlichen faiste*], did not mean that Luther was "rather fat" [*ziemlich feist*], but the exact opposite, that he had a strength that seemed to fit his medium built and his natural age, that is, naturally; it was only later that he became fat.

We also encounter his stately appearance, still youthfully strong despite his forty-some years, in Cranach's paintings of the young bridal couple soon after his wedding with Katie. By this time he had already gotten rid of the full beard he had come home with from the Wartburg. "Luther got married," Desiderius Erasmus scoffed in 1525, "yes, encouraged and urged by his brothers, he even set aside the ascetic's mantle and the philosopher's beard." Already in 1523, in the rooms of his monastery, Luther wore secular clothing instead of the monk's cowl, and on October 9, 1524 he even stood in the pulpit for the first time without his cowl. Since then, instead of the monk's hood, he wore the biretta that came to him as a Doctor of Theology. And instead of the cowl that was held together by a cincture, he wore a wide doctor's robe that came down far past the knee, the so-called *Schaube*. This old garment, with small modifications, is retained in the robe of the Protestant clergy even to our time.

Erasmus was quite well informed when he wrote that Luther had laid aside his cowl only at the urging of his closest friends. Later Luther himself repeatedly said that his cowl was quite threadbare and patched when Elector Fredrick sent him a piece of cloth and told him that he should have a robe or a cap made for himself. And the prince had said to Spalatin, that even if Luther wanted to have a Spanish cap made—Spanish dress had first come into the empire as the latest fashion only with Emperor Charles V and his attendants—then who could blame him for that? But his friends urged him for a long time before he wore secular clothing. Even in this relatively small matter we see his basically conservative character, which required only that he live in accord with all the main points of Holy Scripture and remove whatever was against the will of God. But in lesser matters he wanted to preserve the old and avoid any coercion. In his writings, however, and especially in the Latin treatise *Concerning Monastic Vows*, written while he was still at the Wartburg, he had taken up the right for everyone else to leave the monastery, to lay aside the outward signs of monasticism, and to get married, but no one should be forced into it.

Luther continued to live in the Black Cloister at Wittenberg with his Prior, Eberhard Brisger, even when they were the last two brothers of the Order in the deserted building. For many more years he put up with his miserable strawbed and meager food. It was very difficult for him to make the decision to marry. While others rushed to put his teachings into practice, many with selfish ulterior motives, any thought about this at all for himself was quite distant. He held his followers back, rather than pushing them, for he knew that the seed that was sown needed time to mature. He wanted hearts to be won first; he wanted people to be sure of things, before outward rules might be changed. He wanted to proceed step-by-step. They were actually giant steps, and the ground rumbled and erupted under them.

The Reformation Spreads

From the passing of the old way, however, new life sprang up everywhere, and hearts opened willingly to the teachings that were proclaimed from Wittenberg. With lightning speed Luther's writings flew across the country. Even if the Emperor and Pope wanted to outlaw and ban them and subject them to the fire, and even if zealous abbots and abbesses still wanted to keep the windows of their cloisters tightly barred—still the living Word hurdled the barricades that had been placed on the printed word, and even the printed writings found ways and means of passing secretly from hand to hand despite the supervision of the authorities. If Luther's doctrine made its way even into such a strictly guarded convent as Neuenhelfta, how could someone like Margarete von Haubitz have protected her Nimbschen convent?

A half hour from Nimbschen was the Electoral city of Grimma. The majority of the inhabitants were evangelically minded, and in the Augustinian monastery at Grimma many monks also cheered for their great brother in the Order at Wittenberg. The Saxon nobleman Wolfgang von Zeschau was the Prior of the monastery. He voluntarily resigned his position in 1522 and with a number of like-minded brothers withdrew from the Order. He became hospital chaplain of the Johannite Hospital of the Holy Cross in Grimma, later (from 1531) he was pastor in nearby Hohnstädt. Two of his relatives, however, now lived in the Nimbschen convent, the two sisters Veronika and Margarete von Zeschau, perhaps his nieces. They escaped from the convent along with Katie. Although we have no express testimony that this Wolfgang von Zeschau arranged the introduction of Luther's teachings into Nimbschen, the assumption is that he very likely did. Through his relationship with the two sisters, access to the convent was easier for von Zeschau than for others. However, the alleged underground passage leading from the Cistercian convent in Nimbschen to the Augustinian monastery in Grimma that would have allowed "godless" nuns to meet with "apostate" monks and "wicked" evangelical preachers in Grimma, and the rumored tryst Katie was supposed to have granted Doctor Luther at a spring in the forest near the cloister, the so-called Luther Well—these are all ridiculous fables.

Katie Escapes the Convent

The Nimbschen nuns only dared turn to Luther, who, of course, had more important things to do in Wittenberg, when every other assistance failed them; when in their distress, as Luther himself reports, they knew no other way out than to escape from the convent. Luther's doctrine had taken away everything that had previously given meaning to their lives: the belief that they had done a God-pleasing work with their vow of chastity, the hope of securing for themselves the right to a place in heaven through penitential exercises and monastic discipline, trust in the merit and intercession of the saints and the power of their relics to grant indulgence. What Luther's doctrine promised them—the sure confidence of God's grace and inner peace—they could attain only outside the convent walls in a pious, active life, faithful to their duties. Nine nuns were ready to break their vows and leave

Nimbschen: Magdalena von Staupitz, Elsa von Canitz, Laneta von Gohlis, Ave Grosse, Veronika and her sister Margarete von Zeschau, the two sisters Ave and Margarete von Schönfeld, and Katharine von Bora.

First they wrote to their parents and relatives, urgently asking their help in getting out of the convent since "such a life in order to save their soul was no longer tolerable to them." They would gladly do and endure everything else as obedient children. Their relatives' responses were negative, as was to be expected. The Gospel had not yet grown in the hearts of these simple landed gentry, to the extent that they would daringly and fearlessly be willing to lend a hand to an act that was so risky and so unprecedented as was planned by the nine girls in leaving the convent. Also, for most of them the reason they had intended their daughters for the religious estate was certainly the same as it had been with Katie's parents. For the poorer landed gentry, the convents served as an institution of support for their daughters, and in the Catholic period no one had taken offense at that.

Abandoned by their families, the nine nuns sought Luther's advice and assistance, and Luther regarded it as his Christian obligation to assist them in their predicament. Since their superiors would never voluntarily let them go, they had to be abducted from the convent, secretly and sneakily, because force could not be used, if only on account of the Elector, who for all his gentleness nevertheless would have punished an open breach of the public peace. The operation was dangerous enough anyway, because abducting a nun was threatened with the death penalty.

But Luther knew a man who had enough courage and cunning to bring the risky undertaking to a successful conclusion and who at the same time was protected from every vile suspicion by his prestigious position and his dignified age: Leonhard Koppe. Coming from an old Torgau family, he was fifty-nine at that time and was a universally respected and educated man, having proven himself in several offices. Beginning in 1495, he had studied for several years in Leipzig and in Erfurt, and then he had been councilman from 1504–09 in his home city. Since 1510 he had served the Elector for a while as tax collector in the Torgau district.

We have already heard about his business connections with the Nimbschen convent. With Luther's repeated visits to Torgau in 1519 and in April 1522, he became better acquainted with Luther.

Koppe, however, did not alone feel up to the undertaking and its dangers; therefore, he secured two hearty comrades. One, his nephew, was probably the younger Leonhard Koppe. The Torgau chronicles report that he participated in the raid on the Torgau convent still during Elector Fredrick's lifetime and therefore had to flee because of the prince's wrath. The other, Wolf Dommitzsch, was also a citizen of Torgau and, like the Koppes, he also came from a respectable family who had lived in Torgau for a long time.

We do not know the method Koppe used to communicate with the nine nuns. Perhaps he went to Nimbschen sometime at the beginning of 1523 and secretly discussed the escape with them. Perhaps the hospital manager, Wolfgang von Zeschau in Grimma, took over the arrangements. At any rate, the greatest caution had to be taken, and some notes must have passed back and forth before the day and hour for the escape could be determined. The day when Christ once rose from the dark night of the grave was to bring the poor nuns release from the convent walls. On the night of Easter Eve to Easter Sunday—which in 1523 fell on April 5—they dared the escape, and succeeded, "miraculously enough," as Luther writes.

Later on, people would tell all kinds of stories about the detailed circumstances of the escape, and even into the nineteenth century every visitor was shown a window with the remnants of old sandstone decoration in the rubble of the convent, whose bare walls are now covered with wild grapevines. This is where Katie's cell was supposed to have been. Through this window she supposedly began her journey to freedom. But the size of the window should have cautioned the eager storyteller away from locating Katie's cell in this part of the ruins. The nuns' narrow cells were certainly not in the tall main building, which are the only remnants still standing.

A precious "relic" is still kept in the modest convent inn, and whoever has rested a while under the high linden trees to eat and drink something after visiting the ruins, would not miss going into the lower pub. Here, in a small glass case, a silk shoe is on display, a slipper. Katie is supposed to have lost it when she climbed through the window on her escape. But unfortunately the shoe is too elegant for a poor nun and at least two hundred years too late for the first quarter of the sixteenth century!

In the absence of facts, fables were spun. Since it was known that a contemporary reported that the fugitives had to break through a mud wall before they could gain their freedom, it was imagined that Katie escaped in secular clothes dressed like a dancing girl. Another reported that Koppe would have come to meet them in the convent garden and would have helped them climb over the wall. A third person, as we already heard, has them climbing out through the window beforehand. A fourth thinks that, after they had successfully escaped from the close, they probably would have slipped out through the poorly guarded back gate. Finally, a fifth assumed that the gate girl could have been in collusion with them and could have let them through the gate by night. All of these stories are unwarranted speculation. There were many ways for them to escape.

Nuns and Herring Barrels

Concerning the means of the escape, however, an old Torgau chronicler, who lived around 1600, still had definite information. He writes that Koppe, the liberator, abducted the nine noble young girls "from the convent with particular cunning and agility, as though he were bringing out herring barrels." This chronicler must have known that Koppe drove to Nimbschen rather frequently with herring and that when Koppe arrived with a new shipment, of course, he would have returned to Torgau with the empty barrels from the previous shipment. A more recent Torgau chronicler, who was told about this account of his compatriot, also understood it correctly. He writes in somewhat more detail that Koppe brought the nine nuns out "in a covered wagon, just as if he were bringing the empty herring barrels." The only things that are new in this more recent account are the specific mentions of empty herring barrels and that Koppe alone brought a covered wagon for the escape. We may regard this latter point, in fact, as confirmation that Koppe came in with a regular freight wagon in order to arouse no suspicion en route or near the convent. The statement of a contemporary also indicates that Koppe indeed carried the nine girls away in a single large wagon, and not in several carriages.

This simple and in fact truthful account by the Torgau chronicler was later misunderstood in a strange way. A version of the story attests that Koppe actually loaded the empty herring barrels at the convent gates in the middle of the night and inverted one barrel over each nun. The poor things! Later someone took offense at this means of transportation, but still thought they had to keep the empty herring barrels in the story, and so it was assumed that Koppe probably set the barrels up in the front of the wagon like barricades to keep curious eyes from seeing the fugitives sitting behind them. But the Torgau chronicler doesn't say anything about *actual* herring barrels at all! He is only comparing the live freight, which Koppe had in his wagon this time, with a load of empty barrels he usually transported as return freight from Nimbschen. The nine girls may simply have been pressed close together under the wagon tarp.

When we were young, we still saw people driving these old freight wagons on the country roads. They could be covered with a tarp on semicircular hoops, and if the large tarp was pulled over it and a broad-shouldered wagon driver sat in front on the driver's seat in his blue overalls, one would have to have good eyes to detect what was behind him in the wagon. If the fugitives were simply hidden under the tarp, the only precaution they needed to take was to sit very still if, for instance, they met someone walking, and not to give too free a rein to their innate female talkativeness, which probably had not been squelched in the convent, or to rejoice to loudly over their liberation.

Their rescue was still miraculous, even without the fabled empty herring barrels. The fact that there was no traitor among the many who knew about it, that no one carelessly blabbed the secret, that the exchange of letters in which Koppe had to prepare and discuss everything for the escape was not discovered, and finally that nine nuns were able to leave their cells undetected on Easter Eve and escape from the convent unimpeded—all this might have seemed truly miraculous to the man in Wittenberg who awaited intently the successful outcome of the bold and indeed risky undertaking. How easily another nun or one of the servants could have come in, even at the last moment, and noticed the large wagon that Koppe and his two companions had waiting in the nearby forest or when they were on the dark road at night! When the wagon with its precious cargo finally rolled through the meadowland toward Grimma, the greatest danger was over, because the convent had no horsemen who could have rushed after the fugitives on horseback and returned them by force. And in the villages they had to travel through, they had to be more afraid of encouragement than interference. Their journey led them through electoral territory, first down along the Mulde and then east to Torgau. They stayed the night there and probably even rested the entire next day, Easter Monday, because they had a long distance behind them and because the trip had not been comfortable. It had been a very bumpy ride on bad roads in their covered wagon.

Katie in Torgau and Wittenberg

Katie's stay in the city of Torgau was a strange coincidence. At one time this was the cradle of the convent from which she fled. Here she took a short rest when she entered the secular world, and one day this would be her final resting place. The Nimbschen nuns still had patronage over the city's parish church. Did Katie with her eight companions actually attend Easter Monday service in order to thank the Lord for their marvelous rescue? Perhaps her headstone in the parish church at Torgau is in the very place where she knelt then.

On Easter Tuesday, the fugitives drove on to Wittenberg. One of the Torgau clergymen, Master Gabriel Zwilling, called Didymus in Latin, is thought to have led them. The trip from Torgau to Wittenberg was not as far as the distance from Nimbschen to Torgau. It was probably still daylight when they approached Luther's city through the Elbe floodplain and over the bridge. The city was situated along the right bank of the river in front of them. In the west the stately edifice of the Electoral Castle rose proudly, behind it the Castle Church where just six years earlier Luther's hammer blows on the door had stirred an echo that resounded throughout the world and roused the silent monasteries. In front of them the Parish Church rose above low roofs in the north. Two years later, Katie, who fled as a nun, would attend church here for the first time as a married woman at Luther's side. Further to the east were the high gables of the University and Melanchthon's house situated between homes of other citizens. To the extreme east, bare and plain, was the long structure of the Black Cloister where Luther lived, and thus where Katie, as the Doctor's wife [*Frau Doktorin*], would find the greatest happiness of her life in tenderly caring for her husband and her children.

The arrival of the covered wagon with the nine nuns drew a lot of attention in Wittenberg. Later, on May 4, 1523, the young Austrian Wolfgang Schiefer, who was studying with Luther and Melanchthon at that time, sent a letter to his former teacher, Beatus Thenanus in Basel. At the end of the letter he mentions the arrival of the nuns in Wittenberg as an important bit of news. The wagon was supposedly quite full of nuns, he writes, and with a joking wordplay he adds that they were probably longing for suitors [*Freier*, liberators] as well as for liberty [*Freiheit*].

They were given their freedom again, but what would become of them from now on? Luther bore the responsibility for their escape. To him also fell the provision for their future. And he did not shrink from it either.

With the wonderful candor that was his own, he immediately admitted to the act publicly. He had suggested it; he had advised it; he had chosen the man he thought could do it. The whole world should know it; he would defend it. In addition, everyone should know the name of the brave man who had successfully accomplished the task so that the poor girls would be kept from vile gossip. It was during this time that Luther wrote an open letter to the careful and wise Leonhard Koppe at Torgau, his special friend, and also had it published on Friday of Easter week: *Reason and Answer That Young Women May Leave Convents in a Godly Way*. He calls the act a new work that nation and people will sing and talk about. And if others would say phooey to Koppe and call him a robber and a fool for letting himself get caught up with the condemned heretical monk in Wittenberg, then he, Luther, will instead call him a blessed robber. That he states this and doesn't keep it secret comes from sincere motives: First, because he does what he does in God, and does not shy away from the light; secondly, so that the honor of the young girls and their relatives is not shamed by venemous tongues that would like to allege that they let themselves be abducted by rogues, while in fact they were brought out of the convent with all decency by respectable men such as Koppe and his companions; and thirdly, that it might be an example to others.

Luther knew that many parents wanted to get their children back from the cloister, where only human work was promoted and the Word of God was never preached to them purely and plainly. "But may one break his vows?" some might ask. Others say: "One should not give offense!" Luther answers: "God does not want vows that are unchristian and harmful. Offense here, offense there! Necessity breaks all rules[2] and gives no offense." Therefore he, who had advised and prayed for the undertaking, takes the responsibility for himself and for Koppe and his companions who carried it out, and for the young women who needed to be released; but also for all who want to follow their example: "I am also certain that in this regard we want to stand blameless before God and the world. We have a judge over us, who will judge righteously."

At the conclusion of this open letter—so that everything is freely out in the open—he lists the names of the nine girls. He likewise gives their names in a letter he writes to his friend Spalatin on April 10, and he also expressly emphasizes to his friend that they were brought out by respectable citizens of Torgau so that no malicious suspicion may dare to come near them.

On April 11, Nikolaus of Amsdorf, who at that time was still professor of theology at the University of Wittenberg, also writes to Spalatin. He calls the refugees poor, miserable, and abandoned by their relatives, but in their great poverty and fear, quite patient and happy. "I pity the girls." He adds: "they have neither shoes nor clothing." So even four days after their arrival in Wittenberg the

---

[2] *Not bricht Eisen* [Necessity breaks iron].

nine nuns had to go around in their habits, and certainly not in new robes. So Amsdorf urges his friend to ask the court noblemen and the Elector if they could provide them with food and clothing.

Luther had addressed the same request to Spalatin. He certainly could not feed and clothe the fugitives from his own holdings, which at that time amounted to 9 old *Schock*, that is, 9 *Gulden*, and his Wittenbergers were tough Saxons who kept their cash firmly in their purse. But there were rich lords at the court. Spalatin was to ask for support so that the girls could be taken care of for one or two weeks. By that time he hoped to find ways and means. He would first ask the girls' relatives to take them in. If they were not willing, he would accommodate them elsewhere. Several people had already promised to take one or another into their home and even find a husband for the younger ones. And likewise Amsdorf jokingly writes to Spalatin:

> There weren't nine, but twelve nuns who left. Nine have come to us. They're beautiful, dignified, and all from the aristocracy. I do not find a fifty-year-old among them. The oldest among them, the sister of my benevolent lord and uncle, Dr. Staupitz, I have appointed for you, my dear brother, to be her husband, so that you may boast about your brother-in-law just as I boast about my uncle. If you want a younger one, however, then you are to have the choice among the most beautiful.

Luther had not yet contacted the Elector. Did he simply want to wait and see how the prince would take the news about nine nuns being abducted from a convent that was under his sovereignty? Finally on April 22, in a second letter he did ask the Elector through Spalatin for support for the poor girls: "Oh, I want to keep it secret from him and tell no one!" He did not ask in vain. Fredrick the Wise maintained the same attitude, in this matter also, that had enabled him so far to keep his hand over Luther and his work, protecting him from emperor and empire. Even if he only dared to slowly follow Luther's turbulent progress, and even if in his inmost heart he still might have doubted whether it was possible for a nun to break her vows, it was not up to him as the prince to make decisions in religious disputes. It was his princely obligation to punish only where there was violence. He did not want to intervene in questions of conscience. Some weeks later on June 9, when the abbess of Nimbschen and also the abbott Petrus of Pforte as superintendents of the Nimbschen convent submitted their complaint to Fredrick that the convent was ruined with the help of his subjects, he rejected this, answering on June 13:

> Since we do not know how this happened and who incited the girls from the convent to undertake this, and since we have never dealt with this and similar matters before, we leave it to their own responsibility.

Fredrick also held back when the example of the Nimbschen nuns had the effect Luther expected. The convent in Nimbschen lost half of its residents within two years. Three others escaped almost at the same time as the nine girls who had regained their freedom on Easter Eve 1523. Since, according to Amsdorf's account, they did not come to Wittenberg, they had probably each turned to their relatives. Again, on Pentecost, three girls were demanded from the convent by their own relatives. Others followed. Even Katie's aunt, Magdalena von Bora, left the convent. At the end of 1525 there were only twenty nuns in Nimbschen. From the convent Beutitz in the province of Weissenfels eight nuns had fled; from Wiederstedt in the Mansfeld district sixteen fled at one time.

Throughout the country, the "exodus" had begun. It even reached over into the Ducal Saxony. What use was it that George the Bearded had Heinrich Kelner, the citizen of Mittweida who had abducted a nun from the convent Sornzig, beheaded in Dresden and disgracefully had his body put on a stake above the gallows? After six noble young girls from Sornzig had already fled on April 28, 1523, thirteen more nuns, with Luther's help, escaped from the regions of the Duke on the night of September 29, 1525, and this time also Leonhard Koppe, the "convent robber" and "Father Prior" as Luther jokingly called him, seems to have had a hand in it. And the cases where we have more detailed accounts are certainly only a small part of what really happened. The infection, from which the country was to be protected, was more powerful than all prevention.

In the monasteries for monks, the exodus had already started earlier. Many of the monks and nuns who fled found lodging or a little work in their homeland or with their relatives who fed them fairly well. Many, however, came to Wittenberg. Luther was supposed to help them, and in his poverty he untiringly helped them with advice and assistance. In this regard he was not spared some very bad experiences. Among the defectors were some who had not taken to heart the word about the freedom of a Christian, but only talked about it. Luther unsuspectingly condescended also to help hypocrites and cheats. He must have experienced the most aggravating disappointments. And he learned the meaning of the proverb that says: "the fish belongs in the water, the thief on the gallows, the monk in the monastery."

The Future of the Refugees

What later happened to the nine nuns can show us how Luther provided for those in his charge. His appeals through letters were received favorably wherever their relatives lived in Electoral Saxony and could be assured the protection of their lord, but in the event that they refused, they could expect Luther's repeated and rather sharp reminder of their obligation. Of the nine girls, six were able to leave Wittenberg again after short time.

Magdalena von Staupitz was the oldest of the nine, but according to Amsdorf's account she was not yet fifty years old. She had been in the convent since 1501. She was a sister of the famous Vicar General of the Augustinian Order, Johann von Staupitz, who now lived in Salzburg as abbot of the Benedictine Cloister of Saint Peter. Another brother, Günther von Staupitz, was in Motterwitz near Leisnig. Magdalena lived with him for a while after the escape. At Luther's recommendation, in 1529 "with honor and thanks to her brother Dr. Johann Staupitz" she received from the excise officers[3] a little house in Grimma, which was situated on the

---

[3] *Visitatoren.*

Mulde, south of the old Augustinian Cloister, which had previously owned it. Here she established a girls' school, the first in Grimma. When the Electoral debt-collectors wanted to take the house back again in 1531, Luther forcefully intervened and protected her in her property. She married Tiburtius Geuder, a citizen of Grimma, and died in 1548.

Elsa von Canitz perhaps came from the branch of the family that had lived at Thallwitz (Dallwitz) near Wurzen. Yet in 1527 she was not in Thallwitz, but at Eiche, which is probably the farmstead at Eiche between Leipzig and Grimma, a much-visited place of pilgrimage in Catholic times. Since 1525 it had been the property of the electoral knight and counselor Hans von Minckwitz. On August 22, 1527 Luther writes to the "honorable and virtuous young lady Elsa von Kanitz, now at Eiche" that she is to come to Wittenberg to teach young girls. He offers her room and board in his house—he had married Katie in the meantime—and asks her not to refuse. We do not know whether she heeded his invitation. In 1537 she also had a house in Grimma.

Laneta (Lonatha) von Gohlis, of unknown descent, was close to thirty years old, so she had been in Nimbschen since she was a very young girl. She had a sister in Colditz, found refuge with her, and married a pastor in Colditz on August 24, 1523. However, a shepherd killed her husband just a few weeks later. She was married a second time in 1527 to Pastor Heinrich Kind in Leisnig.

Likewise **Ave Grosse**, raised in the convent from childhood on, came from a knightly family that lived north of Grimma at Trebsen on the left bank of the Mulde. Her brother Magnus had also taken Holy Orders and had fled from the Benedictine Cloister in Chemnitz shortly before her escape. Two other brothers, Reinhard and Christoph, had taken over their father's property at Trebsen, but soon sold it to Hans von Minckwitz. Ave Grosse was later married to Hans Marx (Marcus) in Schweinitz.

Veronika and Margarete von Zeschau. Just a little north of Trebsen to the right of the Mulde lies Obernitzschka, the property of Heinrich of Zeschau. His daughters Veronika (Luther inadvertently calls her Katharine in his letter to Spalatin; it is corrected as Veronika in his open letter to Leonhard Koppe) and

Margarete had been in the convent since 1505. Since Obernitzschka was a fiefdom of Electoral Saxony, the two sisters would have returned to their father's property. Or did they find accommodation with their uncle, the head of the infirmary, Wolfgang von Zeschau, in Grimma? Nothing more about their life is known.

Parents and siblings of the three other nuns were subjects of Duke George the Bearded, and with them Luther's appeal had no chance of success. If they did not want to provoke the anger of their lord on themselves, they had to treat their disobedient children as lost children or at least make it seem to the prince as if they did.

Sisters **Margarete and Ave von Schönfeld** were the daughters of George von Schönfeld at Löbnitz and Kleinwölkau near Delitzsch. Since the two girls could not return to their relatives, Luther had to accept on their behalf eager offers from those who were willing to help. Perhaps both the Schönfeld girls stayed in Cranach's house in Wittenberg until they got married. Luther took a certain fancy to Ave. One time he later publicly stated that, if he had wanted to get married at that time, he probably would have chosen Ave von Schönfeld, because he considered his Katie to be proud; but he wasn't sure about getting married at that time. Ave von Schönfeld soon married the young physician Basilius Axt, who had studied in Wittenberg and at that time managed Cranach's pharmacy. As a doctor of medicine, he was later physician of Duke Albrecht of Prussia, the loyal patron of Luther and his household. Ave's sister Margarete later married the Braunschweig nobleman von Garssenbüttel.

And **Katharine von Bora**? Her father was probably no longer living. The fact that he is not mentioned during these weeks is not especially noteworthy, considering the fragmentary condition of what has been passed on to us. In the contemporary accounts, there is little mention likewise of the parents and siblings of the rest of the Nimbschen nuns at the time of their escape from the convent. The fact, however, that Katie's father is not named even two years later when she married Luther, and also that there is no mention of him at all in the extensive correspondence between Luther and his co-workers and in the abundant collection of Luther's *Table Talk*, leads us to conclude, that it was highly likely that he had died at an old age shortly before Katie's escape from the convent. When Katie came to Wittenberg, probably only her stepmother Margarete and her adult brothers were left, living in poverty at Zölsdorf. Even if Frau Margarete von Bora had dared to defy her lord, Duke George, on account of her poverty alone she would not have been in the position and would hardly have been inclined to suddenly take back her stepdaughter, who, in her opinion, had been best provided for in the convent.

Katie stayed in Wittenberg.

3.

IN MASTER REICHENBACH'S HOUSE

Behind the old venerable Wittenberg City Church, the Parish Church is Bürgermeistergasse [Mayor Lane]. Here Master Philipp Reichenbach lived. A native of Zwickau, he had studied law, first in Leipzig beginning in 1506, and then in Wittenberg beginning in 1510. He had also continued as Master at the University of Wittenberg. Now he had a wife and child, and his own house on Bürgermeistergasse. In 1525 he became city clerk. Cities that could afford it liked to choose a lawyer for the office of city clerk. In 1529 he received his law degree, and in 1530 he became mayor. He administered this office, alternating with Lucas Cranach, Johann Hohndorf, Melanchthon's brother-in-law (Jerome Krapp), and lawyer Benedict Pauli. Wittenberg later had several capable men at the head of its city administration, but never again such a succession of mayors as in those decades. At the end of October 1543 Reichenbach died. The notice, in which the Rector of the University invited his colleagues and students to the funeral service on October 30, calls him a scholarly man and of great merit around the city. The notice praises him for being a lawyer who was regarded more for fair-minded moderation than for severity in pronouncing judgment, and for always trying especially hard to bring matters to an amicable conclusion in order to cure people of the tiresome obsession of bringing lawsuits. So he did not belong to the class of greedy and stingy lawyers who so roused Luther's anger that at one point he said another Luther would have to come to deal with the jurists, just as one had come to deal with the theologians.

This pious lawyer and his wife took Katie into their house. Mrs. Reichenbach and Mrs. Barbara Cranach, in whose house it seems Katie was soon active or at home, must have been proficient housewives, and Katie a diligent student. The business Katie later managed as the Doctor's wife was extensive, and she knew how to handle everything with such insight and care! Where could she have learned it other than in the Reichenbach or the Cranach house? Secluded in the convent walls since age five or six, she had certainly been instructed in everything that was considered as service to God, but foreign to her were the services that formed a woman's true vocation to carry out faithfully. Everything went according to its proper course in the large, quiet convent, except that they did not have to use their hands to touch or think or care about the minutia of daily life. None of the sisters had been instructed about love or about taking care of oneself. Their life had had only one function and goal: to follow the rules of their Order, as if praying and singing and monastic mortification of the flesh was the only way to God. Now the world lay before their eyes, and it was as if a veil had been removed when they laid aside their monastic robes. In secular clothing they were introduced to the obligations and cares of an active life, but also to its joys.

What a contrast to Nimbschen, this Wittenberg! It was really only a small city, but already at that time housed Germany's leading university. The crowd of students was almost as large as the number of the city's residents. From all over, they came rushing to Wittenberg: Germans and foreigners, boys who still had to be prepared for the university, young men who accepted the Gospel with fervent zeal and tried to spread the pure doctrine in their homeland through inspired letters, older men who already held office and prestige and who now, together with the youngest, sat at the feet of Luther and Melanchthon. A new heaven had been opened for them all. Like the sun, Luther stood in the midst of the bustling religious life, inspiring and permeating everything with his strength, the shining star of the day and of its fierce battles.

Luther's Colleagues

With a gentler glow, **Melanchthon** stood beside Luther, like the moon next to the sun, receiving his light from him, reflecting it, and illuminating the darkness of the night with his clear scholarship. Beside these two great lights of faith and knowledge, there were men like **Justus Jonas**, the provost at the Castle Church; and the honest Pomeranian **Johann Bugenhagen** who had been the pastor of the City Church for a year already; the sincere lawyer **Jerome Schurf** who had stood at Luther's side in the crucial hours of the Diet of Worms; and the Hebrew teacher **Matthaeus Aurogallus**, a German Bohemian who was actually surnamed Goldhahn. In addition there was Schurf's brother **Augustin Schurf**, a physician who taught as a professor at the university and who was also active in Luther's home as a practicing physician. The lawyer **Johann Apel** came from Bamberg in October 1523. He had been kept imprisoned for three months by the bishop of Bamberg because of his marriage to a nun; in Wittenberg he lectured on church law. Master **George Rörer**, Luther's faithful assistant, was already in Wittenberg.

But who could name all the doctors, lawyers, and teachers who taught at the university and provided lodging, moral support, and intellectual growth for the young students? Even those young people who had means also sought lodging with one of the university teachers. Master Reichenbach would have had students in his house as well, and Katie probably had to care for and interact with not only his wife and his children, but also young men, for the first time in her life.

Youthful Exuberance at the University

Youthful exuberance and crudeness is hard to restrain and certainly emerged more than once among the motley student body. Parties and commotions, duels and murderous brawls, carousing, wild outbreaks of drunkenness and gluttony and other vices were not absent in Wittenberg, just like other German universities. Which of them were pure and free from such things? Wittenberg couldn't be either. Yet here the moral and religious sincerity and zeal of the professors opposed the students' dissipations more sharply than elsewhere. A spirit that strove for what is noblest and loftiest filled the core of the student body. "By their fruits you shall know them," says the word of the Lord. Luther was not spared several disappointments in this regard, but the large number of the God-fearing theologians and capable scholars who were trained in those decades in Wittenberg allowed him to make a defense in his later years with the bold yet modest statement that his Wittenberg did not need to shrink from being compared with any other university in academics and in moral conduct.

Piety and Entertainment in Wittenberg

Wittenberg was a pious city. But a city of pretended piety it was not, nor should it have been. Where Melanchthon could participate in the round dance with the wife of his friend Provost Jonas, and where Luther himself, along with other respectable men and ladies, wanted to watch the young people dancing and enjoyed their merriment, there was no room either for zealous ascetics or for hypocritical pietists. Even from the pulpit, Luther declared that dancing and inviting guests, dressing up, eating and drinking and being merry, were not to be condemned, but it should be done with decency and without excess. Modesty and merriment indeed could and should go together. Young women shouldn't stay at home all the time like nuns in the convent, but if they walked along the streets, they should do it with manners and with refined, decent conduct fitting for young women. They should not toss their eyes back and forth, as if they wanted to count all the bricks on the roof or all the sparrows under the roof, and they also shouldn't sit around everywhere chatting.

Katie meets Nobility and Royalty

Katie, likewise, would have walked through the narrow streets of Wittenberg with eyes lowered in modesty, greeting people in a friendly house here, helping others there. The close livingquarters in the small city brought the citizens close together both physically and in spirit.

By virtue of his position, Master Reichenbach was already a friend with Cranach. Master **Lucas Cranach**, painter of the Electoral court, councilman, treasurer, and later also mayor of Wittenberg, was fifty years old at that time and at the height of his energy and fame. He was the richest citizen of the city. Besides his art studio, he also operated a pharmacy, a wineshop, and printshop in his large house at the southwest corner of the marketplace. And the extensive building offered plenty of room for the Master's family, the assistants, apprentices, and partners, and could even accommodate guests.

Cranach's highest-born guest was **King Christian II**, brother-in-law to Emperor Charles V. He had worn three crowns: Denmark, Sweden, and Norway. In November 1520 he had tried to restrain the rebellious Swedish aristocracy in the bloodbath at Stockholm, but in the spring of 1523 he had been exiled from his kingdoms. In order to regain his throne, he turned for assistance to the German princes who were related to him, and in the autumn of that year he came to Electoral Saxony because Fredrick the Wise was also related to him by marriage. On October 10 he rode to Wittenberg with two others. He stayed there a few days as Cranach's guest, and here in Luther's city he humbled himself so deeply that he voluntarily carried out services for Deacon Sebastian Fröschel in the Parish Church. What a strange city it was, anyway, that little Wittenberg, where threadbare monks became earth-shattering reformers, idle nuns became proficient housewives, and kings dripping with blood became devout deacons!

Where Katie was introduced to King Christian is not indicated for us, but it was probably in Cranach's house. Cranach and his wife had possibly even taken Katie from Master Reichenbach's house into their own large household. The fact that two years later the Cranachs were present as the only witnesses among the citizens at Luther and Katie's wedding indeed points to the fact that Katie had almost become like their own child. Active in Cranach's house, she had probably waited on Christian II. The king honored her with a gold ring sometime between October 10 and 16, 1523. In those days, princes used rings, medallions, tankards, and commemorative chains the way we might use medals, oil paintings, photographs, and brooches today as honorific gifts.

A second household where Katie became closely acquainted before she married Luther was that of **Philipp Melanchthon**. Five years earlier, Master Philipp was brought to Wittenberg as teacher of Greek. There was general surprise at his appearance, so tender in age and almost weak with disease. But right away, with his inaugural speech, he had been able to turn such feelings into unanimous admiration for his intellectual gifts. Born on February 16, 1497 in the small town of Bretten in Electoral Palatinate, he was last among the Wittenberg professors in terms of age, but by the depth of his erudition, and the richness and clarity of his thoughts, he was second only to Luther. Since 1520 he had been married to Katharine Krapp, daughter of the deceased mayor Hans Krapp. He also boarded young students. In his house he had created his own Latin school, and with the boys and young men he held performances of Latin dramas.

The most talented among his students, **Joachim Camerarius**, a descendant of the old Bamberg family of chamberlains, became his closest friend. Trained at the Universities of Leipzig and Erfurt, Camerarius had studied yet another year in Wittenberg since the autumn of 1521 and had even lectured already at the same time, and through repeated visits and a lively exchange of letters, he stayed in very close contact with those in Wittenberg. (We will meet him several times later in Luther and Katie's house.) During his first stay in Wittenberg he had stayed with Melanchthon, and through daily contact and the liveliest exchange of ideas a bond of friendship had been formed between the two young scholars— Melanchthon was twenty-five, Camerarius twenty-two years old— which defied any change and all the storms of time. Hardly anywhere is there a friendship that was as close and as longlasting. An enduring memorial of this bond is the exchange of letters, in which Melanchthon reveals his most secret thoughts to his friend.

The third person in this bond of friendship was the young patrician **Jerome Baumgärtner** from Nürnberg, born March 9, 1498. After he had studied in Wittenberg from 1518–21, he came back to Wittenberg to visit Melanchthon in the spring of 1523, a short time after Katie had escaped from the convent. Katie and Baumgärtner got to know each other and fell in love in Melanchthon's or in Reichenbach's house.

Not only had King Christian honored Katie, but she was also highly regarded in Baumgärtner's circle of young people with whom he interacted during his visit in Wittenberg. They called her Catherine of Siena. Saint Catherine, whose house can still be seen in Siena today, had consecrated herself as a child to the service of the Lord. Was it this that led the young students to call Katie Catherine of Siena, or were there other similarities in her life and in that of the saint? In any case, this nickname of hers is testimony of her modest behavior in Wittenberg and her piety. And Luther also testifies of Baumgärtner that already in recent years he combined godliness and erudition.

Katie was twenty-four years old when she won Baumgärtner's affections. We would like to have a good picture of her from this time. Was she beautiful? Or even if her face showed no regular beauty, was she graceful perhaps? Did she have a certain charm that fascinated the young patrician of Nürnberg? We cannot give a definite answer to these questions that force themselves upon us. Of course, we have several portraits of Katie from just a little time later, from the years 1525 and 1526, but they are all from the hand of Cranach and his pupils.

Lucas Cranach's Portraits of Luther and Katie

Master Lucas was the leading artist of Saxony at that time. He painted a lot, and he painted a lot of excellent work, even several good portraits. However, one thing he could almost never depict: characteristics of the spirit and the life of the soul, as it is reflected in the eyes. Under most portraits from his hand one could write the words that Albrecht Dürer all too modestly put under his portrait of Melanchthon: "The painter has shown the facial features faithfully, but he could not paint the spirit."

Photo courtesy of Concordia Historical Institute

Painting the spirit and the soul—only rarely did Cranach accomplish that. We sense this deficiency in his art most acutely in his portraits of Luther. We have several contemporary statements, from friends and foes, about what that powerful man looked like, and particularly about the look of his eyes. In 1518, the papal cardinal legate Cajetan, who had negotiated with Luther for days in Augsburg, spoke of the deep eyes of this beast—the one word *bestia* in the mouth of an Italian already proves that this statement has been faithfully passed on to us—and the papal nuncio Vergerio, who was with Luther in Wittenberg in 1535, believed he saw in the glint of his eyes a fire of rage and fury, yes, the very manifestation of the devil, who in his opinion had to be in this monster.

The adversaries certainly did not see the divine and the heroic in Luther's shining eyes, or they did not want to see it. To them the man who dared to take away the pope's triple tiara and free his German nation from Roman paternalism was a sinister personality, possessed by the devil himself. But even a man of the world such as Cajetan, and a diplomat such as Vergerio, could not avoid the impression of Luther's powerful appearance.

And the friends, who were around Luther and were beside him every day, describe for us what was lion-like in his appearance. His eyes were brown, says Melanchthon, with a yellowish ring around the brown, and in his stare blazed the ferociousness of a lion, and the young Kessler, who was with Luther in 1522, even calls his eyes black, but dazzling like a star one cannot look into. And even from later times we still hear that Luther's stare forced the eyes of others down. That is the same thing that is told to us about other great men of history.

How a Dürer or even a Holbein would have shown us Luther's eyes! And what has become of it under Cranach's hand? His best portraits of Luther show us a genuinely German face, and in the forehead, mouth, and chin there is something of the uncompromising will and the irresistible energy with which this fearless religious hero rallied as one individual against a world of enemies. But the eyes, which in Cranach's style are slit and set somewhat askew, look so clear and calm, as if this man could not make a ripple in a pond. We see before us the conscientious husband and father, the faithful curate of souls, even the man who was often tough to the point of being obstinate. But in Cranach's portraits we search in vain for the powerful Reformer who blazed a new trail for faith and knowledge, the Luther who is still with us today in spirit.

And likewise Cranach's portraits of Katie, on the whole, show us the outward forms correctly, including the shape of the eyes, but they give us little of the life in her soul. While with Luther's portraits we can compare the painter's skill against contemporary accounts, with Katie's portraits we don't have this benchmark. One of her contemporaries tells us that Katie was one of the most beautiful of the nuns who fled from Nimbschen. However, comparing this opinion against Cranach's portraits of Katie, one can confidently state: If Luther is condemned for saying that he was fascinated by Katie's beauty, then this condemnation (if being responsive to female beauty can seem to us like a condemnation at all!) is disproved by Cranach's portraits.

Katie was not beautiful, that's what all her pictures show. We do not see before us a regular, classically sculpted face, or even a spicy or beguiling little expression. The dark-blond hair is simply pushed back from the forehead and temples. The outline of the face is somewhat angular. The eyes look clear and deliberate. Only the lips are beautiful—full, sharply curved lips that could not refrain from letting out rapidfire speech, but probably could also form a firm and severe scowl.

Erasmus' Comments about Katie

But even in the kind of German faces that aren't beautiful at first glance, there is often a particular beauty that transforms the face like sunshine when the person is talking, and makes a closer bond than outward charm does, when we get to know the person better. And concerning Katie we have a statement from at least one of her most important contemporaries that seems to point directly to that.

Erasmus of Rotterdam, the Master of Humanism, in a letter from the year 1525, calls her *puellam mire venustam* [an especially charming girl]. (Here, this one time, we must keep the Latin expression.) He doesn't call her *pulchram* [beautiful] or *formosam* [comely] or *speciosam* [handsome], which would describe her physical beauty, but *venustam* [charming]. Our mythology derives the name of the Roman goddess Venus from a word stem that means "dear" [*lieb*] or "lovely" [*lieblich*]. And likewise the adjective formed from Venus, *venustus*, is to be translated as "lovely" [*lieblich*] or "charming" [*hold*]. So, according to Erasmus, Katie was an especially charming girl [*Mägdlein wunderhold*]. Erasmus showed himself to be amenable to every piece of gossip about Katie. Yet, when he later learned the truth, he honorably retracted a wicked rumor about her that he had naively circulated further. And he would have been quite well informed through his Wittenberg friends. Would he really have written the words *puellam mire venustam* unintentionally or without thinking?

Katie's First Love: Jerome Baumgärtner

At any rate, the affection Katie had for Jerome Baumgärtner, the young man from Nürnberg, was not one-sided. He reciprocated. And it became known that the two loved each other. Baumgärtner's friends knew about it; Luther agreed with it. Not until age twenty-four, however, would Katie learn the painful experience that other girls outgrew at a much younger age: first love is usually not the right love. After a short stay in Wittenberg, Baumgärtner already went back to Nürnberg in June 1523, by way of Leipzig and Bamberg, where Camerarius was staying.

He had promised to come back soon. But month after month passed without his return. Katie worried and grieved bitterly and became ill about it before she got over her pain. It had not yet come, however, to an actual engagement. An engagement wasn't as easy to break off in those days as it is now. But when he left, Katie had been allowed to hope that he would keep his allegiance to her. There must have been some insurmountable obstacle that forced him to break it off, because in his whole later life he always showed himself to be loyal and genuine, as councilman of the free imperial city of Nürnberg, in his care for church and school and in all matters of state. This protects him from the suspicion that some might say about him: "Out of sight, out of mind!"

Apparently, his family's resistance was the obstacle that rose up like an immovable wall between him and Katie. To the proud patrician family it seemed unthinkable that one of their own wanted to marry a runaway nun. Even if she might have been of noble blood, and even if the young Baumgärtner might have ignored the barriers that separated him from Katie in Wittenberg under the influence of the Protestant spirit that lived and thrived there, in Nürnberg he would have to acknowledge them and yield to them.

His birth, his family's position, and the work of his forebears decisively showed that he was to work in the service of the city, which was one of the foremost in the Empire at that time, with its wealthy citizens and the region subordinate to it. Marrying an apostate nun would have been the worst advice he could have taken in his life. Religious and secular law had forbidden marriage to a nun under penalty of death. Now, of course, for those who held to the Reformation, the old religious law, with which the popes had bolstered their authority, was revoked, and a Protestant clergyman could with pure conscience marry a nun. But imperial law remained, and it would have been impossible for a statesman to disregard its regulations.

We do not know whether Baumgärtner wrote to Katie herself or to Luther, perhaps even to Melanchthon, during his struggle between the affection that enthralled him and the duties to which he was to dedicate his life. But Luther writes to Baumgärtner on October 12, 1524: "By the way, if you want to hold on to your Katie von Bora, then hurry before she is given to someone else, which is already imminent. She has not yet gotten over her love for you. I would surely be delighted at your union. Live well!" But Baumgärtner stayed away from Wittenberg during these years. On January 23, 1526 he married Sibylle Dichtel, the fifteen-year-old daughter of the Bavarian high bailiff, Bernhard Dichtel from Tutzing, seven months after Katie had moved into the Black Cloister in Wittenberg as Luther's wife.

The friendship for Baumgärtner, which Luther and Katie retained their whole life and stood the test in times of trouble, shows us that Katie soon completely got over the pain of being separated from the man she loved. She did not bear a grudge against him afterwards. Her husband later could jokingly remind her of her first love, without needing to be afraid of hitting a sour note with her. When he sent a humorous letter to Baumgärtner from the Castle Coburg on October 1, 1530, shortly before his return to Wittenberg, he also added to his letter greetings from his Lady, his Katie, for whom Baumgärtner had once glowed, and he promised to tell her about it when he returned home, because occasionally he tended to tease her with Baumgärtner's name. Katie would be devoted to him now with a new love—so he assures the Nürnberger councilman on October 3, 1541—because of his outstanding virtues and would have a kind heart toward him.

One time in the summer of 1543, to his lodgers Luther lauded Baumgärtner's integrity, his piety, his ability, and the fact that he worked with great respect and with great success for the well-being of the commonwealth. When Katie, who had not followed the discussions from the outset, asked whom they were actually taking about, her husband answered her with a verse from Vergil, half in Latin, half in German: "Your flame, Amyntas, your old paramour!"[1] And in 1544 when Baumgärtner was caught in a feud by the Knight von Rosenberg and held in harsh imprisonment for over a year, Luther sent his friend's worried wife a heartfelt letter of comfort and was busy praying and interceding for his release.

,At the time of Luther's correspondence with Baumgärtner in October 1524, Baumgärtner was not the only suitor for Katie's hand. Of course, Luther was not yet thinking about himself; at that time he was still undecided about getting married. It was a doctor of theology who was courting Katie, Doctor Caspar Glatz, called Glacius in Latin. In the summer of 1524 he had been Rector of the University of Wittenberg and on Luther's behalf had gone to Orlamünde where Carlstadt's lectures had confused and stirred up the people. On August 27 he had even assumed the pastorate at Orlamünde. He certainly did not fulfill the hopes Luther had for him, and he had later to be relieved of his pastorate. At that time [1524], however, he was still held in esteem and honor, and Luther supported his courtship with Katie. Meanwhile, Katie could not

---

[1] The Eclogues by Virgil, written 37 BC, Eclogue X.

agree to extend her hand to him in marriage. Her refusal was not based on pride of aristocracy; the high rank of a doctor of theology was at least equal to the aristocracy of a poor young woman of the landed gentry. Rather the reason seems to be the character of this man, whom one of his colleagues called an old miser, and who later showed himself to be unreliable in confidential matters.

The resolution of this conflict came, as is reported, through Nikolaus von Amsdorf. Shortly before he left Wittenberg in September 1524 to assume the pastorate at St. Ulrich's Church in Magdeburg, Katie in her self-confident and determined manner went to Amsdorf, which she could do as a close friend of Luther's. She asked him to arrange with Luther not to have her marry Glatz against her will. She was free and open in explaining that if he or Luther would like to marry her, she would not refuse. Doctor Glatz, however, she could not have.

Was it this outcry in her distress that moved Luther? Did his love arise out of sympathy for the poor, but honest, girl? As we already heard from his own words, he did not love Katie at first; he considered her proud. He would rather have chosen her young companion Ave von Schönfeld, if he had wanted to go courting at that time. The change in his feelings toward Katie seems to coincide, however, with the Amsdorf's interceding for Katie. Out of indifference came compassion; and out of compassion, love. The words he later spoke among his lodgers about Ave von Schönfeld really point to the fact that his inclination toward Katie grew out of his compassion for her. "It was God's will," he says, "that I pitied the one who had been abandoned. And for me—God be praised!— it had the happiest ending, because I have a pious, faithful wife." And he directed his lodgers to the beautiful passage in Solomon's Proverbs, where it says in chapter 31: "Who can find a virtuous wife? For her worth is far above rubies. The heart of her husband safely trusts her; So he will have no lack of gain. She does him good and not evil All the days of her life."[2]

---

[2] Proverbs 31:10–12 (NKJV).

4.

KATIE ENTERS THE BLACK CLOISTER

It was not a very easy decision for Luther to get married, and according to his letters it was also not an act of passion, but the result of careful consideration and severe struggles in his soul. Only gradually was he able to release himself from the old church statutes that had controlled him even into adulthood. While he was still at the Wartburg, it had seemed amazing to him that the people of Wittenberg were putting his teachings into action so that monks were leaving their monasteries, breaking their vows, and getting married. In the long run he certainly could not disapprove of it.

More than four centuries earlier, Pope Gregory VII had obligated even secular priests to celibacy. It was one of the worst instruments of power by which the church had tried to shore up its control. Already in the summer of 1520, in his powerful writing *To the Christian Nobility of the German Nation*, Luther had even attacked celibacy and contrasted the papal prohibition with the command of the Apostle Paul: "A bishop then must be blameless, the husband of one wife, temperate, sober-minded, of good behavior, hospitable, able to teach."[1] He had reclaimed the right of pastors to marry. And yet, during his stay at the Wartburg, he had struggled to come to the conviction that monastic vows are unchristian and therefore not binding.

Then in Wittenberg, in clearer and clearer words, he praised the happiness and the blessing of the married state and the fact that

---

[1] 1 Timothy 3:2 (NKJV).

God instituted marriage for all people. With growing urgency he warned of the dangers of forced celibacy. He himself urged his friends and co-workers to get married, including Spalatin and the head of the Order of St. Anthony in Lichtenberg, Wolfgang Reissenbusch. When Duke Albrecht of Prussia, the Grand Master of the German Order of Knights, wanted to convert his religious dominion into a secular duchy, Luther gladly gave his endorsement, and in a personal meeting in Wittenberg on November 29, 1523 advised the prince himself to get maried. And in a letter on June 2, 1525 he encouraged another Hohenzollern, Archbishop Albrecht of Mainz, to follow the example of his cousin, the Grand Master, and the next day, on Pentecost Eve, he sent a copy of this letter to his friend and brother-in-law, the Mansfeld councilman Dr. Johann Rühel, and authorized him to have it printed and to tell the archbishop on his behalf:

> If my getting married might be a reinforcement for His Electoral Grace, I would gladly be ready to follow soon as an example to His Electoral Grace, since I am still of a mind anyway, before I leave this life, to find myself in the married state, which I regard as required by God; and even if it should be nothing more than an engagement-like 'Joseph's marriage.'

Ten days later he brought his Katie home. So he had considered it a necessity, indeed his obligation, to affirm his teaching by his example. He had not allowed himself to be frightened into this conviction, either by the encouragements of eager followers or by the warnings of nervous friends.

Luther Decides to Get Married

There was no lack of voices advising him against it. Many of those who otherwise were heartily devoted to the new teaching nevertheless took offense at allowing someone to revoke vows of chastity made to God, the notion that a monk could enter into a genuine, true marriage-bond with a nun. Doctor Schurf, the lawyer, who really thought that the old canon law directly supported the

Gospel, harbored the most serious doubts, and he even expressed his fears openly, so that Luther had to have heard them. He is supposed to have said: "So if a monk gets married, then the whole world and the devil himself will laugh, and he will have destroyed all his work himself." While Schurf was still biased toward the old church statutes, other apprehensive friends asked themselves what the world would say about it. They feared the scorn and mockery of the opponents and were afraid of the offense that could develop from it among friends and enemies. Even Melanchthon was among these worried minds.

Far more numerous, however, were the voices that advised Luther to marry. And in the autumn of 1524 a rumor that he intended to marry had already spread as far as the Upper Palatinate to Lady Argula von Grumbach, the faithful confessor of the Gospel, a good writer, who in her letters calls herself by her maiden name, Argula von Stauff or the Staufferin. She was married to Friedrich von Grumbach, an administrator of ducal Bavaria, in Dietfurt, but her husband had remained loyal to the old church. Now when she heard the rumor that Luther intended to get married, she asked Luther through Spalatin by letter what the situation really was. On November 30, 1524 Luther replied to her that he had not yet decided to get married, that even he was not made of wood or stone, but of flesh and blood, and God could change his heart at any moment, but as it was now, he was still reluctant to get married, because he had to be ready to die. It comes out in other accounts as well, that he had thoughts about dying at that time. The flames of the papistic pyre were already gathered for the evangelical martyrs. Luther wished to seal his teaching with his blood. And even on his deathbed he might marry a pious girl and give her two silver tankards as a dowry and "morning gift"—he often received such honorific tankards from high lords, and just as often passed them on to the needy.

While he left the decision to God, good friends were eagerly and actively looking for the right girl for him to marry. He jokes about it himself, and about the mishaps that caused all these well-intentioned plans to fail. On April 16, 1525, he writes to Spalatin that he had three women at the same time and loved them so well that he had already lost two of them, who were now getting engaged to other men; the third he could hardly keep on his left arm, and perhaps she too would soon be torn away from him. We have already gotten to know Ave von Schönfeld. Somewhat later we hear Luther also speak of a young Ave Alemann from Magdeburg. Amsdorf would have been the one who recommended her to him when he came from Magdeburg to Wittenberg in March 1525 to assist him in his tribulations. Perhaps other girls were also suggested, without him taking them seriously. Nobody thought of Katie. That he should court a poverty-stricken runaway nun was not part of his friends' design. They would rather have seen him with a girl from a respectable, wealthy family. And when he chose Katie, all his best friends clamored: "Not this one, but someone else!"

In these springtime weeks that seemed to have been crucial for his getting closer to Katie, he was summoned to his homeland by political unrest. In southern Germany the peasants had already prepared for the great revolt, and also in Thuringia peasant leaders, such as Thomas Müntzer and Heinrich Pfeifer, had laid the groundwork. Luther arrived too late. What could words do now, where callous fists, scythes, and flails had already been wielded as weapons? Luther could no longer feel safe from violent attacks. During these weeks of the bitterest disappointments and the most severe dangers of life and limb, he was with his parents in Mansfeld in the days between April 18 and May 4.

Luther Chooses Katie

For old Hans Luther it was no different than if he had buried a son when the message came that his Martinus had entered the monastery. "My son," he had said when he first saw him again, "don't you know that you are supposed to honor your father?" And when the young monk objected that a heavenly call had led him to the monastery, the old man answered dryly: "What if it was only a ghost that was with you!" What a joy it must have been for him to hear then that his son had left the monastery. With what pride as well, with what concern in quiet Mansfeld he would have followed the earth-shattering path of Doctor Martinus from Wittenberg to

Worms, and to the Wartburg and back to Wittenberg! His son's teachings had grown in his heart. When he was later asked on his deathbed by Pastor Michael Cölius whether he also believed in it, his last words were: It would have to be a very sad person, who would not believe it.

A hard, tough man from lower Saxony, Hans Luther had gotten ahead by a life full of work. And now he was completely content to have a benevolent God for the world to come, and for this world a faithful, industrious wife, and pious, obedient children. He wished the same happiness for his son, and, as we hear from Luther, this desire of his father, yes, his express demand that he should marry, had a crucial influence on his decision. A few days after his visit with his parents, in a letter to Doctor Rühel on May 4, he called Katie *his* Katie for the first time and declared his sincere intent to marry her, to spite the devil, before he died.

The next weeks, however, were not suitable for carrying out marriage plans. They were filled rather with the storm of the Thuringian peasant revolt. But already on May 5 the princes, who nevertheless bore the chief blame for the rebellion by their harsh oppression and abuse of the rural people, were able to squelch them in the massacre of the battle at Frankenhausen, and even afterwards through cruel punishments. In those crucial days also came the death of Fredrick the Wise, who was succeeded as Elector by his brother John the Steadfast.

It had fallen over Germany like a frost in springtime, and although the seed, which Luther had sown already, stood strong enough to withstand the tempest, nevertheless he was afraid of having to start all over. He probably would have waited to marry even longer in this troubled time, when vile gossip induced him to move quickly. Ugly rumors were spread about him and Katie. They were blatant lies, as Melanchthon also attested, but lies can swell like an avalanche. To stop all the slander, Luther married Katharine von Bora on June 13, a surprise to even his closest friends, but carefully observing the usual customs of the land.

Wedding and Wedding Guests

At his invitation a small circle of friends assembled in the Black Cloister in the evening hours of June 13, 1525, a Tuesday: **Justus Jonas**, the Castle provost; and **Johann Bugenhagen**, the parish pastor of the City Church; the lawyer **Johann Apel**; Master **Lucas Cranach** and his wife **Barbara**. Luther had invited no one else. And those present he had selected deliberately. The affectionate concern of his friends was embodied in Jonas, his faithful comrade from the time of the Diet at Worms. With tears in his eyes he observed the married couple on the bridal bed according to old German custom. With wishes that they prosper and be blessed, he prayed for their welfare. In Bugenhagen, the highest clergyman of the city, the evangelical church gave its blessing to the new marriage bond. Although a layman according to the custom of the time could also have validly carried out the marriage, nevertheless it was understood that for Luther, a servant of God would speak the binding words. The University selected Doctor Apel to be the witness of Luther's marriage. Doctor Apel was a teacher of canon law and was also married to a former nun. And Cranach, the councilman and treasurer, represented the city and its citizens. Cranach and his wife probably also acted as Katie's substitute parents and brought her to the Black Cloister, because the wedding and the solemn consummation took place in the Black Cloister.

A later account puts Luther's marriage to Katie in Reichenbach's house and tells in some detail that Katie was surprised by Luther's courtship and at first didn't know if it was sincere. But this account, though it seems true to life, cannot possibly be correct. Luther must have been certain about Katie's love and her consent for a long time. How else could he have called her "his Katie" already on May 4? And likewise the statement that says the marriage took place in Reichenbach's house must be wrong, for Reichenbach's name is mentioned neither by Jonas in his short letter to Spalatin on June 14, nor by Melanchthon in his lengthy letter to Camerarius on June 16. On the contrary, Melanchthon writes: "That evening Luther invited Bugenhagen and Cranach and Apel to the meal, only them, and carried out the solemn traditions as are customary during a marriage ceremony." Thus Luther, not Reichenbach, invited the friends, and as Jonas testifies, Reichenbach was not even present; however, if the wedding had been held in his house, then as head of the house he certainly would have been there.

So on June 13, Katie entered the Black Cloister as Luther's wife. Here, the next morning, she also prepared the small breakfast with which her husband wanted to regale their friends who had served as witnesses at the wedding the evening before. The Wittenberg council provided the young couple with wine for this meal, probably at Cranach's suggestion: a gallon of sweet Madeira wine, a gallon of Rhine wine, and one-and-a-half gallons of Franconian wine. A gallon contained four quarts (liters), and at that time in the Wittenberg *Ratskeller* a quart of sweet Madeira wine cost 5 *Groschen*, a quart of Rhine wine 18 *Pfennig*, and a quart of Franconian wine 14 *Pfennig*.

News of Luther's Marriage, a Wedding Feast, and Wedding Gifts

There would not have been time to arrange a larger wedding feast as well. Luther also wanted to have his parents and siblings and the dearest of his friends from out of town around him at his wedding meal, when they set up their household,[2] as one said at that time. So now he wrote letter after letter announcing his marriage and inviting all who were closest to him to his house in Wittenberg on June 27. This was also a Tuesday, and Tuesday, according to popular belief, was a lucky day for getting married.

But his friends' letters with the news of his marriage flew through the country even more quickly than his own invitations. With sincerity and dignity, Jonas writes to Spalatin, through whom the Electoral court in Torgau received the first news of the great event. Elector John sent 100 *Gulden* for setting up the household and for the first furnishings. Melanchthon, on the other hand, seems to have been completely out of sorts and in a bad mood for some

---

[2] *Wirtschaft.*

days, probably due in part to the disappointment over the fact that Luther had not said a word to him beforehand and had not even invited him on June 13. But the very letter Melanchthon cautiously wrote to Camerarius on June 16 in Greek (very few at that time understood Greek!) clearly shows that Luther was right in keeping this loyal, but somewhat apprehensive friend, from such a commotion as participating in his wedding would have been. This letter is a remarkable testimony as to how little even Melanchthon was able to get inside Luther's heart and spirit and realize the motives for his actions. What he writes about Katie and her companions and about Luther's character, as well as the holy estate of matrimony, about how untimely this marriage was and the dangers it caused, certainly is not false, but nevertheless it arose from a peculiar misjudgment of Luther's real intentions and was obviously dominated by fear of the world's gossip. Yet Melanchthon in his typical uneasiness really believed that he saw in Luther signs of despondency and internal confusion!

Nothing about this is to be found in Luther's letters from this same time. Of course, the opponents mocked and scoffed and threw dirt at him and Katie for many more years, but from the outset he had expected nothing different. He did not even shy away from the supercilious frowns or the awkward shrugs of the wise people, the wiseacres who should know better, nor the sorrow of the faint-hearted and disheartened. In his deepest humiliation, as Doctor Schurf said, the devil should not laugh at him, but he hoped that the angels would laugh and the devils all weep.

The first words he wrote after his marriage are words of defiance. "Now lords, parsons, farmers, everyone is against me," he writes on June 15 to the Mansfeld councilmen Rühel, Johann Thür, and Caspar Müller. "Well then! Because they are crazy and foolish, I will make them even more crazy and more foolish, and all this as a final goodbye and farewell." He asked his three friends to come to his wedding dinner with his dear father and mother if they were not afraid of travelling at such a dangerous time. And whatever good friends they wanted to bring along would be welcome. On June 16 he also invited Spalatin and instructed him to bring venison with him, likewise on June 21 with Marshal Johann von Doltzig.

On June 17 he writes to the honorable Father Prior Leonhard Koppe and his wife, his Audi (Agathe?), and asks him to take part in the wedding. And on June 21 he writes to him again: "My Lord Catherine leaves it up to you"—here he gives his energetic Katie this nickname for the first time—"that my father and mother and all good friends might be the merrier, and I kindly request that you send here at my expense a barrel of the best Torgau beer for us to have a good drink." But the beer had better taste good, or else as punishment Koppe would have to drink the whole barrel himself. Luther again asks him not to stay away with his Audi, and also to bring along Master Zwilling, if it wouldn't cost him anything.

Link in the Altenburg Castle and Amsdorf in Magdeburg are likewise asked to come. Luther also adds, in Katie's name, that Link does not need to bring along a tankard or other wedding gift. He was obviously worried, as even Melanchthon writes to Link, that his dear friends, who, with exception of Amsdorf, were just as poor as he, might overextend themselves to honor him. Melanchthon meanwhile had recovered from his first astonishment; he likewise urgently asks their mutual friend Link to come to the wedding so that Doctor Schurf might receive even further material for debating.

The happiest and most highly honored wedding guests were Luther's parents, Hans and Margarete, both small of stature and thin, bronzed by the sun, weathered by a long life of hard work, but with good, stalwart eyes; simple, decent, pious folk, as they come to us in descriptions from that time and in Cranach's two excellent paintings at the Wartburg. Martin Luther and his siblings grew taller and stronger than their parents.

The wedding meal is also called breakfast (*Frühmahl, prandium*) in Luther's letters from that same time. According to the custom of the time it began at ten o'clock. Before this, the couple was publicly consecrated in the parish church, as Luther's biographer Mathesius testifies: Luther had himself joined in marriage with Katie von Bora in the name and at the word of Jesus Christ in the presence of good people (that had been on June 13, not on June 11, as Mathesius erroneously indicates); soon thereafter (so, on June 27) he also held a public church service and public wedding with her.

For the feast, the Wittenberg council sent an honorific gift of 20 *Gulden* in cash and a barrel of Einbeck beer. At that time Einbeck and Torgau vied for fame in brewing the best beer. Since the records of the finance department indicate 2 *Schock,* 16 *Groschen,* and 6 *Pfennig* for this, which is more than 6 *Gulden,* it must have been a magnificent barrel. At that time the thirty-year-old Johann Pfister of Nürnberg, a former monk, assumed the office of cupbearer.[3] On Easter 1525 he had left the Augustinian Monastery in his hometown, and he had been studying theology in Wittenberg since Pentecost. Later he became pastor at Fürth, and even in 1557, when he wrote down a short sketch of his life, he remembered his busy activity as cupbearer at Luther's wedding.

Perhaps the most precious of the wedding gifts is kept in the University at Greifswald, a large silver engraved tankard, which the University of Wittenberg is supposed to have brought. This magnificent piece of Augsburg workmanship, almost a half-meter tall at the knob of the cover, refined from eighty-four lot of fine silver[4] and lavishly gilded inside and out, bears on the edge of the baseplate the inscription:

> The praiseworthy University of the Electoral City of Wittenberg honors Herr Doctor Martin Luther and his Lady Kethe von Bore with this wedding gift. In the year 1525. Tuesday after the festival of John the Baptist.

Despite the soft *b,* as we Saxons say, in *Babtistae,* the inscription could be genuine, if only it were not so lengthy at the beginning and didn't contain the word "praiseworthy"! Would the University of Wittenberg really call itself "the praiseworthy University of the Electoral City of Wittenberg" in the year 1525? That sounds more like the second half of the seventeenth century than the first quarter of the sixteenth century. Also it is striking that

---

[3] Cupbearer was often an honorary position in the Holy Roman Empire.

[4] Perhaps 2.5–3 pounds of silver.

the inscription is in German in a gift from the University, and in addition the piece itself is too expensive for us to see it as the wedding gift from Luther's colleagues. As we know, the tankard with which the Wittenberg professors honored Luther cost 21 *Gulden* at that time; in the Greifswald tankard, however, the silver alone is worth twice that much, not to mention the gold plating and the luxurious workmanship. So this tankard could not have been the wedding gift from the University of Wittenberg, and the inscription is a forgery. The tankard that Luther and Katie received at their wedding was a more modest piece, at any rate.

In the museum at Braunschweig, where one can see Luther's gold Doctor's ring, Luther's wedding ring is kept as well, a golden double ring with a tall little box. A diamond is inlaid in the upper surface, the symbol of steadfast faithfulness; as well as a ruby, the symbol of pure love. The little box can be moved aside just like the double ring, and then inside, under the diamond, one sees the letters MLD (Martin Luther, Doctor) and under the ruby the letters CVB (Catharina von Bora). On the inside of the two rings are the words:

WHAT•GOD•HAS•JOINED•TOGETHER—
NO•ONE•SHOULD•SEPARATE.

Since this ring and Luther's Doctor's ring had earlier belonged to the house of the Saxon prince, there is no reason to doubt their authenticity. Katie's wedding ring is also genuine, kept in the city-historical museum in Leipzig. It displays a ruby in the center, and on both sides the crucified Christ and the instruments of the Passion. Inside the ring are the words: "D. Martinus Lutherus, Catharina u. Boren" and underneath: "13 June 1525." The story goes that the scholarly patrician Willibald Pirckheimer of Nürnberg had Albrecht Dürer make both wedding rings at the same time as a golden medallion, in order to honor Luther. This account is not credible, at least in regards to Dürer. At the height of his artistic work, Dürer never worked as a goldsmith, and concerning medallions he once said that he did not tend to deal with such things.

Further relics from Luther and Katie's silver treasure and furniture are kept in Wittenberg, Berlin, Leipzig, Dresden,

Nürnberg, and other cities. With some pieces the authenticity is very doubtful; the embroideries, which are shown here and there as Katie's handwork, probably do not all come from her. In the desire to have a keepsake from Luther and his house, people did not refrain from forgeries, even in the seventeenth century. Two more pieces in Leipzig are undoubtedly genuine: a large silver tankard in the council treasury, with an inscription of the Swedish King Gustav Wasa from the year 1536; and from Katie's estate, a silver spoon in the collections of the German Society with the inscription *da gloriam deo* (give glory to God), the interlaced letters DML [Dr. Martin Luther], and the year, 1540.

A Beginning in Poverty

Luther and Katie, however, could not think about collecting a small silver treasury so soon. In the first years of their marriage they were poor, because he had nothing, and she brought him nothing. But his frugality and trust in God, her dauntless courage and industrious hands, helped them out of every need. Their happiness was not seriously clouded by petty concerns. We have no statements from Katie, but her husband gratefully boasted the happiness he found with her already in the first years of his marriage. "I have not fallen passionately in love," he writes to Amsdorf on June 21, 1525, "but I love and esteem my wife." And in a letter from August 11, 1526 he describes his Katie as willing and obedient in everything, more suitable for him than he would ever have dared to hope, and he thanks God for this and adds that now he wouldn't want to trade his poverty for the treasures of a Croesus.[5]

Gossip and Insults

Rather than the hard-pressed conditions in which they had to live at first, it was attacks from opponents that might have disturbed their quiet happiness. Katie was certainly not safe from malicious tongues even in Wittenberg. Already in 1525, Councilman Lorenz

---

[5] Croesus: last king of Lydia in western Asia Minor (reigned c. 560–546), renowned for his great wealth.

Jessner's wife, Klara née Eberhard, had to be summoned to court because she spoke idle words, insulted, and told off Luther and Katie at a wedding and flew off the handle at Bugenhagen's wife. She was fined 2 *Schock Groschen* for this. But neither the Wittenberg Council nor the Elector could offer protection against the hateful gossip of outsiders.

There was an old legend that the Antichrist Paul speaks of in Second Thessalonians would come from the union of a monk and a nun. Now Luther had brought his Katie home, and for the first time the church, even though it was only the evangelical church, had consecrated the marriage of a former monk and of a former nun. Would the Antichrist be born from this marriage? Erasmus, the incurable scoffer, thought that if the fable were true, then the world would have been full of Antichrists a long time ago. Even Luther's old opponent, Archbishop Albrecht of Mainz, didn't seem alarmed about his marriage. He even sent him a wedding gift of 20 gold *Gulden* through Rühel. Luther declined the gold, and when it was too late, he learned that his Katie had gladly accepted the kindly offered gift anyway behind his back.

But others, who seemed almost to excuse priests living together with profligate prostitutes, directed the sharpest attacks and biting derision against Luther's marriage as if it were the most villainous and at the same time the most degrading act of his life. In 1526 King Henry VIII of England, the notorious wife-murderer, accused Luther of disgraceful lust in violating a nun who was consecrated to God. Others tried to do the same. Duke George the Bearded had already criticized him on December 28 1525, saying that craze and ambition had enticed him, that the lusts of the flesh had deceived him, a beautiful Eve had lured him. Indeed, the next year he even insinuated that Luther had driven the Wittenberg monks out of the Black Cloister so that he would have more room to live with his little Katie! Where a whole monastery had found accommodation and food before, there he now revels with another in carnal lust.

If the princes, who only occasionally took to the pen, were already writing in this key signature, what else was to be expected from the actual polemicists! Here, too, Jerome Emser, secretary of George the Bearded, was one of the first. He had already broken some lances against Luther since the Leipzig Debate, until Luther suddenly left him alone and turned against the other opponents as if this "goat" Emser were no longer there. In exchange Emser now wrote a Latin hymn about Luther's wedding with Katie. Johannes Cochlaeus, Luther's biographer on the Catholic side, calls it quite a fine poem, but even if we take into account the crudeness of that time and the bitterness with which they argued on both sides, we must still consider it a very vile poem. At the same time Doctor Eck also seems to have been pleased with it. In spring of 1527 when he published Luther's humble letter to Henry VIII of England and Henry's harsh, sarcastic response, he adds Emser's poem and several similar songs of disgrace for his readers as a welcome addition to his writing.

Soon after this the "Leipzig asses" came onto the field, two young Masters, Joachim von der Heyden who called himself Myricianus in Latin, and Johannes Hasenberg. In German and Latin, in prose and in verse, they attacked Luther and Katie in 1528. Through solemn presentations they tried to confuse Katie concerning the lawfulness of their marriage. But Luther and his Wittenbergers retaliated against them in the *New Newspaper from Leipzig* and in *Aesop's New Fable of the Lion and the Ass* with such coarse ridicule that Myricianus suddenly fell silent, and not until 1530 did Hasenberg come out with a new writing, a Latin drama, in which, at the end of the fourth act, after endless abuse, at least on indulgent paper, he hands Luther over to the stake.

5.

THE MORNING STAR
OF WITTENBERG

At the beginning of the 1530s in the circle of his lodgers, Luther once spoke about allegories and metaphors and took this example of figurative speech: "Katie von Bora is the Morning Star of Wittenberg."

To us her picture is really like a friendly star over the evangelical parsonage, which gave our people an abundance of fresh energy and pious chastity. Luther could not have understood his figurative expression in this way, however. He means rather: As the morning star anticipates the break of day, so Katie is the first one up early in the morning.

The Black Cloister

The first rays of the morning sun strike the Black Cloister, which is at the southeast corner of the city above the green Elbe meadow. At that time it wasn't as big as it is now. The large building on *Kollegienstrasse*, the so-called *Augusteum*, was built only under Elector August in the second half of the sixteenth century. Before that time, the cloister courtyard, the eastern half of which the monks has used as a cemetery, went up to the street. During Luther's time, on the west side of the courtyard, where the hospital adjoined the monastery, there were stables and sheds for Katie's farming, cattle breeding, and the brewing house. Between this and the cloister, a passageway led into the little garden behind the cloister under a tower-like annex.

On the other side, on the eastern side of the courtyard, they began to build a new cloister church in 1502, but, probably from lack of funds, the building was left simply with the foundation walls. And the little old church, still in the midst of the foundation of the new church, of half-timber style, about thirty feet long and twenty wide, was quite dilapidated, so that it had to be supported on all sides. Inside was a narrow, damaged choir loft, which held barely twenty people, and the pulpit, or rather the preaching chair at the south wall, was constructed of rough-hewn boards hardly one-and-a-half yards high. Luther also preached in this little church, which was more like a stable than a house of God.

The construction of the monastery had likewise begun in 1502, the year the University of Wittenberg was founded. On the whole, only the monastery's large dormitory had been built and completed, and it doubled as the dining hall. This is essentially the Luther House. It contains one ground floor, two upper floors, and an attic. The windows, which are larger on the second floor but smaller on the third, open to the south toward the city moat and the Elbe meadow, and to the north toward the monastery courtyard. The large building was not completely finished, but out of necessity it offered accommodation to some forty monks.

Finances of the Black Cloister

After Luther came on the scene, however, one monk after another left the monastery, and in 1523 he and his Prior Eberhard Brisger were the last brothers of the Order. However, they had a number of fugitive monks and refugee preachers with them. They were responsible for supporting them. And supplying food became all the more burdensome for them as the financial circumstances of the monastery fell into the greatest confusion. The Black Cloister had probably never been rich. Now each brother of the Order who left had received a "dividend" of 100 *Gulden*, and the Electoral excise officers[1] had confiscated the income. The "beggar's sack" had a

---

[1] *Visitatoren.*

large hole, as Luther writes in 1523. Also the excise officers canceled his salary of 9 old *Schock*, and compensation was not granted for the time being.

In Luther's letters from this time there are repeated complaints about this oppressive situation. George the Bearded truly believed that Luther was leading a life of luxury! In reality the very opposite was the case: Luther was even afraid he might have to leave Wittenberg. So, at the end of 1524 he asked the Elector, even in Brisger's name, to take the whole monastery for himself as lord, but to leave a room for him and his last comrade in front of the monastery beside the hospital. Here Brisger built a little house facing the street, west of the entrance to the monastery courtyard. Fredrick the Wise allowed Luther and Brisger themselves to live in the Cloister, and perhaps it was at this time that Luther was allotted a fixed income of 100 *Gulden* per year.

Katie in the Black Cloister

After Katie moved in as Luther's wife, Brisger, who also married a few weeks later, moved into the little house just mentioned, and now Luther and Katie were the owners of the Black Cloister, if not by law, then by fact, because Elector John likewise left the large building to their free use. And shortly before his death, he showed Luther his electoral thanks in a legal writ. The document was issued in Torgau on February 4, 1532. In that document the Elector, for himself and his descendants, gave and endowed the venerable and learned Doctor, our dear devout *Herr Doktor* Martin Luther and his wife Katharine and their direct descendants, sons and daughters, with the Black Cloister and all that goes with it, including the garden and courtyard, nothing excluded, as a true and free inheritance, free of all tax and any compulsory service, with the rights to brew, to malt, to sell beer, to keep cattle, and to conduct every other civil matter, with the single stipulation that he, the prince, and his successors retain the option to buy it if they ever sold it.

The Garden

The garden mentioned in this document is the little garden that is also situated behind the monastery toward the city moat. The courtyard in front of the monastery likewise was not entirely without trees. As a monk, Luther had already sat here with his friend Staupitz in the shade of a pear tree. On the courtyard side there was also a covered walk, which was later torn down, and in front of the entrance to the house there was a portico, an atrium.

The Portal with Luther's Portrait and Coat of Arms

The entrance was embellished in 1540 with a beautiful portal of Elbe sandstone. One of Luther's most faithful lodgers, Antonius Lauterbach, Superintendent of Pirna since 1539, had it crafted in his new homeland at Luther and Katie's request of November 26 1539. It bears the year 1540 and the maker's mark of the Pirna stonecutters. Designed in late Gothic form, it is set over the door in a graceful pointed gable. On each side there is a stone seat. How many times Luther and Katie might have enjoyed the cool of the evening here after hot working days! The undersides of the stone canopies above it display Luther's coat of arms on the right, his portrait on the left. His coat of arms, as we know from castings of seals and from his own description, contains a white rose, whose petals encompass a red heart under a black cross on a blue field surrounded by a golden ring.

On the portal the letters V.I.V.I.T. are engraved around the coat of arms. If one leaves out the periods, the result is the Latin word *vivit*, that is, "He lives," namely Christ. Separated by the periods, the five letters form Luther's mysterious motto. According to Luther's statement, they are the first letters of five German words, which comprise our faith and God. The meaning of this, however, will be revealed only on Judgment Day—Luther never told his friends the five words. On the other side of the portal, around Luther's portrait are the indication of his age "*Etatis sue 57*," and in Latin the passage from the prophet Isaiah 30:15: "In quiet and hope will be my strength," one of Luther's favorite passages.

The Luther House

If we climb the spiral staircase in the little tower added on the left, then we are on the second story in front of Luther and Katie's residence. From the landing we arrive first at four rooms on the north side of the house, with windows facing the monastery courtyard: an anteroom, the spacious living room, a rather narrow chamber, which is now designated as a bedroom, and a rather large corner room. There, a narrow spiral staircase under a trapdoor leading to the ground floor where, besides other domestic rooms, there was also the kitchen. On the south side connected to these four rooms there is another little room, a smaller lecture hall, and the aula, rooms that served for lectures and home devotions, where larger festivities could be held as well. Luther's study, "the poor little room," as he calls it, from which he had stormed against the Pope, no longer exists. It was probably situated (a stairway higher?) in the square, tower-like connecting structure that can be seen between the monastery and the brewing house in old depictions of Wittenberg.

But are the other rooms at least the old ones? And has the focal point, the actual Luther room, come down to us in its original state to some extent? We would really like this. The Luther House was preserved in the repeated sieges and bombardments of Wittenberg and was even spared a thorough remodel when an eccentric renovation in the nineteenth century, which was completely necessary but somewhat too elegant, stripped it of its patina. Here we really are standing in Luther and Katie's living room. And alongside these "elders," there were so many young people who came and went in their house, lived with them and sat at table with them, that it would be quite astonishing if the knowledge of where their room was located had not been kept alive even after they died.

In 1671 Luther's study was still regarded as an object of interest, but the study had probably already disappeared at that time. What was shown to visitors was the living room. Even later it was still sometimes erroneously designated as the study. So, October 31, 1717, the bicentennial of the Reformation, it was the living room where the Wittenberg professors met at six o'clock in the morning for a short devotion, and struck up the hymn: "May God Bestow on Us His grace!"

Famous Visitors

There were already a large number of visitors in the eighteenth century. According to a description from 1795, the paneled walls, yes, even the ceiling were written on again and again and virtually whitewashed with the names of those who wanted to memorialize themselves there in chalk. Of all of them, only **Czar Peter**, who was in Wittenberg on October 14, 1712, got his wish. His signature is still visible over the door, mounted under glass.

It is said that the well-traveled Czar Peter at that time angrily threw some beautiful Venetian glass to the ground and destroyed it because he wanted to take it with him as a souvenir and was denied. Pieces of the broken glass are in the cabinet in the anteroom. Five years earlier, on February 21, 1707, his adventurous opponent, **King Karl XII of Sweden**, had been in the Luther House as the renowned victor over Russia and over Poland, whose king was the Elector of Saxony. Five years later the Russian was the victor, and the Swede remained a refugee on Turkish soil, far from the cold north.

The Luther Room

Finally in the eighteenth century, a guest book was set out to protect the walls from further graffiti. The description of the condition of the Luther room from 1795, mentioned before, describes at that time:

> A rather worm-eaten table, whose top must be taken off, if one wants to get into the drawer, a couple wooden chairs on which it was thought he usually sat with his wife, benches that run along the walls with boards facing them, these are the few furnishings one sees there.

Here, too, people were harder on things than time was. From the year 1748, we hear that the Luther room looked bad. The caretaker who lived in these rooms tended to put his flour bags in them. Even in 1802 the Luther room was used "for mercantile things," as a contemporary carefully puts it. Another account from the same time contradicts that statement: That is not the case, at least not with the Luther room, nevertheless even this account must admit that it is correct about using the adjoining hall "for mercantile things." During the siege of 1813, the Luther House served as a military infirmary. To stop the imminent dilapidation, the house was finally renovated under King Fredrick William IV of Prussia during 1844–73 and according to the plans of the Berlin architect August Stüler.

During the renovation, many new things were needed in the Luther room; however, the halls; the paneled walls with the shelf and the hooks for hanging up clothes; the two windows with the bull's eye glass, built-in wooden seats, and beautiful panel cover, are, in all probability, still the originals, or at least faithful copies of what was left of the originals. Scrapings of old paint are probably the basis for the new paint on the ceiling and walls, because, already in 1756, long before the renovation, it is reported that Luther's room was painted. However, it is quite doubtful whether the large, beautiful five-tiered tile stove, and the beautiful fir desk, were both there at Luther's time. The stove looks somewhat more modern, and it is rather improbable that Luther's heirs, when they resold the monastery, would have left a piece like a desk, which is so easy to move. Instead they would have taken the furniture with them. Nevertheless, even though these items come from a later period, they do not destroy the solemn character of the room.

We simply must imagine these rooms somewhat more richly furnished where Katie, with her housework, sat at the window in front of the simple sewing desk, and where her husband joked with his children, drank, and sang with his family, friends, students, and guests, and enjoyed serious discussions and cheerful talks with them, at least in the later years of their marriage.

Pictures hung on the walls: the Virgin Mary with the Christ Child in her lap, a portrait of Katie by Cranach, and over the table a picture of the crucified Christ are mentioned. There was also an hourglass here, and in the room there would also have been a place for one of the two mechanical clocks that arrived as gifts from friends in Nürnberg in 1527 and 1529. Luther admired the clocks very much, and once said that the clock, the firestarter, and the discovery of magnetic power were three of the most important inventions.

Katie Makes a Home

First, however, Katie had her hands full in making the rooms more livable. When she arrived, she found the monastery sorely neglected. Much of the inventory had been dragged off. What was still left of pewter containers and kitchen utensils and other furniture, Luther later estimated, hardly added up to 20 *Gulden*. If he had had to buy it, he adds, he would have bought something better. In the rooms nothing had probably been improved for years, and in recent time he had a real bachelor household with Brisger. He had a student assistant, Wolfgang Sieberger, who was in the monastery already in 1517—a pious, loyal fellow, but he was not the most industrious. Above all, he lacked what was most needed: order and cleanliness. Luther's straw bed, as he himself tells it, had not been properly shaken for a whole year, but he said: "I was tired, and wore myself out during the day and then fell into bed, and didn't notice it."

Here Katie's thoroughness and her love of order quickly fixed things up. Already in the first year of their marriage, the records of the Wittenberg finance department note 6 *Groschen* for two barrels of lime, and 10 more *Groschen* for two-and-a-half wagonloads of lime that the Council supplied to Doctor Martin. The walls, where they were damaged, were probably plastered and freshly whitewashed with this lime.

Luther let his young wife's eagerness put him to work. In December 1525 he even asked his friend Link in Nürnberg to get him seeds for the garden and turning lathes for him and his student assistant Wolfgang. Such tools that turned by themselves would have been very precious to him, while Wolf fell asleep over them. The heavier housework was taken care of by a maid. In 1527 there were already several maids there, and the domestic staff became more and more numerous because little children came along for the parents. The land was expanded through purchases. In the sheds there were horses, cows, and pigs, and in the courtyard, all kinds of poultry. Soon boarders, visiting guests, and poor relatives filled all the empty rooms in the house.

Managing the Household Finances

More than once Luther feared being overwhelmed by his extra large household. Katie alone kept the household going. Fortunately their time in debt was overcome. Income kept pace with expenses. In the end a small fortune accrued.

Income gradually became quite significant. Few professors in Germany at that time had a salary of 100 *Gulden* such as Luther had made even before his marriage. After the marriage, John the Steadfast doubled Luther's salary, and his son and successor, John Fredrick the Magnanimous, added another hundred *Gulden*. Beginning in 1536, the Elector also sent a regular delivery of grain and malt, wood and hay, the value of which might have amounted to almost 100 *Gulden* annually as well. Therefore, in 1540 Luther calculated his salary first at 300, then at 400 *Gulden*. Besides this, Melanchthon also received a salary of 400 *Gulden* beginning in 1541.

Luther had no regular income other than this. When he married, he had considered charging lecture fees to the hundreds of listeners who crowded into his lectures, but since without any effort on his part the Elector granted that first extra pay of 100 *Gulden*, he refrained from this and even continued to lecture free of charge, just as Melanchthon did, until finally, under the infirmities of old age, he had to cut back and finally discontinue his lectures altogether.

He likewise rejected a sum of 400 *Gulden* annually, which the printers offered him for publishing his writings. The good people could have easily offered him even more, because they became rich and carefree by selling his writings, people like Wittenberg printer Nickel Schirlentz, who had a small beginning but soon didn't even want to count the "dirt," the pennies—he simply weighed them. Schirlentz, despite his shining business, in the end came into financial ruin, which Luther perceived as a fair punishment for his wantonness. Luther was pleased with another Wittenberg printer, Hans Grunenberg, who had a troubled conscience due to his excessively rich earnings. Luther himself didn't want to earn anything from his writings.

Gifts of Support and Appreciation

It is hardly possible to put a high enough value on how numerous and extensive, even in their significance for Katie's household, were the gifts brought to her husband as thanks and admiration from princes and noblemen, scholars and merchants, friends and others. The Saxon aristocracy did not have a very open hand and thought more about getting than giving. Among these leeches, centaurs, and harpies, as Luther calls the Saxon nobles because of their arrogance and greediness, a rather upright man of war like Field Colonel Assa vom Kram was as rare as a white raven. Every year until his death in 1528, he donated up to 30 *Gulden* from his affluence to Luther's household.

From more distant places, however, donations, including cash, came with increasing frequency. One of the first, which Luther considered in this way, was Naumburg chancellor Doctor Heinrich Schmidburg, a native of Leipzig. In his will of 1520, he left Luther 100 *Gulden*, to the great annoyance of many Catholics. In 1544 King Christian III of Denmark changed his delivery of natural goods, which consisted of butter and herring, but which did not arrive in Wittenberg in good condition, into a regular donation of 50 *Taler* annually. The king also granted the same honorarium of 50 *Taler* each to Bugenhagen the Reformer of the north, to Melanchthon, and to Jonas. And already Elector John Fredrick had donated a sum of 1,000 *Gulden* in 1541, which was to be disbursed only to the heirs. The annual interest from it, however, was paid to Luther at a value of 50 *Gulden*. On the other hand, when the Elector also wanted to give him a share of the rich Schneeberg silver mine with an annual yield of 300 *Gulden*, Luther thanked him, but he didn't want to take part in shares in mining speculations; it seemed like gambling money to him.

The Elector always led among the donors, as was fair and reasonable, without expecting to be thanked. On January 25, 1536,

John Fredrick replied that no special words of thanks were necessary. Indeed, at Luther's request, he had a wild boar and a barrel of wine sent, and Luther in his letter of thanks nevertheless expressed concern about becoming a burden to the prince, since he had already been so generous in giving, providing, and supporting. One time in 1529, when he and Katie were just out of the deepest debt, he thanked the old Elector John just as candidly for a piece of brown cloth and a black robe that was almost so expensive he didn't want to wear it, but at the same time he also asked him not to believe those who said that he was in need of something: "Unfortunately I have more than I bear in good conscience, especially from your Electoral grace. And it is not fitting for me, as a preacher, to have an abundance, nor do I even desire it." He knew how many put pressure on the landed gentry for themselves, and he knew that their coffers also were not inexhaustible: "Too much rips the bag!" He asked the prince to wait with his gifts until he complained and sent a request. Otherwise he might shy away from approaching his lord on behalf of others who were more deserving of such gifts than he.

To Katie, on the other hand, these gifts were surely very welcome: wine from the prince's vineyards near Süptitz or in Thuringia, cider, all kinds of medicines, food, particularly things that otherwise were not to be had in little Wittenberg, such as venison and fish. The gifts became almost too much for Luther. He hardly ever asked the prince for anything for himself. It almost always dealt with arranging a wedding or some other celebration, and providing venison, which could be supplied only by the lords who held the hunting rights. Requests on behalf of others were increasingly frequent in his letters to the Elector.

He even asked the Wittenberg City Council without hesitation, on behalf of others, while he never made a request for himself. The Council, however, knew how much they were indebted to him. The flourishing of the city and the university was his doing. For almost a lifetime he held the office of curate of souls and preacher without pay, and during Bugenhagen's long absence while he implemented the Reformation in Denmark, Luther even took over the office of the parish pastor of the City Church as well, without any remuneration.

He voluntarily waived the privilege of having his house exempt from any obligation, and demanded to be taxed just like everyone else. In return, however, hardly a year passed that the Council did not send him or Katie a valuable gift for the house. Already at the New Year in 1526, Katie received a "Swabian"—that's what they called a certain type of fine white linen at that time. Her husband, however, got a robe with black fleece, lined with lambskin. The next year he got another robe, this time made of purplish cloth and lined with black linen. The Council's cellar, as well as the Electoral wine cellar in the Castle, was open to him for the rather small supply of wine he needed. In the years 1535 to 1540 very important deliveries of lime, bricks, and roofing tiles are recorded for remodeling and new construction in the Black Cloister, and while he was at the Marburg Colloquy in 1529, the Wittenberg city treasurer entered: "3 *Schock* 50 *Groschen* presented to the wife of the venerable and learned Martin Luther in his absence, since he has hardly been given any gift this year; one was 10 *Taler*, and one amounted to 23 *Groschen*."

The mayors of other cities also showed their thanks and admiration by sending gifts, more often and more lavishly than Luther liked. In the first days of January 1530, when he heard that the Council of Zwickau wanted to honor him with a gift, he wrote to his friend Nikolaus Hausmann, who was pastor in Zwickau at that time, and asked him to prevent it: Gifts of high monetary value were annoying to him. Because of them he could come to be suspected of being rich, while he really despised wealth, and couldn't stand it if he had it, and he didn't even want to have the reputation of wealth at all. "No one has anything to give me for food and clothing; but I have everything to give to everyone."

It is likely that at no other time, even down to our present day, have such quantities of voluntary tribute accrued to one German, as they did to Doctor Martin. In addition to the gifts from princes and cities, countless gifts came from friends and admirers: food and drink, as well as furniture and decoration. Doctor Wolfgang Capito, who had enjoyed Katie's hospitality in May 1536, was certainly not the only one who sent a gift to thank her. The words he attached to his gift and in which he praises Katie as a homemaker because of her sweet temperament, her efficiency, and her faithful care for her husband, may have brought her even more joy than the gift, a gold ring. Luther also had several gold rings with jewels, gifts from distinguished lords, besides his wedding ring and the signet ring that Elector John Fredrick had presented to him in 1530. He hung an honorific gold chain around his neck when he visited the Nuncio Pier Paolo Vergerio in 1535. The number of silver tankards multiplied despite his lavish generosity in giving them away. In 1532 he already valued his tankards at 200 *Gulden*. And the following years brought many new pieces. So in 1540 a valuable tankard, almost too valuable, came from the estate of wealthy Hans Honold of Augsburg, whose son had lived and dined with Luther while he was a student. In his will from the year 1542, Luther valued the tankards and jewels, as well as rings, chains, gold and silver commemorative coins, at 1,000 *Gulden*. We must multiply this total at least five times to approach the monetary value of our time.

Luther's Generosity

With such income Katie would have had an easy time maintaining the household, had it not been for her husband's unrestrained generosity. The passage that says, when doing good, the left hand should not know what the right hand is doing (Matthew 6:3), was completely true of him. He was charitable to the point of self-sacrifice. How often we hear only by chance and coincidence about his rich gifts, yes, for his status, extremely rich gifts, which he directed to the needy! His favorite saying was: "Give, and it shall be given you" (Luke 6:38). His Katie, meanwhile, might have looked at this rather critically, but he comforted her by saying: "God gives enough, and blesses it, and I want to give also. Dear Katie, if we don't have money, then the tankards must go. One must give something, if one wants to have something else." In time of need he even took from their children's christening money in order to keep from turning a poor person away from his door without alms: "God is rich; He will give it back."

One time Justus Jonas donated alms from his full moneybag, which he didn't like to open, and then said: "Who knows where God will give it back to me?" Then Luther laughed and chided his friend, saying that God had surely already given him enough anyway. Luther literally bargained with the Wittenberg Council for 30 *Gulden*, which he needed for a poor fellow, a pious scholarly man: "If there isn't enough, then give twenty, and I will give ten; if not, then give half, fifteen, and I will give the other half. God will surely give it back." When he suspected the Council of withholding grain through a price increase in 1539, he became violently angry so that Cranach as mayor went to him and explained the causes of the price increase. And when he didn't have cash to buy grain himself while the plague was raging in Wittenberg, he borrowed some bushels of grain from the Electoral tax collector and gave it to the poor.

His kindness was often abused by unworthy and ungrateful people, even by asking him to co-sign bonds for them. He certainly knew the proverb: "One should strangle bondsmen." But nevertheless he could be enticed to do it again and again in the beginning, and went deep into debt through his benevolence, and through the large household in which he and Katie in their poverty offered refuge to those who were even poorer than they. As he wrote to his friend Brisger on February 1, 1527, who meanwhile had gone to Altenburg, he couldn't even provide 8 *Gulden* for him. He had debts of over 100 *Gulden* himself, four tankards had already been pawned, and he had no more credit with his rich friends Cranach and the goldsmith Christian Döring, because they were afraid he would ruin himself for the sake of others. Still he comforted himself: "The LORD, who punishes my foolishness in this way, will also free me again." Next to God, "Lord Katie" was his helper in time of need. She held together what her husband acquired. She saved where he scattered with lavish hand. She kept records where he relied on God's benevolent assistance.

Occasionally, even he took a count. Once when he was sitting at the table and eating his dinner roll, it weighed heavily on his heart: A roll for each meal, which was already 30 *Groschen* and 4 *Pfennig* a year for him alone, and 4 *Pfennig* every day for his house beer, which annually amounts to . . . the total seemed too high to him, and he said: "I should never take a count; it makes one cross, it climbs too high. I wouldn't have thought that so much should go for one person!" In 1532 he had ominous thoughts about his household needing 500 *Gulden* for the kitchen alone, while he had a salary of only 200 *Gulden*, and he freely admitted: "I cannot take care of this household. But our LORD God must be the guardian of fools."

And in 1542 when he wrote down his will, he probably sat at his desk for hours making calculations about how much he had accumulated with Katie in the Black Cloister, and what the extra land cost that he had bought, and what they still needed to live otherwise. Then he jotted down a summary of assets and liabilities on individual notes, and the precious documents have been preserved. In the middle it says: "*Nota.* Amazing calculation made between Doctor Martin and Katie in the year 1535/1536. These were two half-years." The first eleven items already amount to 389 *Gulden*, and only then do all the expenses for daily life follow, 130-something, from all the littlest things like parsley and caraway up to the biggest items, the oxen and the pigs.

It is as if we could see Luther sitting at his desk, and Katie coming in with the homemaker's age-old but still timely request: "I need money!" He records "I need money" for grain, barley, hops, wheat, flour, wine, beer, etc. "I need money" for the butcher, shoemaker, tailor, furrier, cooper, blacksmith, tool-maker, pharmacist, physician, bookseller, book-binder, etc. "I need money" for linen, bedding, feathers, pewter pots, bowls, etc. Next in the calculations follow the brewing equipment, wagons, tableware, and under the big items, the wedding gifts. In between, little rhymes like the following are written:

> I, poor man, so keep the house!
> Where I my cash should e'er give out,
> In seven places if I dare;
> I'm always short both here and there.

He describes a good householder by remembering the thriftiness of his own father with the words:

> Do, as your father once had done:
> When looking for a coin, just one,
> Then three he found within the purse;
> And so he paid up all his burse.
> No farthing would he ever owe:
> So house and life both well did go!

But he also knows householders who hardly know either in or out because of their debts, and about them he rhymes:

> Do, as your father once had done:
> When looking for a coin, just one,
> He had to borrow three thereto
> And stayed in debt for coat and for shoe:
> That's keeping house for such a bloke;
> At least in his house there's no fire or smoke!

And while he is adding things up item by item, he asks himself: "Tell me: money—where does it come from? All it does is stink and pile up debts."

Cash was often scarce. Even in 1540 he had to go for weeks without his usual nightcap because the beer Katie had brewed had been drunk up and there was no money to buy any. And actually he was never lacking in debts. But when he noted his debts of 450 *Gulden* in his will in 1542, that was still somewhat different from when he had owed 100 *Gulden* in the second year of his marriage, because at that time he had nothing but debts, and now compared to the 450 *Gulden* he had more than double that in jewels and probably ten times that much in real estate. Nevertheless, Katie felt burdened by these debts. One time her husband tried to calm her down with a joke: "This is how the Hessians pray: Our Father, who art in heaven, we are on earth; if you give us nothing, then we have nothing, so we'll make a downpayment." But where would such economics lead?

And what might Katie have said when her husband demanded something from her, as in a letter of February 27, 1532? While he was in Torgau with the Elector at that time, his student assistant Johann Rischmann wanted to leave his house, and he had intended a decent farewell gift for him because he had served faithfully and diligently. He writes to Katie:

> Just think how often we gave to wicked knaves and ungrateful students and it was all lost. So get hold of yourself now! Of course, I know there's not much there, but I would like to give him 10 *Gulden* if I had it. You must not give him less than 5 *Gulden*, because he doesn't have any clothes. So, do not fail, as long as there is a tankard left; think where you get it! I know that God will surely give another.

And as if he hadn't already demanded that she give away every last item, at the same time he even asked Katie to buy something for the children in Wittenberg, because he couldn't find any appropriate little present in Torgau, even though the annual market was open.

Katie's Frugalness

If Luther was all too generous and too carefree about the necessities of daily life, then Katie had to be all the more frugal and more meticulous. Yes, several contemporaries call her miserly, stingy, greedy. And that is the first complaint raised against her: greed and covetousness. The other accusations are about her large and wasteful household—an accusation that sounds rather strange with her alleged greed, her pride, and her bossiness.

Was she stingy or greedy? The Electoral Chancellor, Doctor Gregor Brück, directed the harshest insinuation against her soon after her husband's death. He suggests that she had pilfered into her own household the money the Elector had sent as annual income to the old Wolf Sieberger at Luther's request. But if that really did happen, then it was surely done with Wolf's consent because the loyal, grizzled old man, who in the end received more of the bread of grace in the Black Cloister than he deserved, stayed with Katie and the children even after Luther's death, while he could have been his own lord by the grace of the prince. He obviously had no reason to complain about Katie. And if we consider how many boarders stayed in their house for many years, do we want to believe the two or three who complain about her, or the hundreds who flocked to her table, who praise her as the best woman, who considered that time of their life as the highest honor and most precious memory when they were Luther's lodgers?

It certainly may have happened more than once that the woman, who was pressed upon from all sides, in the rush of the business or in time of need, forgot to pay for purchases that were under her supervision, and that someone in that situation didn't hesitate to remind her, but still we must not discredit her by generalizing from a single occurrence. And when the same young man who complains about this—that is, Jerome Besold—goes on to say that she kept everything in order and got the necessary payment from the lodgers, then it is really praise for her rather than blame. The only way she was able to balance her books was by holding on to what she could with both hands, to counterbalance her husband who scattered with both hands.

Occasionally she expressed the wish that her husband might have a bit more business sense. Who could blame her? One time when they were talking about a greedy scholar, she thought, if her husband were so minded, he could be very rich, but she calmly accepted Melanchthon's reprimand: Whoever would serve the common good must not think about his own profit. In the summer of 1540 money troubles brought to her lips half-jokingly, half-seriously the common wish: "*Herr Doktor*, now don't teach the young fellows for free!" But even that was simply complaining that she didn't want her husband to dish out the Word of God like an innkeeper selling beer on tap. And that same year, when she brought up for discussion the fact that the King of England had honored her husband with only 50 *Gulden*, but gave Melanchthon 500, she certainly was speaking less out of envy than from insulted pride, because proud self-confidence was one of the fundamentals of her character.

Not a single time do we hear that she seriously opposed her husband's lavish charity. Only, the first year they were married, when he wanted to give away a glass encased in pewter that he had first been given by his friend Nikolaus Hausmann, to another friend whom she also regarded highly, Master Johann Agricola, she felt bad about the beautiful piece. She secretly followed after him, and when he wanted to pack it up, it had disappeared. The worthy *Herr Doktors* Jonas and Bugenhagen had been her fellow conspirators. So she understood quite well how to hold on to what she didn't want to let go, but she seldom did! With self-sacrifice she managed the large household without complaining. She willingly took on the burden her husband put on her of providing for his poor relatives. She would have gladly kept his aging parents in their house as well.

The best testimony to her domestic virtues is her husband's straightforward acknowledgment. Never did he speak of her alleged greed, but he praised her thriftiness. He knew what he needed most, and he drew from his own experience when he spoke about being married: "The man is to acquire, and the woman is to save. So the woman can make the man rich, but not the other way around, because a penny saved is better than a penny earned." In 1542 he says of Katie: "What she has now, she got without me." Of the position of homemaker he thought like Bugenhagen, who gave all the keys to his young wife, but the sword, which is the ultimate authority, he kept for himself. In the same sense Luther says to Katie: "In the house I grant control to you, irrespective of my right."

In and around the house she was the lord. He couldn't be and didn't want to be. Even apart from the fact that by his own admission he was not a skillful householder, he wouldn't have had the time at all to manage the large household. Often enough, Katie had to redirect his restless pen anyway for her big and little concerns about rather important matters. Many of her husband's sharp but also humorous letters would have remained unwritten if she had not stood behind his chair pleading and urging. She did not shy away from calling upon the services of good friends in all kinds of jobs needed for her household, which was in such demand from all sides. She also contacted the Electoral officials when the barn was empty and there was no seed. Through her husband she ordered from friends: seeds for the garden, fruit that couldn't be bought in Wittenberg such as bitter oranges or Borsdorf apples, as well as other food for the kitchen and the cellar, household equipment, and clothing. And if a shipment took longer than usual, she certainly reminded them and asked whether the sea had been drained so that no more fish could come from it.

The Cloister Gardens

In the early years, Luther often walked hand in hand with his dear wife, particularly in the little garden behind the Cloister. He loved the flowers. At the Disputation in the Pleissenburg Castle in Leipzig he had brought along a bouquet of carnations, and while Doctor Eck plucked one quotation after another from the heavy tomes of the Church Fathers, Luther refreshed himself with the colors and smell of the blooms in his hand. He was very sensitive to the beauty and the inexhaustible richness of nature where God's omnipotence and wisdom were revealed to his pious mind in a way he could see and understand, even in the tiniest animal and in the most inconspicuous plant. The area around Wittenberg is not noted for being especially beautiful or lush. On the other side of the Elbe, the Düben heath extends a long way, and on this side of the stream the soil is poor and so sandy that there's a proverb that says all the farms threaten to blow away with a strong wind.

At that time there were some pretty paths just outside the city among the gardens where the nightingales warbled in spring, and they very frequently visited the little grove by Specke Street in the northeast of the city. Even before he got married, Luther is said to have enjoyed wandering out toward a cool forest spring that trickled out on the edge of the woods a little ways east of Wittenberg. It is called the Luther Spring to this day. According to more recent sources, he had this spring enclosed and built a summerhouse over or next to it. But these accounts are based on misunderstandings. A contemporary does speak, about a nice room above the water, where Luther, along with other scholars and distinguished gentlemen, used to drink and enjoy themselves, but that certainly would not have been at a summerhouse far outside the city. Instead, this room was the little study in the Black Cloister with the view of the Elbe. According to one of Luther's letters, he built a well during the spring of 1526, but this was the well in the Cloister garden, which is also mentioned later, and not a well in the forest. Both forest and spring belonged to the city, and Luther might have rested there for a while with his friends in the cool shade, but he couldn't build there.

Close to the river, one might expect it would be easy to find water in the Cloister garden. But in 1542 Luther estimated all his expenses for the garden and the well system at 400 *Gulden*. Larger expenditures from recent years are probably included in this high sum—amounting to double what he received in salary since 1525. The next thing to deal with, then, was simply putting the neglected garden back in order, and watering it better by digging the well. It was certainly Katie's effort that made this happen; at least we don't hear earlier that Luther worried about the Cloister garden in the least. Now, on the other hand, on June 17, 1526, he proudly writes to his friend Spalatin that the well is ready and the garden was blooming most beautifully; his friend would be crowned with roses and lilies, if he wanted to come.

There was no shortage of useful plants. For Katie's kitchen, peas and beans, carrots, herbs, cabbage, lettuce, and other greens were more important than lilies and roses. Her husband also tended the garden, and the eagerness with which he did is the best testimony of how much he enjoyed horticulture. In the first month of the next year, 1527, he ordered all kinds of seeds from his friend Link in Nürnberg. And soon after that, he ordered the seeds to grow Erfurt radishes, which were famous for their size, from Lang in Erfurt, his former brother in the Order. In May he was able to inform Link that they had come up well, but the melons, pumpkins, and cucumbers were not doing as well as other gardens. Later, however, they made up for lost ground and spread tremendously in the little garden. The good harvest was in keeping with the good sowing. On December 29 Luther ordered even more and different seeds from Link, and then joked that he would yet become a gardener, if he lived long enough. His teacher in horticulture was probably that "Mr. Heinrich," a former monastic brother. Luther looked for a job for him in the spring of 1527, and he calls him a good gardener. His name was Baumgart, and in 1537 he was the Elector's gardener in Lichtenburg.

Even from later years we occasionally hear of similar orders for the garden. So, in 1533 Link was supposed to send borage seeds, which is an herb that connoisseurs loved on salad. "It is supposed to taste very good," Luther adds to his order. But more and more, his heavy workload prevented him from putting a hand to the garden himself. The gardening, too, which had become dear to him, he had to leave to his gardener, to his Katie, and to the domestic staff.

But he still enjoyed his garden. Sometimes he was there even before sunrise. There he listened to the songs of the nightingale in the evening, and when the discordant croaking of the frogs on the nearby Elbe meadow throbbed its sweet sound, he said: In the same way the voice of Christ in the world will drown out the shouting of Doctor Eck and Cochlaeus. Here he admired the efficiency and organization of the bees and ignored the useless droning in front of the beehive. He was hardly sympathetic toward the burrowing mice, and the sparrows with their chirping, the "robbers" of grain and fruit. Like the crows, magpies, and ravens, they would have to be declared fair game, he said, and once when his children had caught a sparrow, he spoke to the frightened, peeping little thing with sharp words: "You Franciscan with your thick robe, you are quite a shameful bird!" And the swallows he didn't speak well of, either. He compared them to the long-winded preaching-monks, who wore a white coat underneath and a black cowl over it. He thought caterpillars were so completely destructive and deformed that the devil must have brought them into the garden. For his pious faith, everything bad was rooted in the devil's hatred, everything good in the grace of God. Later, he bought another piece of land, at Katie's instigation, and several gardens for the Cloister garden, among them a large orchard. In the company of his friends he marveled at God's omnipotence, which let the most precious fruits ripen on this dry soil. In later years he occasionally still did some gardening, and he personally grafted the fruit trees.

It had cost Katie several tears before she persuaded her husband to buy the first garden. But when the little Cloister garden was obviously insufficient for their household, she insisted on her wish to expand the property, and she was a woman who carried through on what she really wanted. When they were deepest in debt, in 1527, she had been close to getting her wish, but then the purchase of a small garden had to be postponed. At the beginning of the 1530s, however, they were already working another little garden, which her husband had bought—not of his own free will, as he himself admits, but very much against his will. In the end he was not able to resist Katie's flattering requests and her bitter tears; even he was powerless against such weapons. Connected with the garden was a piece of land, an acreage. The property was situated in the oak pond, or leech pond in front of the Elster gate and had belonged to Andreas Mebes. Since it cost only 90 *Gulden*, it was probably not very large. In 1547 it still belonged to Luther's heirs. It isn't mentioned after that.

The garden Luther and Katie bought from Klaus Bildenhauer on April 19, 1532 for about 900 *Gulden* must have been much larger. It is even celebrated in Latin verse by a contemporary poet. Master Klaus Bildenhauer, or Bildenhain as Doctor Jonas' little daughter called him, was a sculptor, as his name implies, the same one who worked for Fredrick the Wise in 1491. Klaus Heffner was his civilian name, but he is called Klaus Bildenschnitzer in the record books. One time at Luther's table, Master Klaus, who died in August 1539, said that he could still remember the time when Elector Ernst and Duke Albrecht were supposed to have been together in the Torgau court before Saxony was divided in 1485. When Master Klaus complained about the difficulties of old age, Luther comforted him by mentioning his own pains and that he thought they both had eaten Easter eggs too often already. In earlier times, Master Klaus had been well off, and for many years had sat on the city council, but he had given everything away for the sake of his children and now himself suffered poverty in his old age so that Luther reminded him of the old proverb:

> A father who gives up by force what is his,
> Of being beaten to death most worthy is.

So he had even sold his garden. It is probably the same property that is designated as the garden on Zahnisch Street in 1542, and the garden at the hog market in 1553. It was located outside the city, not far from the Black Cloister, somewhat north of the place where the post office is now. A brook, the so-called Lazy Brook, flowed through it and formed a small pond. And when they went fishing in the autumn of 1533, Luther also went along. And then at home he thoroughly enjoyed the great delight with which Katie dished out their pike, loach, trout, perch, and carp, as if she had made a miraculous catch of fish. Her joy would have been no less, when the fruit-laden trees supplied their abundance for kitchen and cellar in summer and fall, and she could offer her husband and children and the many lodgers, cherries, pears, apples, peaches, nuts, and grapes for dessert.

She even started her own little vineyard. In 1544 Lauterbach was also supposed to procure six hundred stakes for grapevines in Pirna at one time. It was impossible to eat all the grapes, so several jugs of vinegar were made from some of them, and sweet mustard was prepared. Rarer plants also thrived. In 1538 Luther was able to send Duchess Elisabeth of Braunschweig a gift of mulberry seedlings in return for a shipment of cheese. And one fruit that had ripened in his garden, he said, was the *Mandragora* or the fruit in the Bible called *Dudaim* [*mandrakes*, Genesis 30:14–16]. It seems that a building that stood in this garden was soon sold again, because the property, which had cost Luther 900 *Gulden*, was valued at only 500 *Gulden* in 1542.

A third and fourth garden, the hops garden on Specke Street and a garden in the Elsholze, were first acquired in 1544 for 375 *Gulden*. Hops were still frequently grown in the area around Wittenberg at that time.

Luther had also bought a small garden for 20 *Gulden*, not for himself, but for his servant Wolf Sieberger. And under Wolf's name, for 430 *Gulden*, he also took over the little house or the cabin where Brisger had once lived. When Brisger had moved away, he transferred control of the small property to his friend Bruno Brauer [Brisger], and then he bought and sold it again to Luther in 1541 when he became pastor in Dobien near Wittenberg. Luther got little enjoyment from it, however, because he had taken it over at too high a price and could pay only a small part of the purchase price. He had to repair it for around 70 *Gulden* as well, and having to find a tenant so that it wouldn't stand empty was a worry and a bother. Despite that fact, he had acquired the little house because he was afraid that after his death Katie would not be able to maintain the large house, which took no end of construction and upkeep, or that the building additions ordered by the Elector, which grew into an enormous embankment right at the southeast corner of the city, would still bring the house to ruin. Then his widow, along with their children, would be able to find refuge in Bruno's little house.

So, gradually, a rather stately property surrounded the heart of the Black Cloister. When Luther assessed all his property in Wittenberg in 1542 for the "Turk-tax," it came to 9,000 *Gulden*. He really doubted whether Katie would be able to draw even 100 *Gulden* annually from it after his death. But without this property Katie would hardly have been able to manage their large household, because a good part of what she needed for the kitchen and cellar grew for her in the gardens, in the fields, and in the stockyard in front of the Cloister.

Farm Animals

Katie had begun raising several pigs right away. So it was a hard blow to her in late autumn 1527, while the plague was raging in the city and the Black Cloister became a hospital, that a large kill struck the pigs at the same time so that five head were taken. But the empty pens in the sty were soon filled again. Luther preferred pork to venison, which he called melancholy. And although he thought the grunting and mud-rooting animals with their insatiable desire for food were like an image of Epicurean life, nevertheless he did not mind also taking time with them occasionally and conversing with his swineherder Johannes. In 1542 Katie had 8 pigs in the stockyard that were estimated at a *Gulden* apiece, 2 sows worth 5 *Gulden* together, and 3 piglets each estimated at 7 *Groschen*, as well as 5 cows that were estimated at 15 *Gulden*, 9 large calves worth 2 *Gulden* apiece, and a goat which, along with its two kids, was estimated at 2 *Gulden*. There were no horses there in 1542. They were probably working at the Zölsdorf estate. But when they were in Wittenberg, they were often harnessed for rides and for the official trips the Doctor took across the country with his colleagues in order to visit the area pastors. In his later years he often used to drive them to church in Wittenberg as well, because longer walks were difficult for him. In the summary of assets and liabilities from 1542, the horse stable is also listed, besides the cowshed and the pigsty, and all three are valued at 20 *Gulden*.

Lots of poultry also populated the courtyard. More than once Katie gleefully brought newly hatched chicks to her husband, and he always praised anew the miracles of creation. Besides the chickens, Katie of course also kept pigeons and geese, perhaps even a peacock, the sight of which reminded her husband several times of the old saying: "The peacock has the garb of an angel, the gait of a thief, and the song of a devil." So the cloister courtyard wasn't as quiet then, as it is now. Here students and guests came and went, children ran back and forth, and cattle were driven in and out. There wasn't a watchdog, just a little dog. Already as a bachelor Luther had had a small dog, a quick thing that sometimes even jumped on the table and chewed up letters of people from far away. Later the children liked to play with the little dog. He was called Tölpel [*Fool*], and in spite of his name he was a clever animal. An Altenburg farmer couldn't be more excited for the end of the sermon than Tölpel, so that he could finally get to the table.

Brewing Beer

Bit by bit, 130 *Gulden* was spent on the brewing house, which was located in the southwest corner of the courtyard, and on brewing equipment. The brewing rights, which the Cloister had for twelve brewings a year, were transferred to Luther and Katie, and Katie understood the business, a brewer notwithstanding. Her husband loved a fresh drink, although he occasionally lamented that noble barley was wasted by brewing beer, and how very few people understand anything about it. He said: Compared to one city that could brew good beer, there were a hundred where the only beer available makes one vomit; and wine was a gift of God, but beer was a work of man. Katie's beer always tasted good to him, and if he didn't have it, he yearned for it. Even at the Electoral Court in Torgau he thought, as he wrote to Katie on July 29, 1534: "What good wine and beer I have at home, and a beautiful lady or—I should say—lord as well." And he thought to himself that he wished he could have had a bottle of her house beer, to get some relief from the pain caused by the kidney stone that severely tormented him for years.

Besides tasting good, Katie's beer had the advantage of being inexpensive. Wittenberg city beer was not cheap; the price went up to 3 *Pfennig* for a small pitcher. And since Luther estimated his daily expense for beer at 4 *Pfennig*, he often would have been too short to have his usual nightcap if he had not had his house beer. He liked to have plenty to drink in the evening and made no secret of it either. At his age and with the work that rested on him, he believed he was allowed his nightcap with good conscience after the burden and heat of the day. And just as he never closed his heart and his house to any unfortunate soul, he also rejoiced with the joyful. Drunkenness, however, he hated, and therefore he duly criticized the wine-red faces of the nobility at the court, and he deplored as the greatest vice of his dear Germans that they would drink themselves poor, ill, dead, and into hell.

Luther's Diet

Already in his lifetime, however, his opponents accused him of immoderation in drinking and eating, without thinking of the words of the Gospel of Matthew 11:19,[2] and even now they jeeringly point to the letter he wrote from Eisenach on July 16, 1540, to his Katie. The salutation reads: "My gracious young lady Katherin Lutherin von Bora and Zölsdorf near Wittenberg, my sweetheart,"

---

[2] "The Son of Man came eating and drinking, and they say, 'Look at him! A glutton and a drunkard, a friend of tax collectors and sinners!' Yet wisdom is justified by her deeds."

and then it goes on to say: "Grace and peace! My dear matron and lady Katie: Your Grace should know that we are hale and healthy here, God be praised. We eat like the Bohemians (yet not much), drink like the Germans (yet not a lot), but we are happy."

Don't the words in parentheses have to keep every unbiased person from understanding this letter in any way other than in jest? Philipp Melanchthon, who was around Luther almost daily and knew his way of life very accurately, writes: "He was by nature very moderate in food and drink, which often surprised me, because he was not small nor weak in body. I saw that he neither ate a bite nor drank anything at all for four days in a row, although he was well. So I have also often seen that he was content for many days with a little bread and a herring each day."

The Electoral physician, Doctor Matthäus Ratzeberger, also talks about herring as one of Luther's favorite foods. When Luther was laid up during his first kidney stone attack, he could neither eat nor drink because of the pain, and he left the most delicious meals untouched until Katie in her worry finally asked him whether he didn't have any appetite at all! He said: "Of course, so make me a fried herring and a dish of cold peas with mustard, but quickly, before I lose my appetite again." And Katie hurried, with great care in her heart, because it was a strange "little soup for the sick" that her husband had ordered, but she brought it quickly, and he ate. Then the doctors came and were horrified, and one of them exclaimed: "Oh, what are you doing, *Herr Doktor!* Do you want to make yourself even more sick?" The *Herr Doktor*, however, was silent and ate, and the physicians left, fearing they would be called the next day to a critically ill patient. But when they visited him the next morning, behold, he was already back sitting over his books in his little study.

Hearty plain fare, or as he says, good, common, plain home cooking was his favorite. And a regular lifestyle was a necessity for him. He felt best when he was early to bed and early to rise. He usually went to sleep at nine o'clock. It is also noteworthy that he removed fasting as a church ordinance, but he wanted to keep one or even two days of fasting a week as a civil ordinance.

With his way of life and his taste, Katie didn't usually dish up any special delicacies, but probably made hearty, good-tasting meals. And on festive occasions such as birthdays and anniversaries, or weddings and doctoral banquets, which he had to arrange and to which a number of guests came, she was his head cook, as he said, and he was also happy when kitchen and cellar gave their best so that it tasted good to the guests. In his household records from 1542 there is record of what things in the cellars cost: 10 *Gulden* from the wine cellars, 50 *Gulden* from the new cellars, taking into consideration the breakage, and 130 *Gulden* from the large cellars, "including the damage." The damage was a special matter. On July 12, 1532, a Friday, shortly before five o'clock in the evening, Luther and Katie returned from their garden and wanted to visit the cellar that was being built at that time. The arch collapsed and both were spared from death only as if by a miracle.

Renovation Costs

The other renovations and new construction in the Black Cloister also cost a lot of money. In the household records from 1542 the following are recorded: 100 *Gulden* for the upstairs living room and bedroom, 40 *Gulden* for the downstairs room, 20 *Gulden* to repair the stairs twice, 5 *Gulden* for Auntie Lena's little living room with chimney and her bedroom, another 5 *Gulden* for the little room in which Crato and Plato (two younger boarder lodgers) lived, and the same for a gatehouse at the entrance into the Cloister courtyard; in addition 100 *Gulden* for boards, 130 *Gulden* for the roof, and 400 *Gulden* for the new building that was built beside the little garden behind the Cloister.

According to the Wittenberg finance department records, the construction work was busiest between 1535 and 1540. That included finishing the installation of the beautiful sandstone portal in 1540, and the addition of a new bathroom, the exact size of which Luther indicated to his friend Lauterbach on September 25, 1541: eight yards square and four-and-a-half yards high. The stones for the bathroom also came from the Elbe sandstone ridge downstream.

While these changes and new construction involved great expense, over 1,000 *Gulden*, at the same time, the Elector's construction of fortifications caused the owners of the Black Cloister great annoyance and some concern for the future. The Wettins were lords who liked to build, and John Fredrick's political intentions were in line with his personal inclinations. Two heavy stormclouds rose up in the south and threatened to let loose over Germany. The siege of Vienna by the Turks in 1529 had strongly agitated the people. And Emperor Charles V, more a Spaniard than a German, had not yet dared to attack the Protestants with force of arms, but his posture made them fear the worst nevertheless.

Wittenberg's lord wanted the city to be able to resist the Turk and the Emperor. The city walls were reinforced and raised higher, and since the protruding corners were most exposed to enemy attack, the southeast corner, where the Black Cloister jutted out toward the city wall, was to be covered by a powerful embarnkment that would surround the new building in the back and the cloister garden in a semi-circle. To Luther's very great sadness, even the little old church in the Cloister courtyard had to come down in 1542. His little study had also been threatened, and he had to give his consent to have the ground floor of the large house filled in on the south side. The Elector had ordered them not to build too close to the Cloister or to damage it, but the Electoral quartermaster, Fredrick von der Grune, nevertheless considered it necessary to add fill up to the second floor—Luther then intervened by letter. Against few did he proceed so vehemently as in his own affairs. He threatens to call upon God and the prince against the quartermaster if he did not remove the fill: "Of this you should be certain, that I will not empty out even a hairbreadth more for your damned construction with which you are emptying out my gracious lord's purse!" Luther wants the damage to the brewery gate to be repaired, he demands to see the garden wall and the new building protected from any damage, and he complains about the embankment workers who smash in his windows and do it maliciously enough. He calls the Electoral official his and God's secret enemy, and he closes with the words: "Herewith I commend you to God who may persuade you and bring about a change!" And

Katie probably had a hand in the extreme vehemence of this letter, because the encroachments of the quartermaster certainly meant the invasion of her domain, and she was even less inclined than her husband to give up her property rights, even just the tiniest bit.

The Farm at Zölsdorf

The property at Zölsdorf, which Luther and Katie had bought in 1540, also caused frustrations. Since the middle of the 1530s Katie had entertained the thought of managing a small acreage where she could operate her cattle breeding more extensively and with richer yield than was possible in the city. She didn't want to buy, but simply lease some property, and she turned her attention to the Boos farmstead, also called Böse, a small piece of property of fifty–sixty acres with good pasture growth. It was located about a mile southeast of Wittenberg across the Elbe. Her husband had already spoken with Chancellor Brück about leasing it, but nothing came of it. Katie however did not lose sight of Boos, and in 1539 she learned that the little property would again be available to rent. On April 28 she wrote a long letter, not to the chancellor, who wouldn't be very favorable to her intention to rent the property, but to her godfather, Hans von Taubenheim, the master of land income. This is the first letter we have from her hand, and we present it here unabridged as an example of her writing style:

> Grace and peace to you in Christ, strict, sincere, dear lord godfather!
>
> Your grace probably remembers that I asked you three years ago if I might obtain the Boos property with its equipment as a normal rental property for my daily household management, as might be allowed to anyone else. At that time my dear lord approached Dr. Brug about the matter; but nothing came of it, that I might have it. Perhaps it has not been gotten rid of yet by its owner, who had it just for the rent.
>
> I am told, however, how the Kruger von Brato who is renting it at this time is supposed to have written off such property. If this should be so, my kind

request to you as my dear godfather is this: that you would be a sponsor for me in regard to such property. I will gladly and heartily take it for about the same rent as anyone else gives, and deliver the rent daily on two places. Please very kindly, if your grace would be of a mind to write back to me, give me the best advice in this case and show where I have desired something unreasonable in this and that you would not want to give place to the suspicion of those who think I want such property for myself or my children's inheritance, the thought of which never entered my mind. I hope to God He will thus grant my children the heritage that they live and keep themselves pious and honorable. I ask only that I might be allowed to rent it at a fairly reasonable rate for a year or two, so that I might be able to keep my household and cattle all the more comfortably, because here one must buy everything at the most expensive prices and such a place close by would be very useful to me.

I didn't want to burden my dear lord now in this matter by writing to you, since you have so much to do otherwise. And it is not necessary that your grace should address my request further to anyone or to my most gracious lord, but that you acknowledge my request as reasonable, that you would arrange it with the tax collector at Seida that I should be allowed to rent such property at a reasonable rate just like anyone else.

Thus I commend you to God.

Given at Wittenberg
Monday after Jubilate in 1539
Catherina Lutherynn[3]

And the master of land income now for the sake of his dear lady and godchild easily did what it seems Chancellor Brück had

---

[3] The original German text of this letter can be found in the appendix.

not pursued seriously or had even prevented some years earlier. Katie received the lease of the Boos at a low interest so that in 1546 Brück still thought she would have been locked in at the prevailing rates at ridiculously high interest.

Almost at the same time that she leased the Boos, she became the "lady of the house" of her own property. Her brother Hans von Bora could not continue on little Zölsdorf with his wife and child and was looking for a buyer for it. It was the last remnant of their father's fortune, the little property and poor inherited shelter or little house Zölsdorf, from whose fields one could see the gables of the nearby court in Lippendorf. So Katie's memory of her childhood and the desire to help her brother combined with her longing for her own land and soil.

In the week before Pentecost 1540 Hans von Bora was with Katie in Wittenberg. During those days she was just recovering from a serious illness that had brought her near death, and in connection with this her husband then spoke these words: "God always gives more than we ask. If we ask just for a piece of bread, then he gives a whole field. I asked God to let my Katie live, and He gives her a good year as well."

The purchase price amounted to 610 *Gulden*. It was rare indeed for Luther to have such a sum in his treasure chest (which was a thousand times too big for his savings). And since it was likely that Hans von Bora urgently needed to have the cash, the Elector gave 600 *Gulden*. He continued to support Katie by supplying building lumber. Obviously the small property was run down, but Katie's brother had not left her in the dark about that. Even before she could go to Zölsdorf, she had already requested and received a statement from the Elector according to which the tax collector of Altenburg was to supply her with the necessary building lumber. East of Altenburg a wide forest stretched toward the Mulde, the Leine Forest, where the timbers were to be taken. Spalatin, who was pastor and superintendent in Altenburg since the death of Fredrick the Wise, received many letters from Wittenberg in this regard.

Katie's dear Zölsdorf was in her thoughts weeks before she could actually see her home country again. So Luther wrote her a letter from Eisenach on July 26, 1540, with the joking title: "To the rich lady at Zölsdorf, Mrs. Doctor Katherine Luther, physically living in Wittenberg, and mentally wandering to Zölsdorf, for the attention of my sweetheart." A postscript authorizes Doctor Bugenhagen to open and read this letter in Katie's absence. So Luther didn't really know whether Katie was already in Zölsdorf or not. But it was November before she could enter her new "kingdom," as her husband calls the little property. Although she stayed there only a few days, he feared large expenses: "Now she'll squander what we've acquired." The year 1540 on her portrait medallion proves, however, that the lady of Zölsdorf not only arranged the much-needed repairs at that time, but also that she was rather careful to arrange a modest refurbishing of the small manorhouse.

The little property probably consisted only of the manorhouse, the stable, a barn, and a few small threshing houses. Already before the middle of the eighteenth century, as we learn from 1753, the manorhouse had "fallen over in a heap on account of age, and nothing more than a few of its old walls is visible." Two portraits of Luther and Katie were first placed in the manorhouse of the nearby Kieritzsch estate, in the so-called Luther Hall. Later they were moved to the church of Kieritzsch. A traveler, who was on that spot in 1793, reports about Zölsdorf, or Zeilsdorf as he calls it:

> Old people in that area still remember having seen the actual old manorhouse, Luther's residence. Now there's not even a single building here in which cattle are raised. The farmstead belongs to the nearby village of Kiwitzsch (sic) where one can see the busts of Luther and his wife brought from Zeilsdorf into the manorial chapel of the church at that time. They are approximately 1¼ yards high. Luther's image is made of sandstone, his wife's, however, is made of plaster.

Soon after that, Zölsdorf became a wilderness again when the very last building was torn down in 1800 or 1802.

Katie also worked in animal husbandry and agriculture at Zölsdorf. On May 20, 1541 her husband wrote to Mr. Ehrenfried von Ende, who was at the Castle at Wolkenburg on the Mulde, and asked him out of neighborly kindness to lend twelve bushels of grain and twenty-four bushels of oats to the new lady householder at Zölsdorf. After threshing she would repay him. From Luther's letters we occasionally learn about Katie's later visits to Zölsdorf as well, such as in the summer and autumn of 1541 when she probably stayed on the property for weeks until her husband called her home. In August 1542 she went back to Zölsdorf, but had to return home soon, however, when her little daughter Magdalena got sick. In August 1544 it seems Luther himself was in Zölsdorf once.

In his correspondence with Spalatin about the buildings, discussion about Katie trying to improve her property is quite frequent and continued for years. Since the Altenburg tax collector had in fact kept the Electoral order in 1540, the logs, choice logs, were felled the next year. But due to a mistake by the forestry officer they were sold to someone else. The letter Luther then had to write to Spalatin on January 12, 1542 contained sharp words against the tax collector that he should quickly pay compensation for the mistake. On August 30, Katie was able to leave Wittenberg with her wagon in order to have the logs picked up. In January 1543 the horses were back in Zölsdorf, in November 1543 for a third time, because eleven more logs were ready in the Leine Forest and twenty-four were still to be felled. However, since a snowstorm covered the roads with snow, the wagon had to turn around again without completing its task. The farm-horses still had to cover the long way between Wittenberg and Zölsdorf many times, although the Lord von Einsiedel at Castle Gnandstein offered his horse and wagon. He also said he was prepared to have the logs cut into boards at his sawmill. Nikolaus von Amsdorf, Protestant bishop at Naumburg since 1542, was also on friendly terms with his neighbors.

The relationship with the neighbors in the village and at Kieritzsch manor was not so good. Conflict had already arisen with them in 1541. The farmers stirred up disputes about pasture rights, and the manor laid claims on compulsory labor and other benefits that probably still rested on the small property even from the time when Zölsdorf had been a farmstead of Kieritzsch. Luther would have been ready for an amicable settlement for the sake of peace and good neighborliness, but then the Elector issued a judgment in Katie's favor. After Luther's death, however, the lawsuit over the Kieritzsch property rights began anew.

The letters in which her husband jokingly addresses her as "the Zölsdorf lady" and the "rich lady" or "the gracious lady of Zölsdorf" show that Katie took great joy in her little property despite this annoyance. He would also soon come to realize that she was not wasteful in acquiring Zölsdorf. If we were to believe Chancellor Brück, then Katie fared very poorly on her little property: Brück is sure it should have gone for 1,600 Gulden or even more, but they hardly got 600 *Gulden* back on it. The second statement, however, is obviously false, and the first is probably false as well. Brück probably calculated the alleged 1,600 *Gulden* as follows: 610 *Gulden,* which the Hans von Bora got for the property; 600 *Gulden,* which the Elector gave "for building the property" as Brück writes; another 100 *Gulden* for building lumber, which the Elector supplied; and a few hundred *Gulden* for wages and acquisitions—which comes to 1,600 *Gulden* altogether. But the 600 *Gulden* the Elector gave was probably not intended for building the property at all. The Elector had already supplied building lumber worth as much as 100 *Gulden* for the buildings on the small estate free of charge. Why, then, would he have given cash as well, and furthermore a sum equal the purchase price of the whole property? The Elector's gift of 600 *Gulden* was rather the purchase price itself, and so we must subtract the second 600 *Gulden* in Brück's calculation. In the end, the property came to be Katie's, not for 1,600, but for 1,000 *Gulden*. This is consistent with the fact that after her death in 1554 Zölsdorf was taken over by Wittenberg mayor Christoph Keller for 956 *Gulden*. So in her hands the property had increased in value about 350 *Gulden,* despite the war that had also plagued this area in 1546 and 1547. In contrast to the spiteful statements of Chancellor Brück, this fact is strong proof of Katie's good management. It would be strange indeed, if the same woman who so carefully managed her extensive household in Wittenberg had managed little Zölsdorf quite carelessly!

Luther praises a pious, efficient homemaker with the Proverbs of Solomon:

> She rises while it is yet night and provides food for her household and portions for her maidens. She considers a field and buys it; with the fruit of her hands she plants a vineyard. She dresses herself with strength and makes her arms strong. . . . Strength and dignity are her clothing, and she laughs at the time to come. She opens her mouth with wisdom, and the teaching of kindness is on her tongue. She looks well to the ways of her household. (Proverbs 31:15–17, 25–27)

He doesn't expressly mention Katie's name in connection with these words, but he could speak each sentence in reference to her.

And a few weeks before his death, on February 1, 1546, he writes from Eisleben: "To my dear wife Katherine Luther, Doctoress, Zölsdorferess, swine-marketer, and whatever else she might be." So did Katie want to be even more than the owner of the large garden at the sow-market, the renter of Boos, the lady of Zölsdorf manor? Indeed, she did. She wanted to buy a large new property, and her husband supported her in this so decidedly that his closest friends believed it was a matter of special concern to him. This is also proof that Katie was quite successful with the properties she bought and leased, and did not at all, as Brück states, risk a lot of money without drawing appropriate incomes from them.

To the north next to Boos and even closer to the Elbe was the Wachsdorf manor. It had belonged to Wittenberg University Professor Doctor Sebald Münster. Luther highly respected this friend. On November 20, 1538 he even extolled him as an honest lawyer. Münster demonstrated his philanthropy when the plague raged in Wittenberg once again in the fall of the next year, 1539. In his home he supported several students who were stricken by the epidemic, but on October 26 his wife died in the plague, and soon after, he succumbed to the epidemic. Ignoring people's apprehensive cries, Luther and Katie took their friend's four orphaned children into their home. Katie would have liked to acquire the Wachsdorf property, which had to be sold to settle an estate. But Chancellor Brück was her strong adversary in this matter too. Not until her husband had closed his eyes in death was she allowed to buy Wachsdorf despite Brück's advising against it, and she owed it to the Elector's intervention.

Wittenberg

At any rate, she was not alone among the wives of the Wittenberg professors in her ambition for her own property. At that time there was no better way to amass a small fortune or secure an interest-bearing savings than by acquiring a piece of land. At the same time, it offered a clergyman the only assurance of knowing that his wife and child would be cared for after his death, for in Smalcald the Elector was able to ensure only that pastors' widows would be cared for temporarily. In addition, a piece of land or a garden was welcome because there was little to buy in tiny Wittenberg and prices were high. "Our market is rubbish," Luther writes angrily, and Fredrick Mekum (Myconius), pastor in Gotha since 1524, describes for us the small town of Wittenberg, as it looked before the Reformation, with these words:

> Before this time, Wittenberg was a poor, shabby city; small, old, ugly, low, little wooden houses: more like an old village than a city. But now people come from all over the world who want to look and listen, and some want to study there.

With the influx of students, the city became more presentable, and in place of the old half-timber houses, some new stone houses went up. At the same time, however, food prices were driven so high that Luther complained that one now had to pay about two or three times as much for everything. The farmers outdid themselves in prices, and the rural pastors who brought their flour into the city even outdid the farmers, sometimes to Katie's annoyance.

Home Industry in Wittenberg

Since most of the larger properties in the city were now provided with a courtyard or garden and farm buildings, everyone who was able to, raised some cattle and did some farming besides their actual occupation. Katie industriously brewed beer and churned butter. Bugenhagen's wife also churned butter with her maidservants, not always successfully. And beginning in 1553, Melanchthon's wife received free malt from the Elector's mill in Wittenberg for her brewing. Jonas had a garden, and Chancellor Brück had four gardens and thirty–forty acres. And when raising goats was forbidden in Wittenberg in 1542, because the animals had caused a lot of damage to the undergrowth, Melanchthon's wife contacted the Elector and on November 7 got permission from him to keep her three goats. Luther's goat and the two kids that he assessed that same year for the "Turk tax" probably received exemption as well.

So Katie's household management differed from that of her friends only by the extent of the operation. Katharine Melanchthon, Walpurga Bugenhagen, and Katharine Jonas also did some farming, but Katie Luther had the larger enterprise. Joy in agriculture and in raising cattle was probably innate to the young lady of the landed genry, and with the autonomy her husband left to her in the household, she enjoyed managing, arranging things, and being in charge. When Brück wrote to the Elector after Luther's death that the widow didn't want to sell her property, but wanted to keep it, "to be able to work, to do business, and to manage it, and therefore not to lose any of her previous reputation," his words described her quite accurately, recognizing Katie's love for work, but also pointing to her pride. To have her own property was, in fact, a necessity for this tirelessly active and self-confident lady. But undoubtedly even more powerful in her was the effort to guarantee the future of her children who were growing up.

Her husband also gratefully recognized this. In his will from 1542, he asks his friends to bear witness for his dear Katie if someone would disparage her after his death, as though she had put aside something for herself to the disadvantage of the children. He clearly emphasizes that it was a particularly wonderful blessing that, with his income, he could afford to build and buy so much, and to maintain such a large and demanding household. Then he bequeaths a large part of his fortune to his dear and faithful wife, with full confidence that she will not use it to the harm or disadvantage of the children, but for their benefit and improvement. He was also opposed to placing a guardian over them, because she herself would be the best guardian for the children. He thanks her for always considering him a pious and faithful husband, always dear and worthy and good, and for having raised the children.

6.

CHILDREN AND CHILD-REARING

Luther and Katie's marriage was blessed with six children, three boys and three girls: **Johannes** [Hans], born June 7, 1526; **Elisabeth**, born December 10, 1527; **Magdalena**, born May 4, 1529; **Martin**, born November 9, 1531; **Paul**, born January 28, 1533; and **Margarete**, born December 17,1534.

While Luther put Katie in charge of taking care of the household, he stood alongside her in raising the children, and he saw to it that there wouldn't be any worry about physical welfare, spiritual food, and moral training in his house. He knew that people were watching him and his family like a hawk. With preposterous ridicule in 1540 he once joked about his enemies' sharp sense of smell, saying that their noses reached from Rome to Wittenberg. An evangelical preacher should not at all leave himself open to his friends either, because even if someone had only one fault compared to ten virtues, people would nevertheless make more noise about his one fault than about his ten virtues.

As he admonished his friends with the words of the Apostle Paul: "A bishop should be a man who manages his house well and has raised his children well." And since he required each of his pastors to have his life open and public, blameless before the adversaries, given to hospitality, and above reproach, then above all, his own house should remain pure and blameless. The Evangelical Church had been founded on Holy Scripture. The Bible and the Catechism should also be the foundation and cornerstone of every evangelical home.

Katie's Christian Faith

When Katie taught her oldest son, little **Hans**, to fold his little hands in prayer, and answered his first childlike questions about God and the dear Lord Jesus, she already had her husband's *Small Catechism*, the *Kattegissema*, as she called the book, because Greek words sounded too strange to her and therefore didn't like to pass over her otherwise eloquent lips. But she knew Latin and interpreted the Greek ending *ismus* in the word *Katechismus* as a Latin superlative form, *issimus*. She understood the content of the book better than the title. In one of his last letters, from Eisleben on February 7, 1546, her husband still writes: "Dear Katie, read [the Gospel of] John and the *Small Catechism*, of which you once said: 'Everything in the book is about me.' "

From the day that she gave up the veil and the carefree life of a nun and boldly faced an uncertain future with renewed confidence, up to the last difficult weeks on her sickbed at Torgau when she fervently prayed for death to hurry its slow progress, we have many witnesses about Katie's piety and her strong faith. Her husband called her strong in faith when she stayed by his side among the sick and dying during the plague in the autumn of 1527, while the professors and the students fled the contaminated city in droves. And when he had been close to death himself that same summer, he did not need to comfort her by referring to God as the Father of the orphan and Defender of the widow; she comforted him instead, resigned to the will of God. She was by no means carefree or easygoing. On the contrary, as her husband writes, she used to worry too much and feared what might possibly happen. But when there was real danger, she withstood it courageously. Even on her gravestone she is pictured for us as a pious Christian, holding an open prayerbook in her hands.

In the Nimbschen Cloister, the Book of books probably remained closed to her. In the Black Cloister it was the book of the house. Her husband compared the Bible to a very large and wide forest in which there were many trees of various kinds. One could pick various kinds of fruit from them, and he added that there wasn't a tree in this forest that he had not shaken and picked a couple apples and pears. He made sure that his Katie was also well-versed in the Bible. On October 28, 1535, he writes to Jonas:

> My lord Katie greets you. She is hauling, ordering a field, pasturing and buying cattle, brewing beer, etc. In between this she also continues to read the Bible, and I promised her 50 *Gulden* if she would finish before Easter. She is really going at it! She is already at Deuteronomy.

And fourteen days later he can report that she is still reading eagerly.

We hear that he directed her to the Bible or individual passages of Holy Scripture as well, particularly often to the Psalter, so that one time on April 14, 1538, she replied to him that she probably had read and heard and understood enough of God's Word now; God wanted her to use it! There are also testimonies about her being well-versed in the Bible in the *Table Talks* where she occasionally throws a Bible passage into the scholarly conversation of her husband and his lodgers. And though he was certainly joking when her called her his "deeply learned" Lady Katherine, he was serious when he said of her one time: "My Katie now understands the Psalms better than all the papists put together."

She also willingly and joyfully took up its teachings with her pious mind, like the earth opening up to the warming rays of the spring sunshine after winter's harshness! Her husband became her instructor. But at the same time he was the instructor of the whole Protestant world: *Doctor Martinus*, whose voice was heard far and wide, just like that of the emperor or the pope. Even if he was her dear *Herr Doktor* and her dear husband, still she never forgot that he was her lord. In the presence of others she didn't usually use the familiar form [*du*], she used the polite form [*Ihr*]. And when she was afraid she was going to already lose him to death in 1527, and when she mourned for him as a widow in 1546, it was a comfort to her in her sorrow that her dear and precious husband had served the whole world, and that many pious Christian people mourned his death with her.

Katie and Martin

Another woman perhaps would have felt oppressed at the side of such a husband, or would have become proud and arrogant. Our Katie certainly has the reputation of being proud, and we will examine these accusations even more closely. In any case, she was self-confident enough to take the place fitting for her as Luther's wife.

In a few words her husband unfolds for us a vivid picture from the first year of their marriage: Katie with her spinning wheel in Luther's study. It sometimes looked chaotic in here, because her organizing hand was probably not allowed to intervene too often here. There among the books lay letters, inquiries, opinions, controversial matters, and requests—on the table, in the windows, on the benches and footstools, on the desks, chests, and shelves—everywhere something could be put. While he sat there writing at his desk, she sat doing her spinning, and he was often so deep into his work that he completely forgot she was there. Then when he looked up, he was surprised that he was no longer alone like before, but with someone.

Katie's Talkativeness

Occasionally a question from his young wife would also tear him from his work, because it was hard for her to be quiet for a long time. While he often still observed monastic silence later on, even during mealtime, she had left that practice behind in Nimbschen along with other superfluous rules, and now she enjoyed being allowed to speak freely as to what was on her heart, which was quite a lot. One of her questions stuck firmly in his memory: "*'Er Doktor*," she had begun to say, "is the Grand Master the count's brother?" Strange question! Duke Albrecht of Brandenburg *was* the Grand Master in Prussia. Since Luther couldn't possibly imagine that someone didn't know that, he suspected that his Katie probably asked it only to have something to talk about. But he was probably mistaken. Where would she have learned such things? Politics and genealogy were rarely spoken about in the Nimbschen Cloister and Master Reichenbach's house, and while her husband dealt with the princes as with his equals, sometimes her head began to swim with the new images, before she started to sort her way through understanding who were all the various princes of the Holy Roman Empire of the German nation.

He liked to tease her about her talkativeness. When words flowed nonstop from her lips, he probably listened to her a while and smiled, but then he interrupted the flow of her speech with the teasing question: "Dear Katie, did you pray the Lord's Prayer before your sermon, then?" To a scholarly Englishman who ate with him in November 1538 and who did not understand German, Luther recommended that he take instruction with his Katie because she was very talkative: "She is so well prepared that she can far outdo me."

Luther was convinced that women were talkative by nature, while men had to learn it through much hard work. A woman who wanted to talk about her household would exceed a Cicero in eloquence. If only the short and sad subject matter of the long speeches was not always: "Give me money!" In addition, women had yet another weapon that was sharper than the tongue, namely tears. What they couldn't achieve by speaking, they got by weeping. If they spoke of something other than their households, however, it was worth little. There would certainly be enough words, but they were short on content. They didn't understand any of these matters, and therefore they talked higgledy-piggledy about lots of things, foolishly, disorderly, and wildly.

Nevertheless he heard and obeyed many of his Katie's words even when she wasn't talking about her household. Not even a quarter year had passed since their wedding, when their mutual friend Joachim Camerarius came to Wittenberg for a visit in August 1525. Despite his youth, Camerarius was already one of the most important scholars of Germany at that time. Respected equally highly by representatives of Humanism as well as adherents of the Reformation, he tried to mediate between the two intellectual movements that opposed each other with increasing hostility. A year earlier Erasmus had opened the already long-awaited attack on Luther with his treatise *On the Freedom of the Will*, and friends and enemies amidst fear and hope dreaded

Luther's answer. Luther was silent. He didn't think his greatest adversary's writing was even worth a response. But the opponents could easily interpret his scornful silence quite differently, and how could agreement be reached if Luther remained silent? Camerarius spoke with Katie about it, and Katie turned and pleaded to her husband, as he reports fifteen years later: "Erasmus believed no one could answer his writing, and I wanted to be silent, but Joachim persuaded my Katie to attend to this matter. It was at her fervent request that I wrote." So it was her doing that he finally did respond. His response appeared in December of that year. It did not meet the expectations of his friends who really wanted the discord between the Reformation and Humanism settled. It is one of the sharpest and most decisive of Luther's writings, the treatise: *On the Bondage of the Will.*

So there was probably a give-and-take exchange, in which Katie got a great deal more than she gave, but Luther didn't remain without return either. Katie brought something new into his life, enriching it and improving it. He was almost forty-two years old when he brought her home. When he was just fourteen, he had left his parents' house where he had spent an unhappy childhood. Since then in Magdeburg, Eisenach, Erfurt, and Wittenberg he had always lived among other people, twenty of those years behind the walls of the monastery. The indulgence controversy had hurled him into a battle against the papacy, in which he had to spend each year standing up for his doctrine with his own life. Attacked and reviled from all sides, he had toughened the powerful weapons of his spirit ever harder and polished them ever more sharply, but other latent gifts in him threatened to waste away. His sunny disposition and the whole depth and warmth of his mind were displayed only in his family life. He, and those who wrote down his *Table Talk,* draw quite contrasting pictures of life in the Black Cloister before and after Katie's arrival: In the past the lonely monk in his patched cowl, working tirelessly all day in the neglected rooms of the monastery, until he sank dead-tired onto his dirty straw mattress in the evening—now the husband and father, still tirelessly busy for others, but at the same time taking care of house and yard and, after work was done, sitting at his Katie's side in the evening hours, soon joking with the children until they were put to bed, soon having serious discussions and cheerful conversations with friends and loyal pupils.

Luther's Table Talk

Those discussions and conversations are Luther's famous and infamous *Table Talk*. Written down right away during the conversation by eager lodgers and then carefully collected, they were published in 1566 in a thick tome by Aurifaber, one of the youngest lodgers, although they were intended only for a narrow, trusted circle, and not at all for the public. They contain some superfluous material that has hardly any value for us, some harsh and loose words that may offend a sensitive mind, some opinions and some expressions that arose from a momentary disagreement or a temporary disturbance. Luther himself would have been against publishing these speeches. But how much pure gold there is beneath the dross, nevertheless! Just think if these tomes were removed from what has been handed down to us about Luther's life and his way of life! The picture would be much poorer and less colorful! Not that his stature would be diminished by this; his greatness lies in what he accomplished, and in his writings. But in his *Table Talk* we get closer to him as a human being. And we owe these conversations to the evening leisure hours, which he didn't allow himself to have regularly until he got married, and we owe them to the comfortable homeyness his Katie knew how to create.

Some hoped that marriage would make him much more mild-mannered and even not so severely harsh and rough in his writings. Yes, already on Christmas Day 1525, Erasmus believed that he could assert: "Luther is getting milder now and no longer rages so much with his pen. Nothing is so wild that it will not be tamed by a little woman." The old scoffer probably meant that very seriously.

But very soon Erasmus was bitterly disappointed in his expectation. Luther's character didn't soften with his marriage at all. His anger in controversy and the extreme fierceness of his language stayed the same. Even the Protestant side complained about this. People wince with sensitivity when someone attacks and doesn't hesitate to use terrible words that should be strictly forbidden, or when he speaks openly about things we would rather keep silent. We wish that he had dealt somewhat more politely in his polemic with the opponents. But it is hardly appropriate to complain when Luther behaved simply the way he really was. That does no more good than condemning the thunderstorm because it tore down a fence in the storm here or threw a lightning bolt at a straw roof there while at the same time clearing the air and bringing long-awaited rain. Without thunder and lightning there is no thunderstorm!

Luther's character did not change, not even with Katie, but she added to his character. One time he had learned a saying from noble Frau Cotta in Eisenach:

> Nothing dearer on earth can there be,
> Than the love of a woman, for whomever it can be.

The truth of these words became apparent for him in Katie. Now he wrote these words in his Bible translation as a side-comment next to that beautiful passage in Proverbs 31:10, a passage that at the same time shows how he understood the words of Frau Cotta and how he wanted them to be understood by others. And to his lodgers he said: "Children are the loveliest pledge in marriage; they bind together and maintain the bond of love."

Son Hans (Johannes)

With happy, and at the same time nervous, expectation, he awaited his firstborn, the child of a monk and a nun. He asked friends to pray for Katie. Already on April 25, 1526 he had offered the scholarly Strassburg Professor Nikolaus Gerbel's wife to be godmother if it was a girl. Gerbel, however, should be the godfather if it were a boy. It was a boy. On June 7 the day that was defined on the calendar (the so-called *Cisiojanus*) with the little Latin word *dat*, i. e.: "He gives," at noontime God gave Luther a healthy little boy who, according to the custom of the time, was baptized in the parish church on the very same day at four o'clock by Deacon George Rörer. Pfister, who had attended the child's parents at their wedding dinner, was also present at the ceremony of Holy Baptism. The good Wittenbergers believed the father would give his firstborn a rather exotic name, perhaps a completely new one, but Luther was of the opinion that common names were the best. The little one was baptized Johannes because that was the first name of Parish Pastor Bugenhagen who baptized him. Besides, his grandfather's name was also Hans Luther. The other sponsors were Jonas, Cranach, and the wife of Mayor Hohndorf in Wittenberg, as well as the Electoral Vice-chancellor Christian Baier, the Mansfeld Chancellor Müller, and Nikolaus Gerbel, the last three *in absentia*.

This little Luther was a miracle child [*Wunderkind*]. What firstborn child isn't? He showed up in letters to his father's friends, giving and receiving greetings and gifts, before he was even a week old. Although he didn't tolerate milk well at first and Katie could give him only a little nourishment, in one year he thrived and developed into cute and strong little Hans, so that his father could proudly write about the *homo vorax ac bibax*, the little man who heartily gobbles and gulps. In good time, at six months, his first little tooth had come, and his mumbling became more intelligible so that it soon sounded like scolding, but sounded delightful indeed.

The father's pride must likewise give us a measure of the mother's joy. Because all we learn about her is that it went well for her. Now that is the way of the world; such a little screamer pushes father and mother into the background. Good and bad were reported about little Hans. On October 19, 1527 he had accomplished a great feat, as Luther writes to Jonas: There were unmistakable traces that the little one, without any help, had crawled into all four corners of the room when no one was looking. Then Katie had bathed him and put him to bed, so now he couldn't have his father greet his godfather. But at the end of the month he became bedridden from teething, and for twelve days he could take only a little liquid food, while at the same time the plague broke out in the Black Cloister threefold, and a new member of the family was expected. Then Luther almost despaired. It cut him to the heart when he saw how the child fought the pain and tried to lift his head to show his parents a happy little face, and yet he couldn't do it because he was too weak. But fortunately, this danger also passed, and New Year 1528 brought little Hans a silver "Hans" (a coin with the picture of the Elector) from Doctor Jonas who was happy that his godchild was now jumping around again. And in the summer a rattle came from Nikolaus Hausmann, which the little one held up in the air.

Daughter Elisabeth (Elsa, Elslein)

The girl who was born as Luther and Katie's second child in 1527, in the first week after the plague, got the name Elisabeth after the mother of John the Baptist. Luther's letters don't say much more about her than the day of her birth, December 10, 1527, and her death on August 3, 1528. Her little gravestone can be seen in the wall around the old cemetery in front of the Elster Gate to the left of the entrance. The simple Latin inscription reads in translation:

> Here sleeps Elisabeth, Martin Luther's little daughter.
> In the year 1528, August 3.

In the deepest pain Luther came to know what he would not have considered possible before: that a father could be so tenderhearted concerning his child.

Daughter Magdalena (Lena)

He regarded the little daughter born to him on May 4, 1529 as replacement for little Elsa [*Elslein*] whom God had taken back. She received the name Magdalena at her Baptism. Only one of the godparent letters still exists, the one directed to Amsdorf with the news of the girl's quick and extremely happy birth.

Little Lena Luther was not yet a half-year old when her father travelled to Marburg in September 1529 to negotiate with the Swiss and the Strassburgers concerning the Lord's Supper question. "Kiss little Lena and little Hans for me," he writes to Katie on October 4. He was back with his family already by the middle of the month.

Diet of Augsburg, Castle Coburg

His absence lasted much longer the next year when he stayed at the Castle Coburg from the middle of April to the beginning of October, accompanied only by one lodger, Veit Dietrich, who had been with him in Marburg the year before, and his own nephew Cyriacus Kaufmann. The Elector along with Melanchthon and his advisors participated in the Diet of Augsburg. The actual negotiations lasted a long time since the Emperor arrived late and agreement was difficult. Meanwhile, in seclusion in the secure castle high above the city Coburg, in the realm of the birds (as he called it), Luther himself was still the focal point in the thoughts of the negotiating parties of the Diet, but impatience often took hold of him when he went for a long time without word from Augsburg.

After the first week of his stay in Gruboc,[1] as he twisted the name Coburg at that time, he wrote to the lodgers who stayed in Wittenberg that humorous letter in which he describes the Diet held by the jackdaws and crows that nested below the Castle in a little forest, the so-called Haine. Early each day amidst deafening "caw, caw" they prepared an enormous meal of wheat, barley, oats, and all kinds of grains and cereals. But boldly this man could joke so innocently during the weeks when his life's work was to stand the test before Emperor and Empire! And how pure and deep the mind from which came such a precious letter as the first letter to little Hans!

Luther certainly didn't leave his Katie alone with the two little children without being concerned. Even greater joy was brought to him by the message that one of the oldest lodgers, the pious theologian Jerome Weller, had kindly taken on Luther's family and had moved his brother, the lawyer Peter Weller, into the Black Cloister to support them. Jerome became little Hans' first teacher. He could only write good things about the child to Luther at Coburg, for which Luther heartily thanked him on June 19, and he even wrote to little Hans that same day as well, for further reward and encouragement:

---

[1] Gruboc is Coburg spelled backwards.

Luther's Letter to Hans

To my dear son, Hänschen Luther at Wittenberg.

Grace and peace in Christ, dear son! I am glad to hear that you are studying well and praying diligently. Keep doing that, my son. When I come home, I will bring you something beautiful from the fair.

I know a pretty, beautiful garden, where lots of children go. They have golden coats, and pick beautiful apples under the trees, and pears, cherries, and plums. They sing, jump, and are happy. They even have beautiful ponies with golden bridles and silver saddles. Then I asked the man whose garden it was, whose children they were? He said: These are the children who like to pray, read, and be good. Then I said: Dear sir, I also have a son, named Hänschen Luther. Might he not also come to this garden so that he too can reach such beautiful apples and pears, and ride such beautiful horses, and play with these children? Then the man said: If he likes to pray, study, and be good, then he too can come into this garden; Lippus and Jost too. And when they all come together, then they will also have fifes, drums, lutes, and all kinds of stringed instruments, and they will dance, and shoot with little crossbows.

And he showed me there a beautiful meadow in the garden, set up for dancing, where there were hanging pure golden fifes, drums, and fine silver crossbows. But it was early enough that the children had not yet eaten. So I could not wait for the dancing and I said to the man: But dear sir, I will rush and write about all this to my dear little son Hänschen, so that he will study, pray, and be good, so that he too may come to this garden. But he has an Auntie Lena, whom he must bring along. Then the man said: It will surely be so. Go and write that to him.

Therefore, dear little son Hänschen, study and pray confidently, and tell Lippus and Jost too, so that they also study and pray. Then you will come to this garden together. With this I commend you to the almighty dear God. Greet Auntie Lena and give her a smooch for me. Year 1530.

Your dear father, Martin Luther. [2]

Lippus and Jost, little Hans' playmates, are Philipp Melanchthon the younger (born February 21, 1525, died as notary of the University of Wittenberg, October 3, 1605), and Justus Jonas the younger (born December 3, 1525, beheaded in Copenhagen on June 20, 1567 because of his participation in the Grumbach matters).

Auntie Lena

Auntie Lena, however, to whom Luther sent a *Puss* (kiss) by way of little Hans, was Katie's Aunt Magdalena von Bora, who once was a nun in Nimbschen, but now was the good "house spirit"[3] in the Black Cloister, as she was appropriately called. She was at the same time the children's Auntie and Katie's support in running the household. The little ones apparently clung to her with great affection so that their father became almost jealous of her. But he also loved her and esteemed her highly. He probably named his second little daughter Magdalena after her. Again and again in his letters he added greetings to her. Even Doctor Jonas sent her greetings by letter. And as Luther from Coburg teased and shocked his Katie with the message that the papists in Augsburg wanted to put virtually all the monks and nuns back in the cloisters from which they had escaped, he even occasionally asked Auntie Lena in Wittenberg whether she wanted to go back into the convent. In doing so he got her so riled up that she answered in Latin. She was still alive at the beginning of 1537. When Luther had gotten over the serious illness that had come upon him in Smalcald, in a letter

---

[2] Another translation of this letter is in *Luther's Works: American Edition* 49:323–24.

[3] Or "house ghost" *Hausgeist*, a play on the word *Hausgast* (house guest).

he asks his Katie to thank God and he included the dear little children along with Auntie Lena to thank their heavenly Father that He let them keep their earthly father. The faithful old woman died that same year. Luther was at her bedside even in her final hours, comforting her. But when he saw her peace and devotion, he went over to the window and prayed quietly and then left her with the words: "It is well for you, for it is not death, but a sleep."

Luther's Father Dies

A gentle death had taken his father after he had been bed-ridden for a long time during Luther's stay in Coburg. At the beginning of 1530 gray-haired Hans Luther sensed his end approaching, as Luther's younger brother Jacob from the Mansfeld valley wrote to Wittenberg. But the old man's firm, tough body resisted for months yet. Luther, to his regret, could not travel to Mansfeld to fulfill a child's last duty to his father, but on February 15 he sent his nephew Cyriacus Kaufmann with a long, heartfelt letter of comfort and with the task of checking into whether father and mother could perhaps be brought to Wittenberg. He writes:

> It would make me really happy if you and mother could possibly be brought to us. My Katie also tearfully wishes so, as we all do. I hope we can expect what is best for you.

But he probably suspected that it was already too late, and that he and his Katie, little Hans, and little Lena, Auntie Lena, and the whole house could do nothing more than pray for him in his sickness and send their final greetings.

Then on June 5 at the Coburg he got word in a letter from his schoolmate, Hans Reinicke, that his father had quietly fallen asleep with faith in Christ on Sunday, May 29. There in Wittenberg Katie sorrowfully worried about how her dear husband would take the news. Veit Dietrich, therefore, calmed her on June 19:

> Dear Mrs. Doctor, I ask you not to worry about the Doctor. He is fine and healthy (God be praised!), and in the first two days has gotten over his father,

although it was very bitter for him. Immediately when he saw Hans Reinicken's letter, he said to me: Indeed, my father is dead too! Then immediately he took his Psalter, went into his bedroom and wept to himself so much that he was still out of sorts the next morning. He didn't let any of the flood of tears show.

In her compassion Katie wanted her husband to have a surprise that would bring him a little happiness in his grief. She sent him a picture of little Lena. It was not from Cranach's masterful hand, for it turned out very dark, but Katie achieved her goal, as Veit Dietrich writes to her in the same letter of June 19:

Kind, fair, dear Mrs. Doctor. Know that by God's grace your husband is still fine and healthy, and we with him. God grant you and your children everything good as well! You have done a very good deed in sending your Herr Doctor the portrait, because the picture helps him forget a lot of [sad] thoughts. He hung it on the wall above the table where we eat, in the prince's room. When he first looked at it, he didn't recognize her for a long time: 'Oh,' he said, 'Lena is so dark!' But now he really likes it, and more and more as time goes by he thinks it is little Lena. She really looks a lot like little Hans in the mouth, eyes, and nose, really in the whole face. She will be just like him.

Also from other messages we learn of Katie's concern for her husband while he was away. Unfortunately, however, in each case there are only the letters of Luther and his friends that tell about her. Not a single one of the letters she wrote to her husband still exists, although they may have been quite numerous. Not only did she have to answer her husband's questions but also carry out his assignments: instructions for the friends who had stayed with her in Wittenberg and who were also supposed to read and translate for her the most important letters written in Latin. She had to send reminders to the printers Nickel Schirlentz, George Rau, and Hans

Weiss who let Luther's writings sit around as though they were fruit in a warehouse instead of quickly putting them to press, and reprimand the goldsmith Christian Döring, for Luther said that in his whole life he hadn't seen any worse eyeglasses than the ones he had sent to him.

But even more, she would have had things to tell about the children, the lodgers, and the household. A letter he wrote to her on Pentecost Day ends with these words: "Greet, kiss, hug, and be kind to all, each according to his station." And she had all kinds of jobs for him as well. Once or twice he forgot to order the bitter oranges she wanted in Nürnberg, but when letter after letter reminded him, he finally did it. When his return was delayed from month to month, news came to Wittenberg one time that he was ill—a false report in the middle of summer, but how frightened Katie must have been! We know for sure that despite her courage she was a woman who worried. He finally returned home in the middle of October. For his little Hans he brought a big beautiful book made of sugar. Cyriacus Kaufmann, whom he had sent to Augsburg in August so that he might get to see some of the splendor of an imperial Diet, had bought it in Nürnberg on the way home.

Luther's Mother Dies

Luther's mother Margaret had also run the course of her life. She survived her husband by just one year, one month, and one day. Again a letter from Jacob Luther prepared them for the loss and put both parents and children into deep mourning—both their own children and the foster children who were being raised in the Black Cloister. This time, too, Luther had sent a long, heartfelt letter of comfort and commended his mother to God's mercy. The address reads: "My dearest mother," and the conclusion: "All your children pray for you and so does my Katie. Some cry; some eat and say [this at table grace]: 'Grandmother is very sick! God's grace be with us all.' Amen." On June 30, 1530 the gray-haired lady died, in whose facial features and posture in her younger years Spalatin had noticed amazing similarity with her great son.

Luther's Siblings

With his father's death Luther became the oldest one in his family, as he wrote to Melanchthon on June 5, 1530. But he left the arrangements of the estate to his younger brother Jacob. It didn't come to be divided up finally until July 10, 1534. The inheritance amounted to 1,250 *Gulden* and was divided five ways so that each received 250 *Gulden*. Besides the two brothers, Martin and Jacob, there were also three sisters, who were married to Mackenrod, Kaufmann, and Polner, citizens of Mansfeld. The last two were already deceased. Luther had brought their adolescent children back to Wittenberg with him in order to raise them along with his own children. Even now he had the sad experience of having his blood relatives try to cheat him in dividing the inheritance. In 1531 he spoke very vehemently in the circle of his lodgers concerning their greed and their ingratitude: If they dealt this unfairly already during his lifetime, what would they do to his children if he were dead? They would keep the money for themselves in the name of all the devils! If God grants him, as His servant, so much each year, then he would also commend his children to Him. His son would be rich in God, even if the relatives were poor as beggars.

Son Martin

From the content of these remarks, it is clear that they were spoken at a time when little Hans and little Lena were still the only children. On November 9, 1531, one day before the father's birthday, a second boy was born who, on his Baptism day, got his father's first name, Martin. Of the godparents we know only the young count Borziwog von Dohna, who at that time was studying in Wittenberg and living in Luther's house, and the Electoral treasurer Johann von Rietesel, who had been particularly close to the old Elector Hans, but who also, as the prince's favorite, had had some secret enemies. Now when John Fredrick had come to power, Rietesel, out of envy, felt threatened, and Luther was also afraid that Knight [*Junker*] Neidhardt might become dangerous to the dear lord godfather; therefore, he consoled him on December 6,

1532. To his Katie's greetings he even adds: "Your godfather will be a busy man; he will seize the opportunity to have your advice."

In his son Martin, Luther learned anew the truth of the saying: "My youngest child is my greatest treasure," and the fact that parental love shows itself more strongly and more powerfully the more the child is dependent on their care: "Little Hans, little Lena can talk now and don't require such close attention." The charming, devoted patience with which Katie took care of the little one and gave him terms of endearment, even if he might not have deserved them, caused his father to think about God's patience and mercy. But he also enjoyed it when Katie or Auntie Lena would change the little one's diapers and he would fight them with his little hands and legs. "Cry right out and defend yourself!" he said then. "The Pope would have bound me too, but now I am free."

Soon little Martin played with Tölpel, the family dog, who patiently enjoyed all the tugging and pulling, and when he was a little older, he had a doll that was his avowed favorite, which he groomed wonderfully and stood up for against his own father. But early on there was an "attitude" in the little one that seriously seems to have worried his father. Already when he was holding him in his arms as a very small child, he said half jokingly, half seriously: "If you become a lawyer, I'll hang you on a gallows." He repeatedly expressed his wish that none of his sons should want to become a lawyer, but he also feared that Martin might become one. He regarded the jurisprudence as worthless knowledge that did not want to sever itself from the old canon law, and many other things displeased him in its representatives as well. On January 8, 1538 he said: "My last will is that none of my sons join this profession. Hans will become a theologian. Martin is a little rascal I worry about. Paul will go against the Turk." He doesn't seem to have noticed an inclination toward medicine in any of his three sons.

Son Paul

But his youngest and most capable son, Paul, would indeed become a physician. Born on the night of January 28–29, 1533, he was baptized on the twenty-ninth at the Electoral Castle.

At the baptism dinner Master Anton Lauterbach tended to the guests. The godfathers were Duke John Ernst of Saxony, a younger brother of the Elector John Fredrick, the Electoral hereditary marshal Hans Löser, Jonas, Melanchthon, and the wife of the Electoral physician Caspar Lindemann. We still have the godfather letter that the father wrote to Herr Löser at one o'clock in the morning. At the baptism dinner Lauterbach would hear friendly conversations, because Jonas was talkative, and Melanchthon liked to tell little stories best of all. Among other things in the letter, Luther said he named his youngest son after St. Paul the Apostle at his Baptism, because he was so indebted to him that he could easily have named two sons after him. And he went on to speak about his sons' futures, and that he did not want to keep them for himself, but that they should have the best instructors. Whoever wanted to become a soldier should learn from the lord marshal, whoever wanted to study should do so with Jonas or Melanchthon, and whoever wanted to be a farmer should learn about it from a farmer.

Martin and Paul were probably not completely accepted by little Hans and his little friends Lippus and Jost, but they found the best playmates in each other. They were the most delightful little clowns, the finest "playing birds," as Luther calls the little children. Martin was a wild boy. He ran and jumped around the big house, which was sometimes too spacious for their father, but never for the children. When he was eight, he went outside with five-year-old Paul, armed with wooden swords, and while little Hans had to sit over his Latin, Martin and Paul got up on little wooden horses, shot their little crossbows, beat their drums, and blew the fifes, which were not made of gold or silver as the father described them in his fairy tale letter from Coburg, but they were no less beautiful because of that. Sometimes things did not go on without argument and controversy, but just as quickly the two were good to each other again. "Dear God," said Luther on August 17, 1538, "how well-pleasing to You is the life and play of such children! Yes, all their sins are nothing but forgiveness of sins."

Daughter Margarete

On December 17, 1534 Luther and Katie's youngest child was
born, a girl, who was baptized the next day with the name
Margarete, probably after her deceased grandmother. These were
harsh winter days. Luther was not allowed to go out and even
doubted whether the most distinguished of the out-of-town
godfathers, Prince Joachim von Anhalt, would be able to get to
Wittenberg from Dessau in this weather. Prince Joachim accepted
the sponsorship although he didn't come in the harsh, rough
weather. His court preacher Nikolaus Hausmann represented him.
Likewise godfather *in absentia* was Doctor Jacob Propst, once
Luther's monastic brother in Wittenberg, now pastor and
superintendent in Bremen. To him, as his loyal friend, Luther
entrusted his Margarete, his Maruschel as he lovingly called her,
and from his heart he repeatedly wrote about this, for he suspected
that he would not live to see his children taken care of. Therefore
after his death Propst was to choose a good husband for the girl. He
also had to write godfather letters to the godfathers who were in
Wittenberg, since he was not able to invite them in person. Only
the letter addressed to the wife of Master Göritz still exists.

"Train Up a Child . . . "

Luther often worried about how his widow and minor children
would fare after his death, but his firm confidence in God lifted
him above such thoughts again and again. He could not leave riches
to his family, but he wanted to leave them a rich God. Prayer was
the first thing the little ones in his house learned, and he praised the
pious, childlike simplicity in which they babbled without doubt and
without mistake about their dear God as their heavenly Father and
how they beautifully imagined eternal life in their own way, as if
streams full of pure milk would flow there and bread-rolls would
grow on the trees so that the little angels could eat and dance all
day long.

Through his children he saw some passages of Holy Scripture
brought closer for his understanding. In Psalm 2 we read the words:
"Rejoice with trembling!" Doesn't the one exclude the other? How

can one who is afraid still rejoice? When Luther occasionally let his little Hans play with him in his study, he understood the word of the psalmist. There the little one sometimes forgot where he was, started to sing with his bright little voice until his father scolded him a little. And then he didn't stop completely, but continued to sing his happy little song, but he sang softer and looked at his dear father with big eyes to see whether or not he was disturbing him: That is how we should always have God before our eyes.

At cherry-picking time the children certainly enjoyed the richly-laden trees much more than their father did. And if they were brought peaches, how the children's eyes gleamed in joyful anticipation! In seeing this, Luther wished for himself and his family: "If only we could think of Judgment Day with such joy in our hope!" And once when he jokingly asked his little Hans: "What do you think you cost me each year" and the little one answered in all seriousness: "O father, you don't buy food and drink, but apples and pears take a lot of money," then he compared the childlike lack of understanding to how adults foolishly think little about what God gives us each day and what we couldn't ever go without, but we highly regard what are pure trifles.

Luther made his *Small Catechism* the basis for the religious instruction of his children and foster children. Although he was an old Doctor, he nevertheless took it up with them daily. "When I get up in the morning," he said in a sermon in 1530, "I pray with the children the Ten Commandments, the Creed, the Lord's Prayer, and then some psalm." Since the spring of 1532 he conducted home devotions on Sundays with his wife and children, students and servants. Veit Dietrich later wrote these down and published them in 1544 as Luther's *House Postil*. When the children got older and could read, they had to read a paragraph aloud from Holy Scripture after the table prayer and before the meal. We can take it for granted that Auntie Lena also prayed with the children, and that Katie read the Catechism with them, even if it isn't expressly attested.

Music

Next to God's Word, Luther gave the highest honor to music. He himself knew how to compose music. He played the lute, and sang second voice [alto]. He often enjoyed singing with his lodgers in the evening. Actually he never got tired or weary of singing, as the Electoral *Kapellmeister* Johann Walter from Torgau testifies. He put many of Luther's pious songs to music and sang with him for many enjoyable hours. Capable musicians, singers, and lute players were always welcome guests in Luther's house. Of his children, Martin and Paul were musical, but all of them were instructed in music early on because their father considered the art of music indispensable. Little Margarete already sang religious songs when she was five. For his children he also composed the lovely Christmas hymn in which the angel announces to the children the birth of the Savior:

> From heav'n above to earth I come
> To bear good news to ev'ry home;
> Glad tidings of great joy I bring,
> Whereof I now will say and sing:

And the children gleefully greet the dear Christ Child:

> Welcome to earth, Thou noble Guest,
> Through whom the sinful world is blest!
> Thou com'st to share my misery;
> What thanks shall I return to Thee?

Luther making music with his children—this scene is often depicted by artists in more recent times. A beautiful oil painting by Gustav Adolf Spangenberg in the Leipzig museum takes us to about the year 1538 and shows Luther sitting at a large table in the living room with a lute in his hands, Melanchthon behind him, Katie in front of him, holding their little Margaret, gently sleeping in her lap. In front of the table, however, are Hans and little Lena, Martin and Paul; the three oldest with music in their hands and singing from it, while Paul, the younger, who can't read yet, sings along by heart. Heinrich Stelzner—in whose picture Hans is missing, for he was at boarding school for a while in 1537—takes us to a somewhat earlier time. And Otto Schwerdgeburth, Gustav König, and Bernhard Plockhorst, whose pictures show the Christmas celebration in Luther's house and also depict old Auntie Lena among those present. In all these pictures Luther is playing the lute.

Christmas

The Christmas tree that the artists place on the table is certainly artistic license, because at Luther's time no Christmas trees were lit yet. And the Christmas gifts in reality were also not as plentiful as in the pictures, because the day on which Luther and Katie gave gifts to the children was not Christmas Eve, but St. Nicholas' Day, December 6. In Luther's house register there is no record of expenses for "Christmas," but "annual fair" and "St. Nicolas" are next to each other. There were, however, also small gifts in Luther's house on Christmas Eve. "Little Lena, what will the holy Christ Child give you?" he once asked his little daughter. Christmas gifts were New Year's gifts at the same time, because, according to old church custom, Luther began the New Year not on January 1, but on December 25, on the day of Christ's birth. That's why it says in the last verse of his Christmas hymn:

> Glory to God in highest heaven,
> Who unto us His Son hath given!
> While angels sing with pious mirth
> A glad new year to all the earth.

Another celebration in which the children participated by praying and singing and reciting was the so-called "Kingdom," which was celebrated with jokes and dances and games in secular-minded homes, while Luther and Melanchthon tried to give it deeper meaning. Friends were invited to a festive meal, but a kind of test was arranged beforehand, and the king and queen, who were chosen each year, were to impose very strict assignments upon the rest of the houseguests: to recite portions from the gospels, to recite a psalm, to pray the Catechism, to make a little speech. Many would sigh if the task was difficult, and would stand there like a poor sinner, and Luther thought: How much greater will our responsibility and our timidity be on Judgment Day!

Discipline

Luther often thought of his own youth when his children were growing up, and raising them became more difficult. His parents had raised him with the best intentions, but they were overly strict. Once his mother beat him bloody simply over one nut. And one time his father flogged him so much that he almost lost all confidence and love for him, so that even his father was frightened by the effect of his harshness. Although they had sincerely meant it for his good, they had only succeeded in intimidating him, without ever supporting him. Therefore, he warned parents and educators about being too severe lest they should only make a child timid. And he would have considered it an even greater wrong for him if his Hans had become alienated, as Luther once was from his father. It couldn't be done without the rod, but one had to chastise in such a way that the apple went along with the rod. About raising children, he borrowed a saying that Nürnberg councilman Anton Tucher had made concerning political life: "Praise and punishment belong to good order."

Also, boys should be raised more strictly and treated more roughly than girls. Boys would only be spoiled by indulgence, he said in 1539. He still joked with little Lena then, but no longer with Hans; with him it didn't matter if he was five or thirteen. But even here he differentiated between lesser and more serious offenses. If a child happened upon some apples or pears, one should scold him, but not rush in with the rod right away. However, if money was taken or if he reached into pockets and coffers, that would be the time to punish. Where father and mother didn't straighten something out, the executioner would have to remedy it.

Above all else, he required children to have good manners, obedience, and respect. He beat his young nephew Endres (Andreas) Kaufmann with a stick because he had said a bad word at the table. Another nephew, Martin Luther, his brother Jacob's son, brought him so much grief by his disobedience that one time he was deathly angry and almost lost control of himself. He was so vehemently angry with his oldest son Hans because of an offense, that he wouldn't see him for three days although the boy asked him for forgiveness in writing. "I would rather have a dead son, than an ill-mannered one," he said as Katie, Melanchthon, Jonas, and Cruciger interceded for the boy. And when Katie's nephew Florian von Bora, who went to school with Hans at Torgau in 1542, took a knife from little Paul before he left, and even lied about it after he arrived in Torgau, Luther ordered three days of harsh corporal punishment for the boy as a thief and a liar. He deplored the fact that much was concealed from him: "Whatever is bad in our house, we are the last to learn about it. We only learn about it when all the people have dragged it through the streets."

Education for the Children

Naturally, the proposition of entrusting others with his sons' further education happened first with his oldest. It began promptly with Hans Luther's academic instruction. In the summer of 1530, the four-year-old received Jerome Weller as his first instructor. Weller certainly introduced him to the basics of Latin, unusually early in our method of education, but boys at that time generally had to begin learning at a tender age, and Latin was not yet a dead language, but actually was important as a world language necessary for scholars and the educated of all nations.

At any rate, Luther could have expected Hans to understand him in 1533 when he wrote down for him in Latin a warning against Erasmus, the enemy of all religion, the special adversary of Christ, the veritable image of Epicurus and Lucian. In that same year, 1533, on June 8, one day after his eighth birthday, Hans was pre-enrolled at the University of Wittenberg, an honor which at that time was often shown to the sons of professors and respected citizens in all German universities in their boyhood.

Luther himself could only be occasionally involved in the instruction of his children. He had to leave it to his lodgers, and the instructors and tutors appointed for this. We will get to know some of them later on. Despite good instruction, Hans seems to have made poor progress. The house was probably too noisy and the distraction of his younger brothers and sisters much too great. So the parents thought more and more about sending their oldest away to school. Their friends in Strasbourg: Wolfgang Capito, Gerbel, and Martin Bucer, learned about this, and Capito wrote to Luther on July 20, 1536 and asked him to entrust the boy to him and his friends. They would try to do their best for him. But Strasbourg was probably too far away for the parents, and Tübingen, where Camerarius was teaching at that time, was completely out of the question for the same reason. At the beginning of 1537 Hans was away from home, not in Strasbourg or Tübingen, but in a city near Wittenberg, so that on January 27 Luther allowed the boy, who had now shown better progress, to come to Wittenberg with his instructor and his wife for Shrove Tuesday. Auntie Lena was particularly pleased about his visit. She even sent a greeting to him through his father, indeed her last.

Since Luther in this letter speaks of the forthcoming completion of his son's studies, he would soon return to Wittenberg again. Now he actually studied at the University. In October 1539, at the same time as his young friends Lippus and Jost, he received his first academic degree, a Bachelor's, and now he no longer seemed like a child to his father. At his graduation in 1539, he gave a Latin speech in public. The Aesop-like fable, which Luther wrote down for his son in German in 1540, was probably intended for a Latin speech, the fable of the crab that traveled across country with the snake and became friends with it only when he had crushed its head. That same year, 1540, Luther wrote a short and precise introduction to dialectics for Hans. From the next year we have a very cordial and complimentary Latin letter, which twelve-year-old Electoral Prince John Fredrick from Torgau wrote to fifteen-year-old Hans Luther. The praises, which the young prince strews with lavish hand, were not completely deserved, however. Hans was actually still deficient in grammar and music. He also lacked discipline and initiative.

So his parents decided to send him away again, and in fact to a school that was considered one of the best in the country, the Latin School of Rector Markus Krodel in Torgau, which Luther highly regarded. On August 25, 1542, he wrote the cover letter for him. And with this letter he sent his son Hans and his nephew Florian von Bora to Rector Krodel. With Florian, Luther considered rather strict discipline advisable. He also commended his son to *Kapellmeister* Walter, because he, Luther, could train good theologians, but he really wanted to have good grammarians and musicians as well.

Magdalena's Death

Hans hadn't been in Torgau four weeks when, on the evening of the sixteenth or the morning hours of the seventeenth of September, his parents' coachman stopped his winded horse in front of Krodel's house and brought the rector a letter. He was supposed to keep the contents of it secret from Hans: Magdalena, her parents' joy, Hans' favorite sister, was ill and near death and wanted to see her brother again. The two loved each other deeply. Luther kept a faint hope that seeing Hans again might boost his daughter's dwindling powers. But also so that he would not have to blame himself later, he had sent the carriage and asked Krodel to send the boy to Wittenberg as quickly as possible, but to conceal from him the sad reason he was being called home.

Hans arrived at his parents' home in time. For four days Magdalena struggled with death, days of the deepest concerns, hope sometimes flickering and then going out again. These days were bitterly painful for the parents, because the girl had grown up to be so charming, gentle, and good—everyone's favorite. Not a single time in her young life had she made her father angry. And now he stood at her deathbed and said:

> I love her very much! But if it is Your will to take her, dear God, then I will be glad to know that she is with You.

And he went on:

> I would like to keep my dear daughter, because I love her so much. If only our Lord God would let me keep

her! But Your will be done! Nothing can be better for
her—nothing could be better.

And he asked the sick girl:

Little Magdalena, my little daughter, would you like
to stay here with me, your father? And would you also
like to go to your Father above?

Then she answered: "Yes, dear father, as God wills!" "You dear
little daughter!" he then said, and turned away to hide his emotions.
And his Katie, who was weeping out loud, he comforted with the
words: "Dear Katie, just think of where she is going! It will be well
with her!"

She had no pain and no fear of death. In the end she gently fell
asleep. On the night of September 19–20, Katie dreamt that two
handsome young men came and took her daughter to a wedding.
Early in the morning Melanchthon asked about little Lena's
condition, and Katie told him her dream. But the faithful friend,
who highly regarded signs and dreams, was terribly frightened
because he suspected and even told others that the two young men
were the dear angels who would come and take this young girl to
the kingdom of heaven into the true wedding.

Shortly after nine o'clock on September 20 she passed away in
her father's arms. While she was breathing her last, the big, strong
man at her bed sank to his knees and wept bitterly and prayed, not
that God should let him keep her, but that he could let her go.
Katie, however, stood behind him, speechless because of the pain.
And the pain also overwhelmed him when they lifted the dead child
from the bed into the coffin and found that the coffin was a little bit
too short. "The little bed is too small for her!" he said, and then he
broke into intense weeping and quickly left. At the funeral,
however, he showed himself to be comforted and resigned to the
will of God before his household and the friends and acquaintances
who carried his Magdalena to her last resting place. On the way
home from the cemetery he said:

My daughter is now taken care of, both in body and
soul. We Christians now have nothing to complain

about. We know that it should and must be this way,
for we are all the more certain of eternal life.

Of the two Latin couplets that he wrote down as his daughter's epitaph, only the first was engraved on her gravestone. An old German translation reads:

Here I, little Lena, Dr. Luther's daughter, lay my head,
And, with all saints, rest in my bed.
Though I too in sin was born,
And would forever be forlorn,
Yet now I live and have it good,
LORD Christ, redeemed with Your dear blood.

The loss was too great for the parents to ever get over it. Little Elisabeth, who died in 1528, flesh and blood of their flesh and blood had already passed away, but with Magdalena's death they felt as if they had been killed. Their daughter's image would not leave their hearts. They kept seeing her face, hearing her voice, feeling her hands, in death just as in life. Katie sobbed for weeks in bitter pain when she thought about her dear child. Three years later Luther still writes: "It is an amazing thing how much the death of my Magdalena torments me. I cannot forget her." In the eyes of their friends her death remained an example of a blessed death in Christ. One time, a half-year later, when they were talking about Luther's father and the confident answer he had given to the preacher in his last illness, Melanchthon said to Luther: "Blessed are those who die thus confessing Christ, just as your Magdalena died."

While the pain was still fresh, new uneasiness arose in Katie's anxious heart when she had to let her oldest return to Torgau. When he left, she said to him: "Come home if you aren't feeling well!" Hans took a long time getting over mourning for his sister. And while he had enjoyed it in Torgau before, where Krodel and his wife treated him well (better than he had been used to at home), now he was consumed with homesickness, and since Christmas was coming, he wrote to his mother and asked to be allowed to return home. Although Katie herself might also have personally longed for her son, she nevertheless agreed with her husband that Hans should stick with his duty in Torgau, and she also left it to her husband to reply to Hans. Luther's two letters, to Krodel on December 26, 1542 and to Hans the next day, still exist. He tells the rector that Hans should stay with him. But if he became ill, the rector should inform Luther. He admonishes his son to bear his pain manfully and not become a new worry to his mother. She did not want her parting words to be understood as he had taken them, and it was her wish that he should put aside his mourning, and happily and calmly continue his studies.

Sons Mark and Paul

Luther later had thoughts about also sending both his younger sons, Mark and Paul, to Markus Krodel at Torgau, but nothing came of it. Hans probably returned to Wittenberg in the fall of 1543. Melanchthon, who already had Justus Jonas the younger in his house, seems to have taken on Hans Luther and his younger brothers as well.

Foster Children

At the same time a whole series of foster children grew up in the Black Cloister with Luther and Katie's own children and nephews and nieces, who all wanted to be fed, clothed, and brought up. One time in 1542 they were talking at Luther's table about King Solomon, of whom Holy Scripture reports that he had countless women in his palace, and Luther said that among them were probably many poor girls from David's family. They all came to King Solomon and he had to supply food for them. He imagined the palace of the Jewish king about a hundred times bigger than the Black Cloister, because all the poor relatives from his father's family had come to him as well: Andreas, Cyriacus, Fabian and George Kaufmann, Elsa and Lena Kaufmann, Hans Polner who had at least two more siblings, Martin Luther from Mansfeld, and Anna Strauss. We hear Luther talk about these eleven foster children only occasionally. And there may have been even more.

George Kaufmann

George Kaufmann and his wife, Luther's sister, both died young, it seems. The George Kaufmann mentioned in Luther's estate settlement from July 10, 1534 was not the father, Luther's brother-in-law, but the son of the same name, because Luther calls him his "cousin." Since he represented his brothers and sisters during the distribution of the estate, he was probably the oldest of the six "Kaufmanns" [*Kaufleute*, "merchant people"]. In the autumn of 1536 he was still in his uncle's house, and one time Luther violently flew off the handle at him when he came home with his carousing comrades. "Drink so that misfortune can come upon you!" he shouted angrily, and more calmly he added: "These people will not live to be old. Most people ruin themselves by their craze for drunkenness."

Cyriacus Kaufmann

Cyriacus Kaufmann, likewise, was already grown when he was registered at the University on November 22, 1529, because the next year he was able to travel to his grandparents in Mansfeld on behalf of his Uncle Luther, and in 1530 he accompanied him to Coburg. He was later mayor of his hometown Mansfeld.

Andreas and Fabian Kaufmann

Andreas and Fabian Kaufmann were enrolled at the same time as Hans Luther, June 8, 1533. Andreas was probably the nephew Luther recommended to Camerarius. The letter that deals with this is not dated, but probably belonged in the time when Camerarius was teaching at the University of Tübingen, because Andreas Kaufmann was registered in Tübingen on June 22, 1541. At his matriculation in Wittenberg, Andreas, or Enders as Luther calls him, would still have been a boy, one whom Luther once had to beat with a stick. Fabian liked to lie in the clover in the summer and to take his midday nap there, despite the snakes; once he found a whole nest full. When he got secretly engaged later, Luther was fiercely angry with him. In 1548 Jonas recommended him to Prince George of Anhalt for a job.

Lena Kaufmann

The two sisters, Elsa and Lena Kaufmann, were of marriageable age in 1538; likewise Anna Strauss, who was related to Katie. The three girls surely were efficient in helping Katie with the domestic work and taking care of the children. To some extent they filled the gap that the death of the old Auntie Lena had left.

But the fosterparents nevertheless had to keep both eyes open as well. As a rather young girl, Lena already wanted to get married too much. Her fellow tenant, Master Veit Dietrich, had won her heart, and she returned his affection, and the young, pious, and capable theologian would have been welcome to Luther and Katie as a suitor if only Lena had been somewhat more settled. Luther did not regard young girls as storable fruit, but still they should properly mature first. He also did not yield to his family's inopportune and unwise wishes as softly as Melanchthon, who let his oldest daughter Anna marry at age 14, to her misfortune, and to his ever-recurrent pain and his neverending regret. Luther said to Dietrich at that time:

> I know, of course, that my cousin would be taken care of with you. I don't know, however, whether you would be taken care of with her. She still has to be raised better. If she will not obey, then I will give her to some dark farmhard and not deceive a pious scholar with her.

And when Lena wouldn't give up thoughts of marriage, he thought she should be punished with a good stick, so that the idea of taking a husband would pass from her. For it would not be advisable for young people to court so early in their first passion and so suddenly; otherwise there would come regret, that little dog that bites many people.

Veit Dietrich soon found another girl who suited him better than Lena Kaufmann. And a few years later, without hesitation

Luther was able to arrange the wedding of his foster daughter who was now old enough. The suitor was Master Ambrosius Berndt, professor at the University of Wittenberg, a widower. He had already been married twice. His first wife had died at the beginning of 1532. His second marriage had also ended after a short time when his wife died in November 1537. And on November 10, 1538, Berndt publicly asked Luther for Lena's hand in marriage, in the presence of the guests who were celebrating their Lord Luther's birthday. The present guests were Jonas, Melanchthon, and Cruciger; also Martin Bucer and Camerarius, who at that time were on a visit in Wittenberg, and the vice-chancellor Dr. Franz Burkhardt. Berndt's "matchmaker" was the Wittenberg tax collector. Luther delivered the girl to him with the words:

> Dear Lord Tax Collector and dear godfather, I have always dealt with the girl, knowing that I will answer to God who has bestowed and given her to me. God grant them His blessing and benediction that they may live together well and as Christians. Amen.

Then when bride and bridegroom had worrisome thoughts about their wedding and were discussing whom they should invite as guests, Luther said to them: "Be of good courage! That's no concern of yours." What were he and Katie there for? Katie provided almost too generously for her foster daughter. Lena's wedding dress was filled at the neck with edgings of interwoven gold, such as even King Solomon and Julius Caesar never wore, in Luther's opinion: "Everything has to be gold now! What in the past would have been given to decorate the church now hangs on her neck!" But even he was eager and busy with preparations for a magnificent wedding. He had already scheduled the nuptials for November 27. Even before this time he often warned against letting a lot of time pass between engagement and marriage, because false friends and the devil, who were enemies of a happy marriage, liked to come between them.

Katie certainly had the most work. She had to bake and cook. But her husband held the wine tasting on November 20 in order to give the guests a good drink so that they would be happy. And he joked with the Englishman who was his guest at that time and to whom he had already recommended his Katie as a master of language and asked him: "How does one get wine into the cellar without rolling it in? Answer: Roll the must[4] in, and it becomes wine. And again: Which waters are widest? Answer: Snow, rain, and dew, which cover the whole country." Two days later he asked Prince John of Anhalt to send him a young boar or a pig's head since he was supposed to provide for his little orphan, his sister's daughter.

He also joked with the bridal couple, and when he saw the two whispering in a dark corner, he teased them: "It surprises me that a bridegroom would have to talk with his bride so much! Don't they get tired of it? But one shouldn't upset them; they have a special right that goes beyond all law and custom." He also asked why one always says "bride and bridegroom" in German, and never "bridegroom and bride." It's the same with cheese and bread, where cheese always comes first, and the main thing, bread, comes afterwards. Then he had the schoolmaster John Kalkofen perform with his musicians. The guests came from Mansfeld and from Eisleben, Luther's brother Jacob, and his father's brothers Veit and Heinz Luther, and other relatives and friends, such as the Mansfeld Castle preacher Michael Cölius, as well as the whole group of Wittenberg friends. And the City Council of Wittenberg sent a gallon of Franconian wine and four quarts of Jüterbog wine; Jüterbog even at that time had a very significant winery.

Lena became a widow quite early. Master Berndt died in January 1542. Luther and Katie took their niece back into the Black Cloister with them. The young widow became a great nuisance for them, however, when she got involved with a twenty-year-old medical student in 1545. Luther hardly knew the young man. His name was Ernst Reuchel or Reuchlin and came from the little Saxon mountain town of Geising. His father George Reuchel was, as we shall soon see, a pastor in Maxen in the Pirna district. Luther suspected Reuchel was only out for Lena's small fortune, but for other reasons he very keenly disapproved such secret engagements

---

[4] "Must" is the juice of the fruit before it is fermented into wine.

without consent of parents or guardians. Since Lena refused any advice, he asked his friend Lauterbach to check with Reuchel's family. They were not to think that he, Luther, wanted to give his consent; on the contrary he would prefer that Reuchel's parents remove him from the University of Wittenberg before he was forced to proceed against the young man more severely.

George Reuchel, the pastor in Maxen, whom Lauterbach immediately went to see, had already received a letter from his son Ernst, in which he wrote that even Melanchthon had sternly admonished him, and he would be glad to be free of the widow, but she wouldn't leave him alone. The very next morning the pastor promised to call his son home from Wittenberg. Lauterbach reported this to Luther. But Lena was as under a spell and said that what Lauterbach wrote about Reuchel's father was false. She couldn't let go of the young Reuchel, and he wasn't letting her go. They didn't dare to get married while Luther was still alive, but after his death they tied the knot. They had to struggle in deepest poverty until Ernst Reuchel finally found employment as a medical practicioner in Stendal in 1549 and gradually came into income and respect as well. He lived into his seventies as appointed physician of the city of Lübeck.

Elsa Kaufmann

We do not learn whether Lena's sister, Elsa Kaufmann, got married. In 1542 she was still unmarried in the Black Cloister.

Anna Strauss

Already in 1540 a rather respectable suitor had asked for Anna Strauss, but he was somewhat notorious in Wittenberg: Doctor Jacob Schenk, the Electoral court preacher at Weimar, a highly talented man, but unsettled, proud, and vain. He had already had a controversy with Melanchthon earlier over the Lord's Supper, and at that time Melanchthon had given him the nickname Cuckoo because of his ingratitude. Now with a bold, fatal step he went beyond Luther's doctrine and preached that it was enough to proclaim the pure Gospel, and it was quite unnecessary to keep expounding the Law to the people and to hold their sins before them. Luther foresaw that there would have to be a public divide with little Jacob Schenk, this Jake [*Jäckel*], as he called him, and when Schenk asked for Anna Strauss's hand in the spring of 1540, he and Katie rejected him. "I wouldn't give my daughter to Doctor Cuckoo," said Katie. "He doesn't preach the Gospel purely." Schenk was likewise turned down flat by Bugenhagen and Mayor Krapp, Melanchthon's brother-in-law.

Anna Strauss, it seems, was more docile than Lena Kaufmann, at least we don't hear that Luther had serious trouble with her. Since she still had blood relatives left in her home territory, for the time being it would have been their obligation first, and not Luther's task to overcome her defiance. "If my Strauss wanted to marry," he said soon after Schenk's request, "and if I saw that the marriage would not be in her best interest, I would send her to her relatives."

The young girl stayed in the Black Cloister, however, until the next year when a Master Heinrich Schillingstadt from Kölleda in Thuringia courted her. The engagement was on December 18. For the wedding, which was celebrated on January 30, 1542, Luther asked the princes Joachim, George, and Johann of Anhalt for venison. The Anhalt princes, who lived near Wittenberg, were happy to provide for their pious and learned neighbors. But this time Luther had pangs of conscience for turning to them again so soon, because Prince George had just sent venison to Wittenberg on September 13, almost too much at one time, and he invited Luther to eat well with Melanchthon and Bugenhagen and other good friends. Some weeks later a wild boar had arrived again from Dessau, which would have been quite a delicious wedding roast had it come in December, but it had already been eaten by that time. Luther's request was quickly fulfilled, so that he had enough chickens and meat for his guests and did not need to fill them up with sausages and tripe, as he feared.

Nephew Martin Luther

Martin Luther from Mansfeld, Jacob Luther's son, was enrolled at Wittenberg in April 1539 and was still a student in 1547. He didn't do well, as we already learned, at least not at first. Later he seems to have been active in public service in Wittenberg. He died in June 1558.

Hans Polner

And Hans Polner, who had come to Wittenberg and enrolled at the same time as Cyriacus Kaufmann, caused concern and trouble for his uncle. While Luther was staying at the Coburg, it seems Katie already had difficulties with the young man so that her husband sent a letter putting him under Peter Weller's control and Bugenhagen's supervision. Polner studied theology, but had inherited his father's craze for drunkenness. And since he was also prone to impulsive anger, Luther once angrily explained to him that people of his nature had to stay away from wine as though it were poison. If only he would think about what disgrace he could bring on himself and his household, on this city and the church, if he ever got carried away and did something wicked while he was drunk!

Polner seems to have improved. In 1542 he was still an assistant in Luther's house and had already ascended into the pulpit. One time after going to church, Katie said that she understood Polner better than Pastor Bugenhagen, because he sometimes got too far off topic. Then her husband smiled a little when he replied: "Polner preaches the way you women tend to talk because they say whatever comes to their mind." And he added a comment that Jonas often made: "A person shouldn't talk to all the soldiers he meets." It might be true that Bugenhagen sometimes took up several thoughts. His sermons might have been somewhat too long. So a woman who had to dish up a tough Sunday roast apologized with the words: "Oh, I thought Dr. Pommer [Bugenhagen] would be preaching today!" But preachers who wanted to say everything that came to mind were like girls who were sent to the market and if another girl met them, they had a chat, and if a second girl came, they held a conversation with her, too, and then with a third and fourth, and they would take so long to get to the market.

Later on, Polner was a schoolmaster in Zahna near Wittenberg and on March 15, 1534 was ordained into the ministry at Jessen.

His siblings are mentioned only in the will from 1534. One of the girls, Magdalen Polner, was the niece Katie sent to take care of her husband in 1537 when he was very ill in Smalcald.

Hanna von der Saale

Poor relatives on Katie's side besides Anna Strauss found accommodations in her husband's house as well. Already in 1527 a Miss Hanna von der Saale was staying in the Black Cloister. On December 28 she got engaged to an Evangelical clergyman, Peter Eisenberg, who came from an honorable old family from Halle and was closely related to the Dresden pastor of the same name, a staunch opponent of the Reformation. The wedding took place on January 1, 1528.

Katie's brothers also repeatedly turned to Luther's intercession. On the other hand Cousin Lena was a support rather than a burden for Katie. But, even when she was widowed, Katie had to worry about her nephew Florian von Bora.

Family Life

The concerns, the frustration, the disappointments that Luther and Katie experienced in their children and foster children, put together on paper, seem bigger and worse than they really were. Based on the amount of material that has come down to us, we learn more of the exceptions than the regular routine of family life in the Black Cloister. The lodgers had no reason to take up their pens if the children were well behaved and good. But if Luther had to punish or scold, they eagerly wrote that down and preserved the offense of the little sins for posterity.

Similarly, when everything is going well, there isn't much in Luther's letters. They usually include only short greetings from Katie and the children. If events in the family are told in more detail, the reason is almost always illnesses, wishes, concerns, and complaints. But isn't that the case in every family with lots of children? And if we gather together everything like this that we hear about Luther's house, how insignificant it is! What speaks to us much louder and more urgently than his concerns are the joyful words in which he praises marriage as a blessed state, and thanks God for the good fortune He has bestowed on him.

Neither of the parents experienced the joy of seeing their sons in office and dignity. Only Paul, the youngest, came to higher honors, but the two older brothers did not dishonor their parents' memory either. But Martin was of poor health, and Hans was probably better suited to some career other than academics. If Luther had lived longer, perhaps he would have led his oldest son to a different profession, because even if it was his favorite wish that his sons should like to study, nevertheless he was not one of those blinded fathers who would force a child to do something to which he was not suited. In 1543 he even said that if one saw that a child couldn't learn anything, he shouldn't be beaten to death, but rather pointed in a different direction.

The goal of education was not knowledge, but Christian training. Even when he was a monk Luther had preached to his congregation that parents could deserve either heaven or hell by the way they raised their children. Indeed, the fact that children turned out well was not in the power of parents, but in the hands of God. As head of the house for his wife, his children, and his household, he prayed this prayer:

> Dear heavenly Father, since You have placed me in the honor of Your name and office and also willed that I be called and honored as father, grant me grace and bless me so that I direct and provide for my dear wife, children, and household in a godly and Christian manner. Give me wisdom and strength indeed to guide and raise them well, and give them a good heart and the will to follow and be obedient to Your teachings. Amen.

7.

MEMBERS OF THE HOUSEHOLD

When Prince George of Anhalt wanted to visit Luther in the spring of 1542 and stay in his house for a while to engage him in religious discussions, his trusted advisor, Luther's loyal admirer Master George Helt, advised him against staying in the Black Cloister: Luther's house was the lodging place of a motley group of young people, students, girls, widows, old women, and quite young boys. Because of the huge commotion there, many sympathized with the venerable father Doctor Luther, because not everyone in the house was alive with his spirit. And earlier Luther had already lamented: "If I fit in the registry of the poor, it is because I have too large a domestic staff."

Boarding House (*Bursa*)

His large domestic staff was just one consequence of his large household, but this went along with his position. University teachers were expected to run a *Bursa,* or *Porse* as Luther writes, in their house, a kind of arrangement in which the members of the *Bursa*, the "lads" [*Burschen*], would receive room and board for a boarding fee. Often they received academic assistance as well. From this arrangement the professors gained a substantial subsidy to their small salary. With some the annual payment climbed to 40 *Gulden*, so that in 1538 the Elector set 30 *Gulden* as the limit. Of course, it was also a heavy burden, but with the conditions at that time and the large enrollment at the University of Wittenberg it was a duty that was difficult for Luther himself to carry out, even if he sincerely wanted to do so. Many out-of-town friends wanted Luther to take in a young relative or acquaintance of theirs as a favor.

There was already a kind of *Bursa* in place when Katie arrived in the Black Cloister, but a quite extraordinary sort of *Bursa*. It was not on a reciprocal basis; rather, Luther had opened his house and a place at his table to every needy person, expecting no reward except from God. When he got married, the only change that was made was that now, except for exiled clergy, he and Katie had to take only poor relatives and former nuns at their table and under their roof. At the same time if more affluent lodgers came, it was not Luther's, but Katie's doing.

Arranging and managing the household accounts was in Katie's firm hand. We have already heard how Katie was criticized for insisting on correct payment for room and board. She took these small annoyances off her husband's hands as much as she could. She also had to set the number of the lodgers and decide whether to accept or turn away new applicants. When Chancellor Müller, little Hans' godfather, at the beginning of 1536 asked them to accept a young Mansfelder named Matthew Kegel, Luther would have liked to accept his young compatriot as a boarder, but the table was full and he couldn't displace the older lodgers in the middle of the semester. But he hoped a place would become available after Easter; then he would willingly accommodate his friend—if Lord Katie would be gracious about it otherwise.

The number of lodgers was always quite large. There were always many who longed to be accepted into Luther and Melanchthon's homes. Mathesius, who ate at Katie's table for a while in 1540, also describes for us how things were at Melanchthon's house at that time. Lippus prayed a Latin prayer before the meal, and his little sister Magdalena read aloud from Luther's German Catechism. Then came the boys, one with a story, another with Holy Scripture, a third with a portion from the gospels, a fourth with Livy, a fifth with some ancient Greek, perhaps it was Thucydides, the sixth with the Psalter, and all of them—all of them—stood around Lord Master Philipp, as if he were an oracle they had to consult. One of Luther's lodgers once reluctantly said that the young people should go easy on the great man a bit more, but Luther replied: "Philipp is now at once the servant of the whole world and a menial of all menials."

The young lads, of course, did not presume to approach Luther as easily as they did Melanchthon. The veneration with which Doctor Martin's most trusted friends treated him, their honorable father, set the standard for the conduct of outsiders. When the Herr Doctor kept his monastic silence at mealtime, no one dared to speak. But everyone eagerly waited for him to begin to speak, for his *Table Talks* were the most precious spices of their meal. He used to give his lodgers the floor with the question: "What's new?" But they waited until he added: "You prefects, what's new in the country?" And only then did the older ones at the table begin to speak and carry on the conversation with questions and interjections. But the younger lodgers listened carefully, not daring to speak, and we learn that they belonged to the "Round Table" only when Luther deigned to address them with a joke or directed a word of warning to them.

Games and Entertainment

Luther also liked to take time with these, his youngest lodgers, who were at the same time playmates of his own boys as they were growing up. So in 1531 he announced an "invasion" to the Lochau preacher Michael Stiefel: He was coming to take a look at his cherries with many cherry-loving boys. On the bowling green, which he had built for the young people, he sometimes showed his own skills and, as Doctor Ratzeberger reports, one time he bowled around the pins, another time sideways or over the corner. When the boys wanted to race each other, he would offer them a little prize. And just as he used to shoot the crossbow at a target and practice music in his loneliness at the Coburg with Veit Dietrich, so also in Wittenberg he liked to see his students fill their free hours with musicmaking or innocent games, so that they were not tempted by idleness into drinking, playing dice, and cardplaying. But he loved the noble game of chess, and he himself was a good player.

Table Companions

The Wittenberg friends comprised the core of the table company. We will get to know them more closely in the next chapter: Melanchthon, Bugenhagen, Jonas, Cruciger, Rörer, Aurogallus, and others. They were not regular dinner guests of Katie's, but were there quite often, or they came for a cool drink after supper, which in those days was taken at an earlier hour than now. Often there were out-of-town guests present, friends and colleagues, but also high-ranking officials and princely personages.

Tutors

Among the actual lodgers were adult men, young tutors, and half-grown boys. The younger ones were stood under the discipline of the older ones, as we occasionally hear, and one of these, as Luther's representative, "vicar" (*Stellvertreter, Vikar*), supervised the whole group of lodgers [*Bursa*]. At the beginning of the 1530s, Veit Dietrich held this position. The Pomeranian nobleman Martin Weyher, who left Wittenberg in August 1541 and died at Cammin in 1556 as an Evangelical Bishop, succeeded him. Under the vicar's supervision, individual tutors had young pupils with them. So in 1540 Mathesius was at Katie's table with several "disciples," and Dietrich already had two in 1530; there were six young boys under his supervision when he left the circle in 1534. Among such a crowd and with the considerable turnover of those in her care, Katie had every reason to keep the payments in order.

Cordatus: Table Talk Recorder

But when we speak about Luther's lodgers, we usually understand this to mean not the whole large group of those who entered and left his house, but only the narrower circle of those who recorded and collected his *Table Talks*. The voluminous collection of Luther's *Table Talks,* of which there are many thousands, is unique in its kind. Of course, eager pupils at Melanchthon's table and in his lectures also recorded all kinds of anecdotes, little stories, recollections from his life, but these *Colloquia* [*Conversations*] with which the *Praeceptor Germaniae* [*Teacher of Germany*] entertained his guests or spiced his lectures are still quite poor in content, and superficial, and can hardly be compared with Luther's *Colloquia*. And from later times, of course, we have records of statements from famous men that resemble Luther's *Table Talks* in copiousness, variety, ruthless sharpness, and openness, but they really take a back seat in how accurately and immediately they were passed down. What puts Luther's *Table Talks* above all similar records, besides the inexhaustible abundance and depth of their content, is the fact that they were recorded by pious, knowledgeable men right as they were being said.

The first person who tried to do so, Cordatus, actually had a bad conscience at first while he sat at the common table with tablet and pencil in hand. And Melanchthon, who once gave him his notes, disapproved his undertaking and wrote him a Latin couplet in the margin:

It isn't profitable, Cordatus, to write everything down.
Let many things just quietly be forgotten!

But since Luther himself raised no objection to it, Cordatus continued to put on paper everything that seemed important to him, and other lodgers soon followed his example. It may be remarkable to us that they all were writing, right at Luther's table, as if they were sitting in the lecture.

In time, these sayings were divided into three large groups. The old group of the lodgers comprises the five years from 1529–33; to these belong Cordatus, Dietrich, Schlaginhaufen, Lauterbach, and Weller. The middle group comprises the six years from 1534–39; from this time only Rabe, Weller, and Lauterbach left extensive transcriptions. The most recent group comprises the seven years from 1540–46; here belong Mathesius, Plato, Heydenrich, Besold, Stolz, and Aurifaber.

Doctor Konrad Cordatus, born at Weissenkirchen in Austria in 1476 to Hussite parents, was older than Luther. After he had studied in Vienna, Ferrara, and Rome, he held a very profitable position at Buda in Hungary, but was imprisoned because of his

Evangelical confession and finally had to leave the country. He was in Wittenberg in 1524 and 1525, then again in 1526 and 1528, and Luther took him in, as with so many other exiles. "Cordatus, if you have no money," he often said to him, "I still have a few silver tankards." From 1529 until 1531 Cordatus was active as preacher beside Nikolaus Hausmann in the rich city of Zwickau, but conflicts with the city's council moved him to leave this place again. In the years 1531 and 1532 he lived as a guest in the Black Cloister. And as parish pastor at Niemegk between Wittenberg and Belzig he often had opportunity to see Luther in the following years. In fall 1540 he got a call to Stendal in Altmark as superintendent; he died here in the spring of 1546, soon after Luther.

Undoubtedly Cordatus was a significant person, learned, eloquent as few others, and loyal beyond reproach, but he was also contentious, a know-it-all, hot-tempered, irritable. He gladly drew Luther, the University, and the Elector into the controversy that he raised against Cruciger and Melanchthon in 1536 on account of the doctrine of justification through faith alone. Thus he showed himself to be a forerunner of those fighters who wanted to be more Lutheran than Luther himself. Even within his record of Luther's *Table Talk,* he occasionally added a derogatory note against Melanchthon, Jonas, and . . . Katie.

With regard to Katie, he didn't like her long speeches, and the fact that she, as a homemaker, didn't refrain from interrupting her husband in the middle of the finest conversations if the food was going to get cold. So, one time she abruptly stopped a long discussion with the words: "What would it mean if you talked non-stop and didn't eat?" She was obviously of the opinion that there would still be enough time for discussion after dinner. Then, in the meantime, Cordatus himself directed a question to Luther that he hardly thought worth answering. But with relish he writes down the account of Luther discussing with Katie how God had created men with narrow hips and broader chests as the seat of wisdom; in women it was the opposite. Three times, twice in almost the same words, he notes Luther's impatient complaint that sometimes he has to be patient with his wife. Cordatus was astounded that her requests and tears had so much power over her spouse. Luther once spoke a harsh word about this to Katie, which is also recorded in Lauterbach's larger collection:

> You persuade me to do whatever you want. You have complete control. In the household I am under your lordship, despite my right, for the rule of women has never accomplished anything good.

And when Luther jokingly greeted a guest: "Indulge a meek host, for he is obedient to the lady," Cordatus grimly wrote: "This is most certainly true!"

His voluminous collection of the *Table Talk* for the most part belongs to the time from August 1531 until February 1533. Some talks were possibly written down already in the 1520s; others can extend up to 1540. His records are valuable, yet often they give us only short excerpts from Luther's long talks and are not free of misunderstandings.

Veit Dietrich: Table Talk Recorder

In the same time period Dietrich, Schlaginhaufen, and Lauterbach kept more dependable notes. Veit Dietrich was born at Nürnberg in 1506 to poor parents and he had been studying medicine in Wittenberg since 1522, but under Luther's influence he transferred to theology. From 1529–34 he was Luther's houseguest and student assistant. The vast majority of his records likewise fall in the years 1531, 1532, and 1533. Since he recorded several *Table Talks* at the same time as Cordatus, by comparing the texts we can conclude that he is more reliable than Cordatus. He also gained respect for handing down Luther's sermons, lectures, and correspondence. Already in Marburg and at the Coburg he began to collect Luther's letters as his assistant and secretary. He was also very close to Melanchthon.

He doesn't, however, seem to have gotten along with Katie. This certainly has to do with the large number of pupils he had with him, and from whom he received an income of 100 *Gulden* in 1534. Under these conditions, disputes between the lady of the house and the young teacher were inevitable. Yet she always offered him her hand in reconciliation. One time when he had left the Coburg to go to his hometown, Luther wrote to him that his Katie had sent very particular greetings to him and that he shouldn't think that she was mad at him. Later came his inopportune courting of Lena Kaufmann. This didn't improve his relations to Katie. When he left the "Round Table" in the middle of October 1534, he wrote to Baumgärtner that he had done it on account of his students, and because the lady of the house was not favorably disposed to them. Even this time the conflict couldn't have been too bad. Luther and Katie retained their goodwill for him. In 1535 he became the preacher at St. Sebald in Nürnberg, but remained in close contact with Wittenberg through lively correspondence, and especially with Melanchthon. He shared the church, political, and literary news from southern Germany. In those days letters had to report what the press would now cover. After a blessed career he died in Nürnberg in 1549.

Johann Schlaginhaufen: Table Talk Recorder

Johann Schlaginhaufen, from the Upper Palatinate, whose name was soon Latinized into Turbicida, then Graecized into Ochloplektes or Typtocholios, was in the Black Cloister from November 1531 until September 1532. He often suffered difficult anxiety and emotional afflictions. Many words of comfort that Luther offered to get him out of his troubled mood are recorded in his notes. Katie had special confidence in him. When her husband suffered a fainting spell on May 1, 1532, she had one of her servant girls call Schlaginhaufen first. He repaid the good that he had received in their house with true loyalty, even if he could show his gratitude only through small gifts such as a shipment of very ripe crabapples. In 1532 he became parish pastor in Zahna and the next year pastor in Cöthen. But in 1536, through Luther's mediation, he was offered the pastorate in Wörlitz, because he was sickly and could not tolerate the air in Cöthen; also he wanted to be even closer to Wittenberg. Yet Prince Wolfgang of Anhalt retained him in his residence at Cöthen.

As one of the representatives of the clergy of Anhalt, he took part in the Diet of Smalcald in 1537. And when Luther was deathly ill and had left town on February 26, he was one of the few who were allowed to accompany him on his painful journey. But when Luther made an unexpected improvement in Tambach, Schlaginhaufen could not contain his joy. He hurried back to Smalcald with a letter from Luther to Melanchthon quickly jotted down on paper, and in front of the place where the papal legate was staying, he joyfully shouted in Latin: "Luther lives! Luther lives!"

Schlaginhaufen got married, and in the free hours allowed him by his spiritual office, he eagerly practiced beekeeping. When Melanchthon visited him from Zerbst in February 1547, Schlaginhaufen showed him his beehives, which the winter had destroyed as much as the war had done at the University of Wittenberg. And soon Melanchthon sent him a letter inviting him to visit, because he wanted to hear about the bee colony, more than what was to be found in books.

Anton Lauterbach: Table Talk Recorder

Anton Lauterbach, born in Stolpen in 1502, was also Luther's lodger, probably as early as 1531 and certainly in 1532. He recorded during that time that his father had once wanted to put the indulgence-preacher Tetzel on the spot by asking him whether the *Groschen*, which was the cost of a letter of indulgence, could also be a *March-Groschen*. The *March-Groschen* were forbidden coins in Saxony, and whoever mistakenly received a gold coin like that certainly wanted to get rid of it again. But the wary Dominican monk, who already had some bad experiences with the pious people, smelled a rat and first wanted to find out the value of the *March-Groschen*. "Come back tomorrow," he said to Lauterbach's father: "then I'll tell you."

Lauterbach had already begun his studies as a boy in 1517 in Leipzig. He was first entered in the Wittenberg register in 1529. He was a big person and had a pious, sincere spirit. In 1533 he left the Black Cloister in order to marry a former nun. We know her first name, Agnes (Nisa), from Luther's letters. That same year, despite the objection of the bishop of Meissen, he was installed as deacon in Leisnig, but he returned to Wittenberg in 1536 and now worked here, in the "holy" city as he called his beloved Wittenberg, as second deacon at the City Church until 1539.

Already during his first stay in Luther's house, he had recorded things said at the table. Yet he was more eager in the years 1536–39, when he likewise was a regular guest of Luther's in the evening. Of the collected notes of the lodgers, Lauterbach's diaries from the years 1538–39 are the most valuable, most extensive, and most reliable. Lauterbach also collected the notes of other lodgers. When he proved successful in his office, a great amount of work was soon entrusted to him, but he was so closely attached to Wittenberg that only with heavy heart did he decide to take over as parish pastor and superintendent of the Pirna district in the summer of 1539. Even then, he hardly let a year go by without visiting Luther in Wittenberg.

Untiringly he carried out Katie's assignments, and he thanked her for her hospitality by sending her butter and cheese or fruit. "Sometime a return-gift will be required from us," Luther wrote to him on October 19, 1545. "You embarrass us when you serve us in so many ways without remuneration and all too lavishly." Numerous letters of Luther, which only rarely do not include greetings to Lady Agnes and their little daughter Elisabeth, and even more numerous letters of Melanchthon, bear witness of the friendship that even later connected Lauterbach with the Wittenbergers. After thirty years of work, he died at Pirna on May 18, 1569. In the reports of the Pirna chronicler his comings and goings were extraordinary. His first ministerial act was the baptism of triplets. And as his body was being lowered into the tomb in the parish church, a strong thunderstorm raged for hours in the Elbe valley, and the pious man went to heaven in a storm, just like Elijah.

Jerome Weller: Table Talk Recorder

Likewise, in the district of the rich mountain city of Freiberg, Jerome Weller carried out the Reformation, beginning in 1539. Weller was a native of Freiberg, born in 1499, a member of the old family of the Wellers from Molsdorf. His father had died at an early age, and for lack of means he had to discontinue his studies in Wittenberg, and he turned to teaching. But when he demonstrated splendid intellectual gifts, wealthy relatives sent him to Wittenberg for a second time in 1525. He wanted to become a lawyer, but as a student he led a freewheeling and godless life, until 1528 when he was gripped and shaken within by a Catechism sermon of Luther, and he turned to theology. He also had to suffer severe tribulations all his life, and Luther, who had taken him into his house, often had to comfort and console him.

Weller celebrated his promotion to Doctor of Theology on September 14 1535 in Luther's house. Luther and Katie prepared the doctoral banquet for him, and Katie brewed a lot of beer, for there were many scholars invited as guests, seven or eight tables full. And through her husband she sent a shiny *Taler* to Jonas with the request that he buy all kinds of poultry; only he should get ravens, for they had enough sparrows, but rabbits and similar delicacies would be welcome. Attending the banquet were Jonas, Melanchthon, and other friends from Jena, where the University was in recess at that time due to the plague.

The next year Weller married the young Anna am Steig from Freiberg. The wedding, at Luther's advice, was celebrated, not in Wittenberg, but in Freiberg. For in Wittenberg Luther and Katie would have had to take over the hosting again, and since Weller was a doctor, he would have to invite the whole University, the whole kit and caboodle, and Luther would have had even more duties as host. There would have been more than twelve tables of guests and a hundred *Gulden* would not have covered it. So Weller limited himself to celebrate by bringing his wife home to Wittenberg with a smaller meal in the Black Cloister. It is only then that he moved into his own house in Luther's neighborhood.

Beginning in 1538, he worked as professor and lecturer of theology in his hometown of Freiberg. Here, next to the superintendent, the oversight of the whole system of church and school was entrusted to him. He was not a good preacher and therefore seldom ascended the pulpit. But he was more capable and successful as teacher and expositor of Scripture. He died at Freiberg, March 20, 1572.

With the year 1534, the information from Luther's *Table Talk* begins to become sparser, and there must have been a time, as Cordatus laments, when no one was taking notes any longer. Schlaginhaufen had already left in 1532, Lauterbach was in Leisnig from 1533–36, Cordatus in Niemegk from 1533–40, and Dietrich left Luther's house in 1534 and Wittenberg in 1535. Only Weller was still with Luther in the following years until 1538, and Lauterbach lived in Luther's closest company again from 1536 until 1539.

Ludwig Rabe: Table Talk Recorder

Besides Weller and Lauterbach in these years, we know only the Halle councilman and treasurer Ludwig Rabe as recorder of Luther's *Table Talk*. He had to flee from Halle in 1535 from the persecutions of Archbishop Albrecht and was accepted as Luther's lodger and houseguest in the Black Cloister. So he now sat at the table, as Luther writes, like a "virgin" and said only good things about the church-prince who persecuted him. Later he was chancellor of Prince George von Anhalt.

Johannes Mathesius: Table Talk Recorder

The younger group of lodgers is more prolific in their records. At the forefront is Johannes Mathesius, one of the best-known pupils of Luther and Melanchthon. Born June 24 1504 at Rochlitz in Saxony, a son of the Councilman Wolfgang Mathesius, he then attended the trivium school in Mittweida, and from 1521 the Latin school in Nürnberg. From 1523–25 he studied in Ingolstadt. The next years still kept him in Bavaria, but here he was already won for Protestantism, and in 1529 he traveled to Wittenberg to hear Luther and Melanchthon. Yet he didn't get any closer contact with Luther at that time. In 1532, after he had been a teacher at Altenburg for a few years, he was called as schoolmaster, that is, rector of the Latin school in the flourishing mountain city of Joachimsthal in the Bohemian Ore Mountains. Until 1540 he expanded the blessed activity of this position, gathered numerous students around himself, and developed the reputation of his school as one of the best in the country. But by serving in the school, he felt more and more drawn to the vocation of clergy, and in 1540, when he was already in his mid thirties, the gratitude of some fellow citizens afforded him the means to follow his inclination.

And immediately in the first weeks of his second stay in Wittenberg, by recommendation of Jonas and Rörer, he had the good fortune of becoming Luther's lodger, which he himself cannot extol highly enough. He stayed here from the beginning of May to the beginning of November 1540, and during this time eagerly wrote down what he heard at Luther's table. He also copied for himself the observations of the older and younger lodgers, and assembled a considerable collection of Luther's *Table Talk*. After he took his Master's degree on September 23, 1540, he was informed by a delegation of seven men in 1541 that his Joachimsthalers had chosen him as their deacon. He was Katie's guest, along with those seven. And in order to honor them Luther took an expensive crystal glass, which was once supposed to have belonged to Saint Elisabeth, the unfortunate countess of Thuringia, poured it full and sent it around the table. In April 1542 Mathesius left Wittenberg and returned to Joachimsthal. He died there as pastor on October 7, 1565.

Among his numerous works, Mathesius' biography of Luther stands out. This consisted of seventeen sermons in the years 1562, 1563, and 1564, in which he presented to his Joachimsthal congregation the life and works of the great Reformer. Printed at Nürnberg in 1566 and then disseminated in countless reprints and editions, these sermons are the first actual biography of Luther on the Protestant side. Both sections in which he leads his hearers into Luther's house rely almost entirely on his great collection of the *Table Talk*. But even in the other sermons he includes much of what he himself heard from Luther or he had learned about him from other lodgers, skillfully woven into his presentation. Because of this, his biography of Luther has enduring value. Unfortunately, his actual life's work, the flourishing of the evangelical Church in northern Bohemia, was destroyed by the Catholic Counter-Reformation.

George Plato: Table Talk Recorder

We learn little about George Plato, born in Hamburg. He took his Master's degree in 1537 and was in Luther's house in 1540, at the same time as Mathesius. In Luther's summary of assets and liabilities from 1542, "Plato's little room" is still mentioned.

Caspar Heydenreich: Table Talk Recorder

Caspar Heydenreich (or Heyderich), born in Freiberg in 1516, succeeded Mathesius in 1540 in the rectory at Joachimsthal, but already gave up this position in 1541 and returned to Wittenberg where he took his Master's degree on September 15, 1541. His records of Luther's *Table Talk* fall in the years 1542 and 1543. On October 24, 1543 he was called from Wittenberg to be court preacher for Duchess Katharina, the widow of Heinrich the Pious. He accompanied her to Torgau in 1553 and was active there for a long time as superintendent. Not until his death on January 30, 1586 did he follow the other lodgers, who had all passed away before him.

Jerome Besold: Table Talk Recorder

Jerome Besold, born in Nürnberg, had studied in Wittenberg since 1537, but first came into Luther's house in 1542, and not without concern about Katie, whom Dietrich, his countryman, described to him as a bossy and greedy lady. He is the lodger who complained that Katie had sent him to Nürnberg on an errand, but forgot to pay him. But he was still at her table in 1546. Not until after Luther's death did he move over to Melanchthon's house, because Katie, in her sorrow, thought about discontinuing the *Bursa*. But he returned to Nürnberg that same year. He served his home city faithfully in church and school, but died in 1562 when he was only forty-two.

Johannes Stolz: Table Talk Recorder

Johannes Stolz from Wittenberg was in Luther's company at the University as docent in the 1540s and already at that time was collecting Luther's *Table Talk*. In 1548 he was court preacher at Weimar. He died on June 15, 1556.

Johannes Aurifaber: Table Talk Recorder

The last was Johannes Aurifaber, born in 1519, who was Luther's lodger and student assistant in 1545 and 1546. He also accompanied him on his last trip to Eisleben. From 1550 he was court preacher in Weimar, from 1566 pastor in Erfurt, where he died on November 18, 1575. He was the first to publish Luther's letters and Luther's *Table Talk*, of which he had gathered a very large collection. He collected other writings of Luther as well; however, he did it almost "commercially."

Other Recorders of the Table Talk

Besides these twelve men, others had occasion to record things at Luther's table as well, especially George Rörer, who was around Luther almost daily. Mathesius reports that someone even less known, Ferdinand von Maugis, had written Luther's explanation of numerous passages next to them in the margin of his Bible. Joachim Mörlin, deacon at the Wittenberg City Church until 1540, an eloquent preacher, later put down from memory many additions in his handwritten copy of Aurifaber's printed collection of the *Table Talk*.

Johann Crafft, who was born on November 20, 1519 at Breslau, and died there on October 19, 1585, also appears to have had a larger collection of the *Table Talk*. This man, who later, as Doctor Crato von Crafftheim, was one of the famous physicians of his time, came to Wittenberg in 1534 as a needy student with the support of the Breslau Council. He stayed in Luther's house for six years. As high an honor as he later also achieved, he always confessed the greatest happiness of his life was that he had been Luther's lodger. Biographies about him even maintain that the main part of the Aurifaber *Table Talk* collection went back to Crato's records. But that can be shown to be wrong. A manuscript from the Breslau City Library can give us an idea of the condition of his *Table Talk* collection; there are probably few of Crato's own records in it. Even less can it be true that the Ohrdruf parish pastor Jacob Weber, whom Aurifaber names among his sources, could have taken notes with his own hand at Luther's table, for he was just a boy at Luther's death.

Collections of the Table Talk

But of the twelve who make up the inner circle of the lodgers, Lauterbach and Aurifaber are the most important. In fact, for a long time their great *Table Talk* collections were all that were known. The Lauterbach collection (*Lutheri Colloquia*) was already revised and published once in the sixteenth century by Pastor Heinrich Peter Rebenstock, but it doesn't come to us in a reliable edition until 1863. That edition gives us the text of the *Table Talk* approximating the original version, the way Luther was accustomed to speak in the circle of his friends: Latin and German mixed together. On the other hand Aurifaber, whose collection (*Luthers Tischreden*) was printed in Eisleben in 1566 and later reprinted and revised many times, translated all the Latin into German, and thus inserted a lot of his own thoughts and expressions in-between Luther's main words.

Both collections group the *Table Talk* together from purely practical considerations. Originally the individual speeches in the notebooks of the lodgers were in chronological order, just as they were recorded at Luther's table day by day. Aurifaber and Lauterbach, however, took the individual speeches out of the chronological context and simply arranged them according to their content. Statements that belong together simply by virtue of content, but were spoken in various years, are now put side by side under the rubrics: God, angels, devil, Christ, Antichrist (that is, the pope), cardinals, bishops and monks, kings, princes and lords, etc. For a clergyman who wanted to spice up his sermon with a word from Luther, this arrangement was certainly practical, but for us it is much more important to know in which year Luther said such and such, and what was the original wording of his statement. In this connection, the manuscripts of the individual lodgers that had been neglected earlier are infinitely more valuable than Lauterbach

MEMBERS OF THE HOUSEHOLD

and Aurifaber's collections. What make them valuable is the original text and the definite chronological references they offer us.

Robert Barnes

Of the large number of other lodgers, there are two men who stand out next as doctors of theology and because of the role they played for a while at the princely courts: Barnes and Schiefer.

Robert Barnes, who was born in 1495 and earned his doctorate at Oxford in 1523, had to flee England when King Henry VIII was still on the pope's side as "Defender of the Christian faith." He lived in Wittenberg at the beginning of the 1530s under the assumed name Antonius. He also matriculated on June 20, 1533 as Antonius Anglus, yet Melanchthon added in his own hand his real name, "Robert Barnes." When Henry VIII turned from the pope to the Protestants from a very secular motive, Barnes was called back to his homeland, named as the king's chaplain, and repeatedly entrusted with many important matters. So, in 1535, he was a member of the English delegation that was supposed to produce a favorable *Opinion*, so that Henry VIII might with just cause be able to divorce his wife Catherine of Aragon, the aunt of Emperor Charles V. The Englishmen negotiated persistently with the Wittenbergers in the first months of 1536, yet without achieving everything they wanted.

Later Barnes again lost favor with the king. He ended up at the stake in July 1540. His death was not really a martyr's death. Rather, all kinds of political and even personal conflicts played into the religious troubles to which he fell victim. But to those standing at a distance, Barnes still seems like a martyr. Luther published the confession of faith that Barnes made before his death with a preface.

Wolfgang Schiefer

Wolfgang Schiefer, Latinized as Severus, came from the Upper Austrian Schiefer family from Freyling, which was situated between Steyr and Linz. Beginning in 1518 he studied in Vienna. Already at that time he was drawn to Basel, where Erasmus and

Beatus Rhenanus were teaching, but the news that the plague was raging in Switzerland held him back in Vienna. When the epidemic moved to Bavaria and finally even to Austria, he set out for Basel in the spring of 1521 despite the long distance. Here Rhenanus took him on. After he survived the winter of 1522–23 in his homeland in Everdingen, he studied in Wittenberg for two years, beginning in the spring of 1523. Then he was the teacher for the children of his countryman, Hans Hofmann, the influential Protestant-leaning councilman and treasurer of King Ferdinand I, and in the end Hofmann brought him to the royal court in Innsbruck.

Archduke Maximilian's training was entrusted to Schiefer. As a result of the teachings that Schiefer sank into the young prince's soul, later, as Emperor Maximilian II, he was very favorably-minded toward the Protestants. Yet his actions could not continue unopposed at the strict Catholic court and under the eyes of the papal nuncio. Already in 1538 or 1539 he had to give up his position. He went to Wittenberg for the second time and stayed there in 1539 and 1540 as a welcome and very respected guest in Luther's house. Mathesius reports that Schiefer sat at the head of the table and often told about what he had seen and experienced at the king's court. Luther and Melanchthon wanted to keep him in Saxony, but in vain. In the fall of 1540 he returned to Austria with a written recommendation from Melanchthon.

Michael Stiefel

Michael Stiefel had to flee repeatedly on account of his faith. Born at Esslingen in 1486, he had entered the Augustinian monastery in his hometown, but already in 1522 he had to escape from the persecution of the Austrians who at that time were the lords in Württemberg. After he had served with Knight Hartmut von Cronberg, the faithful self-sacrificing confessor of the Gospel, Stiefel came to Wittenberg for a short time, found acceptance with Luther, and won his friendship. In 1523 he became court preacher in Mansfeld, but on June 3, 1525 Luther sent him as preacher to Upper Austria, where the young nobleman Christoph Jörger at Tollet confessed the Gospel, along with his mother Dorothea and his siblings. The accompanying letter in which Luther recommends his friend to the young lord Jörger as a pious, educated, virtuous, and capable person, was later followed by many more letters with repeated thanks from Luther and Katie, for the Jörgers showed their respect for Katie's husband with rich gifts and donations to his house and the University.

Christoph Jörger, who died in 1578 as advisor to Emperor Maximlian II, remained faithful to the Lutheran confession his whole life, but in the long run he was not able to protect his preacher Stiefel from the persecutions that threatened him as a heretic. Stiefel had to flee once already in 1526. After he returned to his position, he had to flee a second time in 1527. In the early days of 1528 he was back in Wittenberg, where Luther and Katie gladly granted him refuge in their house. In fact he was already acquainted with Katie before her marriage, for he was one of the first ones with whom Luther had shared the news of his wedding to her, and at that time he had sent her a letter from Tollet with heartfelt best wishes.

In the fall of 1528 he became pastor in Lochau near Wittenberg, so that Luther could "attack" the cherries with his boys and could invite him as a guest at the home of other friends. But some years later, sharp words came between them. Stiefel, who was a good theologian and at the same time a splendid mathematician, had calculated from Daniel, Ezekiel, and Revelation that the world would end on October 19, 1533 at eight o'clock in the morning. The people started to get uneasy out of fear and anxiety, and while Stiefel himself gave away his books (without thinking about what someone else would begin to do with them after the end of the world), his farmers twiddled their thumbs. In vain, through letters and spoken words, Luther tried to bring his friend back to reason from his enthusiastic and foolish thinking. The "ethical" man literally ranted, criticizing Luther, saying that the Spirit had left him, calling him a second Pilate and Herod. Nine years later, Luther still said that during his lifetime no adversary had said such evil things about him as Stiefel had.

When the predicted day came, many hurried to little Lochau from far and wide, even from Schleswig, to die with the great prophet. The evening before, Peter Weller came from Wittenberg with a few friends in order to observe on Luther's behalf. And behold, at daybreak there was no mighty trumpet blast of the Last Judgment, but rather the sound of a cowherd's horn, for Stiefel had prophesied that the oxen and cows would have to believe first. And in order to spare his farmers this painful sight, he had the cattle driven out to the village as early as possible. After that he preached a long sermon in his little church, and then the hour had arrived, amidst the loud wailing of the women, but Judgment Day did not come. Instead, at about nine o'clock, delegates from the Elector came and put Stiefel in a wagon and took him to Wittenberg. He had to be deposed from his spiritual office for some time until he had calmed down again, yet Luther did not hold a grudge against him for his error. Already in the spring of 1535 Stiefel had the gainful pastorate in Holzdorf near Wittenberg. From that time on, he spared the Bible from his mathematical studies. He died at an old age as professor of mathematics and deacon at the City Church of Jena in 1567.

Matthias Dévay

Shortly before his death, Luther told an amazing story about the Hungarian reformer Matthias Dévay, who had free room and board with him as a student in 1529 and 1530. Having returned to his homeland, Dévay preached in Buda, and because of that a Catholic clergyman accused him before the governor. But the governor passed a judgment of Solomon. He had two barrels full of gunpowder brought to the marketplace and said to the accuser and the accused that each should sit down on a barrel of powder, then he would light the fuse, and whoever came out of the explosion healthy and standing on his feet, his doctrine would be the right one. Dévay then jumped onto a barrel right away, but the papist couldn't be moved to take his place on the other barrel, and the governor punished the papist priest and allowed the Lutheran to preach freely. Ten years later, however, Dévay had to flee Hungary with fellow believers. In the winter of 1541 and 1542 he was back in Wittenberg. From there he went to Switzerland. Here, however, he accepted the doctrine of the Reformed on the question of the Lord's Supper.

Peter Weller

Two lodgers, Peter Weller and Hineck Perknowsky, suffered an early death in Jerusalem, far away from Wittenberg. Peter Weller, a younger brother of Jerome Weller, had been in Wittenberg since 1529, holding a scholarship from Duke Albrecht of Prussia, and he was Luther's lodger from 1530–34. He studied law and therefore he got to hear many titillating words from Luther. He had a dog with him in the Black Cloister, which sniffed out every bowl. Luther said he wished people were as devout at praying as Peter Weller's dog was at eating.

During these years a younger brother of both Wellers, Matthias Weller, organist in Freiberg, was visiting in Wittenberg, a man who had to suffer afflictions just like his brother Jerome. Therefore, Luther sent him a letter of comfort, and Weller thanked him for it by sending Borsdorf apples and the dedication of a song. In a humorous letter of January 18, 1535 Luther again expresses his thanks for this, and jokes about the "sows" (mistakes) that were made in singing the song, but that was not the fault of the composer, but the singer. And he closes with the words: "My dear Katie [*Kätha*] asks you to take such a joke; and she greets you very kindly."

Also Johannes Jöppel, whose father was court organist of Duke Heinrich the Pious in Freiberg, belonged to the circle of friends of the Wellers and was a happy, pleasant guest in the Black Cloister, as Luther writes. He died at a young age as court musician of the Earl of Hesse.

After Peter Weller had finished his studies in Wittenberg in 1534, his patron Duke Albrecht also granted him the means to attend the famous Italian universities. It was an unpleasant surprise to the duke when news came that Weller had left Italy to go on a pilgrimage to Jerusalem. Luther also would have disapproved of his lodger taking this trip, for he didn't like to see curiosity, even a devout curiosity, always driving people to the holy sites. Instead of going on pilgrimage to Rome, Jerusalem, and Compostella, they should rather walk through the Psalms, the Prophets, and the Gospels!

Hineck Perknowsky

Weller's traveling companion, the Bohemian nobleman Ignaz or Hineck Perknowsky (in the Wittenberg matriculation in the winter of 1530–31 he is recorded as Hineck Perknousky von Berknaui) belonged to the Bohemian Brethren congregation and stayed in Luther's house as court master of the young earl, Borziwog von Dohna. In the *Table Talk* he is commonly called only by his first name, sometimes with the addition, "a Bohemian lord." He was probably already in Italy along with Peter Weller and now accompanied him to the Holy Land as well. But here, like so many German pilgrims, they both were snatched away by fever in Jerusalem at the end of 1535 or the beginning of 1536. The books that Weller had bought, as a beneficiary of Duke Albrecht, remained in the Black Cloister for a long time. Not until 1538 did Katie ask the duke, through Melanchthon, to give these books to her three sons, and the prince granted her request.

Heinrich and Johann Schneidewein

The two brothers Heinrich and Johann Schneidewein from Stolberg am Harz were in Luther's house at the same time as the Wellers. Both studied law. Heinrich, born in 1510, is mentioned among the lodgers in 1530. In 1534 he went to Italy with Peter Weller. After his return as Doctor of both civil and religious law, he was at Luther's table again in 1538 and often spoke about his trip. Then he was the electoral councilman at Torgau and Weimar, later professor at Jena, where he died on May 7, 1580. He was married to Wolfgang Reissenbusch's widow Anna (*née Erzäger*).

His younger brother Johann Schneidewein, born in 1519, came to Wittenberg in 1529 as a boy. He was one of Dietrich's "disciples." At a young age in 1539, he got engaged to Christian Döring's daughter Anna. His mother, the widowed Frau Ursula Schneidewein in Stolberg, didn't seem to be very pleased about this. But as vigorously as Luther intervened against unauthorized and unwise betrothals, this time everything seemed to him to speak for a marital union between the two young people, and on that account he wrote three times on behalf of his lodger to his obstinate mother. Doctor Johann Schneidewein later taught as professor of law in Wittenberg, and his wife gave him sixteen children. He helped to settle the estate among Katie's children. He died on December 4, 1568.

Wolfgang Sieberger and Other Student Assistants

Luther used to choose his student assistant and the teacher of his children from among the older and more mature lodgers. He seems to have preferred the poorer ones for this position.

His first student assistant, Wolfgang Sieberger, born in Munich, whom we already met in the Black Cloister in 1517, was obviously not up to the increased workload from year to year, and although he had already studied in Wittenberg for a while, since 1515, he was probably not skilled, educated, or able to write well enough for Luther to entrust to him his writings and letters. His place in the Black Cloister is shown when Luther mentioned him in one breath with Katie's cook, Dorothea [*Orthe*]:

> Servants and maids in the house have it better than their lords and ladies, for they have no worry about the household; they only carry out and do their work. My Wolf and Orthe, my assistant and my cook, have it much better than my Katie and I.

The tasks Wolf sometimes received from Katie when Luther was gone, such as caring for the mulberry plants or bottling the wine, also had to do with business matters. Sending books went through his hand. He was also sometimes sent out with an important letter to hire an express messenger. But when Luther went on his first longer trip to Marburg in 1529, he didn't take his Wolf with him as his assistant and secretary, but Veit Dietrich.

What Wolf lacked in spirit and knowledge, he made up for in loyalty. He is a worthy counterpart to Melanchthon's servant Johannes Koch, who dedicated his whole life to the service of his lord. So Wolf Sieberger served in the Black Cloister until Luther's death, yes, even until his own death. Occasionally we hear about him being blamed for something. One time he even managed to doze off over his work. He didn't always find the right time to converse with his lord. If something went wrong, no one wanted to blame him for it. But in spite of his little errors, under Katie's supervision he was still over the whole household, and in business matters he had an important word to put in. That's why Luther once jokingly said that he was worse off than Aaron, for Aaron had only a Moses over him, while he had three overlords: Rörer, Wolf, and his Katie, who were three Moseses all at once.

Luther gained the loyalty of his servant by his fatherly intervention. In 1535 he thought about giving him a "grandparents' cottage" by buying Brisger's little house for him, out of the grace money the Elector had given him. Wolf had a feeble, weak arm at that time. But he never seems to have considered leaving his lord. When Luther once asked him: "What will you do, Wolf, if I should die soon? Do you also want to stay with my wife?" Wolf answered: "I don't know, but I would wish to die anyway, when you, my father, are dead." And when we read the letter Luther wrote to Wolf in the autumn of 1534, we can feel for the old, loyal man that it was sincere love and honor for such a lord that kept him in the Black Cloister to his end.

This letter, one of the humorous ones Luther wrote, is about Wolf's bird trap. Wolf was in the little garden his lord had bought for him for 20 *Gulden*, to make it into a bird snare. Now when he lay in wait for the birds to fly into his old net in droves, and when only four or five had fallen into the trap, he didn't move a finger but thought: "Oh, I'll wait until more of you come!" But his sated guests flew away in the meantime. Occasionally he caught some, and when he had rebuilt his snare in the fall of 1534, he got a long letter from Luther, which the blackbirds, thrushes, finches, linnets, and goldfinches, along with other little birds who wanted to travel south over Wittenberg, had sent to their "favorable Lord Doctor Martin Luther, preacher at Wittenberg." In it they complain that someone named Wolfgang Sieberger, the lord doctor's servant, was trying to take their life with some old broken nets that he had paid a lot for. They let him scatter grain in the evening, but they wished he didn't get up before eight o'clock in the morning—poor Wolf!—and go out to the trap. But if he outrageously kept resetting it on them, then they would ask God to put frogs, grasshoppers, and snails in his net in the daytime, and mice, fleas, and other vermin in his bed at night. He should go out to the field for sparrows, swallows, magpies, jackdaws, ravens, mice, and rats, rather than against good, respectable birds.

We cannot reproduce here a complete list of those who served Luther in the position of his student assistant. There are insignificant men among them, such as Johannes Rischmann from Braunschweig who resigned his office in February 1532 and became deacon in Husum. But there were also very capable scholars such as Dietrich and Aurifaber. Perhaps the most influential was Jodokus Neuheler, called Neobolus, born in 1504 at Ladenburg in the Upper Palatinate, a student in Wittenberg since 1532 and Luther's lodger from 1536 until 1538. Several letters from Bucer of Strasbourg and Capito and Martin Frecht, the pastor of Ulm, indicate that Neobolus had a position of trust in dealing with the concord between the South Germans and the Swiss and the Wittenbergers. He was also the first who showed Luther the heretical doctrinal statement of his friend Agricola at the end of March 1537. Later he was pastor at Endingen in Württemberg and proved himself to be a very capable theologian so that in 1552 his Duke Christoph sent him to the Council of Trent in the company of the Swabian Reformer Johann Brenz. He died at Endingen on July 28, 1572.

Tutors for the Children

The tutors and teachers of Luther's children are also only mentioned occasionally. At the same time as Jerome Weller, who was the first to take on the young Hans Luther, George Schnell from Rothenburg ob der Tauber was in the Black Cloister, a poor fellow. So Luther on his behalf asked his hometown council for support at the beginning of 1533: "It's your hometown boy who has brought you no shame. He's learned and pious, my companion daily in my house and at my table. I must give a good report and testimony of him." Three years later Schnell calls himself the *paedagogus* [tutor] of Luther's children. On October 7, 1537 he was ordained as pastor for Herzberg. He was a good preacher, and his people of Herzberg reluctantly let him go when he returned to the University of Wittenberg in 1540. Later he was active as a clergyman next to Schlaginhaufen in the principality of Anhalt.

His successor may have been Master Johann Sachse, *Saxo, Saxonius*, also called Holstein because he was from Ditmarsch, a farmer's son from Hattstedt in the Elbe duchy. On account of his fire-red hair, Lemnius teased him in several epigrams in 1538. Already at the beginning of the 1530s he lectured as a young master at the University, and in 1533 and again in 1539 he was dean of the philosophical faculty, even rector for the summer semester in 1544, but he waited in vain for a regular professorship. Like Dietrich and Mathesius, he had several boys around him in Luther's house. Perhaps he also instructed Luther's boys for a while. Luther described him to the Elector as being of an honorable, pious disposition. The more remarkable thing is that Besold calls him an immoral and quite Epicurean person, but the young Besold seems to have been somewhat careless with criticisms and rather indiscriminate in his expressions. Sachse finally turned to law studies and still spent time in the Black Cloister in 1544 without employment. In a confidential conversation at that time, all the blame for his lack of professorship was laid on Melanchthon: Melanchthon preferred to see his countrymen, the South Germans, promoted rather than a Saxon. Katie did not shrink from discussing this delicate matter with Melanchthon herself, but he was very much troubled and concerned about the criticism that was unjustly raised against him. Sachse was later active in various occupations as a lawyer, historian, and theologian. He died on March 16, 1561 as cathedral dean at Hamburg.

Finally, Franz Bock from Flanders and Ambrosius Rudtfeld from Delitzsch are also expressly mentioned as tutors of Luther's children. Bock was already with Luther at the beginning of 1539 and left Wittenberg after his Master's promotion in the spring of 1541 in order to return to his homeland. He took the long way round across upper (that is, southern) Germany, where at that time the Emperor and Empire were in session at Regensburg. Rudtfeld accompanied Luther on his last trip to Eisleben and stayed with Katie and the children for a while even after Luther's death.

Katie's Boarding House (*Bursa*)

We have had to pass quickly over a large number of names and dates in order to make a presentation of Katie's *Bursa* to some extent. But without these details, the picture of her life would be incomplete. The boarders and the Wittenberg friends formed the circle at the center of which she herself stood next to her husband as the Lady Doctoress. If individuals mumble about her strict control, in her house she was still the lady of the house, the *domina* and δέσποινα [*despoina*], as Melanchthon also calls her. And she had to be, in order to maintain the complex household in discipline and order.

Taking care of her lodgers demanded a good portion of her energy. There was also no lack of grief and sorrow. Again and again Luther's letters report epidemics. And sickness might often have entered the Black Cloister without our hearing about it. Katie's duties were certainly also dedicated to the young boys who, along with their tutors, lived in her house. Wittenberg at that time was not a healthy city. Childhood diseases such as measles and pox and plague-like epidemics broke out again and again, and malaria, which was native to the damp Elbe lowlands, afflicted not only Luther and Katie and their own children, it also put many of the other boys into the sickbed, and Doctor Augustin Schurf's skill was not able to help in every case.

On April 20, 1532 one of Dietrich's pupils died: Johannes Zink, a dear lad, whose death hurt Luther very much, for he had been rather quiet, modest, and especially diligent in his studies, and around the table in the evenings he had sung so beautifully with a clear voice. Luther and Katie, of course, never allowed a lack of care, concern, and medicine. And Katie had sat many an hour at the boy's bedside so that during these days her husband once said: "Where there is no woman, a sick person sighs, for woman is born to take care of people." But despite all the care, the sickness prevailed, took him away, and brought him home to our Lord Jesus Christ in heaven. For four weeks he lay sick, as Dietrich reports, and the day before his death he still stretched out his hand to say goodbye to his tutor: "Dear Lord Master, I say to you: Farewell!" "Where will you go then?" Dietrich asked the boy, and the dying one replied: "To Christ!" His fellow pupils, who stood at his deathbed, he exhorted, even with his faltering voice, to all good things, then he fell asleep in steadfast faith in God's grace. Luther wrote a heartfelt letter of comfort to the poor father, Thomas Zink at Hofheim.

On the other hand, there is a letter of comfort, which in December 1544 Luther directed to the Mine-Scrivener George Hösel in Marienberg in the Saxon Ore Mountains, and in it he speaks of the death of three young students, misunderstood as though these three or at least two of them were Luther's lodgers. The first one, a young lad from Lüneburg, had died in August 1544; the second, Mastor Theobald Fontejus from Strassburg, on October 27; and the third, Jerome Hösel from Marienberg, in December that same year. The three announcements, in which the rector of the University called upon the students to show their fellow students their last respects, clearly show that none of them had lived with Luther and Katie. But in September 1548 the rector did announce the funeral of a student who had lived in the Black Cloister. This time the one who died was a member of the *Bursa* that Katie had gathered for herself again after her husband's death.

Domestic Servants

Finally, belonging to the members of Katie's household were the many domestic servants. Mentioned are several maids or servant girls (in May 1538 two were laid up with a fever at one time), the cook Dorothea, the coachman, the swineherd Johannes, and several farmhands or day laborers. It was bad enough that one of them suddenly left her service and took up with a girl with a bad reputation in the city. Worse yet, in 1538 one of Katie's day laborers left—a very capable and good man, gentle as a lamb when he was sober, but a real fighter when he was drunk. On February 10, a Sunday, he boasted around town all day that he was Luther's servant, and finally in his drunkenness he beat someone to death.

When he came to his senses, he tearfully left his wife and ran away, abandoning the poor woman with three boys.

The worst of all was an adventurous girl who introduced herself to Luther and Katie as a girl of the nobility, Rosina von Truchsess, and pretended to be a nun. It soon came out that it was a lie, and when Luther himself dealt with her, she confessed to him that she was from Münnerstadt in Franconia, the daughter of a citizen who had been beheaded as a rebel in the Peasants War. She fervently asked him to have pity on her and to forgive her for God's sake for taking a false name. And Luther in his boundless kindheartedness granted this impostor free accommodations in his house on the promise that she wouldn't lie any more! But she continued to lie and deceive. She stole things in the kitchen, cellar, and cupboard and secretly took to an immoral life. Luther was glad when Katie finally found out about her tricks in August 1541 and showed her the door. But when all her shameful actions gradually became public, then he almost complained that Katie had sent her away so quickly, for such a lying, thieving rogue deserved to be drowned in a sack and the Elbe wouldn't have enough water. His anger was rekindled when the vagrant woman went from parish to parish, lying and stealing and not being stopped anywhere. Finally, when word came that she was in Leipzig, on January 29, 1544, he wrote to the city magistrate Johann Göritz, whom he knew, and asked him to keep a sharp eye on the alleged Truchsess woman. On account of "another Rosina" he asks Katie whether this deceiver and rogue had been put into prison yet. It seems that a man in the Black Cloister acted the same way Rosina had four years earlier.

The reason Luther and Katie repeatedly experienced terrible disappointments in their domestics was because they were apparently all too trusting. Luther admitted that he too easily let himself be duped and deceived, because he regarded all people as good or believed they could improve. In fact, now he said that his bad experiences had made him wiser, but again and again he let himself be deceived through fervent petitions and hypocritical promises. Seldom did he show himself as prudently cautious as he did toward the sister of Hartmut von Cronberg, Lorichia or Lorche. In her first marriage she was married to the noble lord Wolf

Kämmerer from Worms, called Dalberg, and as a widow she had eloped with a rich Jewish man named Jacob whom she loved dearly. Then her relatives picked up her tracks again in Erfurt. They sent riders to bring her back. They happened to meet the Jewish man on the street; he came in mounted on horseback like a nobleman. They recognized him and ran him through.

Lorche, who meanwhile had fled to Silesia, was called back by her relatives, but on the way she unexpectantly gave birth in Wittenberg in the summer of 1535. Luther took her into his house. He was even baptismal sponsor for her child. But after several months had passed, he no longer wanted to have her in his house, for she didn't tell him who she was, and he even recognized that she was an aristocratic woman. Therefore he sent her to Justus Menius in Eisenach with a warm letter of recommendation, but with the admonition to be cautious as well. Not until her brother Hartmut came to Wittenberg looking for her was everything made public, and only now could Luther finish what he had earlier wanted to do for the severely tested woman, obtain full pardon from her brother.

There is no more splendid testimony to Luther and Katie's compassion than the fact that they did not let the most bitter disappointments deter them from again and again helping others. Luther did often bemoan the ingratitude of the world, but he expected no thanks for himself. Ready and willing, he took on every new burden that no one else would want to be burdened with, and he comforted himself: "Luther has a strong back; he'll carry this load too." And once, when Katie complained about the disloyalty and disobedience of her household, he comforted her with the words: "A pure and true servant is a splendid gift of God, but a rare bird on earth."

We occasionally hear about lesser offenses as well, when Luther speaks impatiently about the negligence of his people, or when he jokes with Link in Nürnberg about ordering a very large unbreakable and self-cleaning candelabra that the maids couldn't hurt either awake or asleep. But being too quick-tempered around the house would be just as bad as being too lenient. "You know, of course," he adds, "the kind of manners and character the domestics have now." So here, too, there is no lack of frustrations; yes, there are more complaints than words of praise. But what has come down to us here is just as one-sided as what is said about raising the children and foster children. Every bad experience is recorded; we seldom hear about the good, and yet the good was certainly the rule, and the bad only the exception. How would such a large household have been able to thrive otherwise? To be sure, Katie kept close ranks on her domestics just as firmly as she did the rest of the house, and as lady of the house she provided her servants with the best example. Therefore her husband writes: "The eyes of the lady of the house cook better than maid, servant, fire, and coal."

8.

FRIENDS AND GUESTS

Isn't it a completely shameful thing and the devil's deceit in us that we trust a human being more than we trust God? I entrust myself to my Katie, to Philipp, to all of you for more good than to Christ, and I certainly know that none of you would suffer for me as much as Christ suffered.

Philipp Melanchthon

Luther spoke these words to his lodgers at the beginning of 1532, and his whole life is with filled and supported by the adamant confidence he had in his closest friends and co-workers. Yes, it was more than friendship that bound him with Philipp Melanchthon. Since that August day in 1518, when that great "little man" entered Wittenberg from Bretten and stood at his side, he felt that they had grown closer. Without envy he marveled at his mastery of ancient languages, his deep penetration into Scripture's doctrine of salvation, his clarity and consistency in developing a thought. The ardent love for his newly attained friend culminated in the hope that he himself would be only the forerunner who would prepare the way, and that Master Philipp would be called to complete the work.

This hope was frustrated by Melanchthon's wishy-washy behavior while Luther was at the Wartburg. Melanchthon was not suited to laying the foundation for the new church and erecting the pillars that should bear the arch. But he was the right man for internal development. Luther once even compared himself to the lumberjack who fells the trees in the forest and works on the rough parts, but Melanchthon was like the carpenter whose plane smoothed out the unevenness. Luther marveled at his co-worker, and knowing Melanchthon's weaknesses didn't diminish his admiration. Time after time and with splendid words he spoke well of what Wittenberg, Germany—yes, and even the whole known world—had to thank Master Philipp for. He resisted all attempts to alienate his friend. Yes, at times he was even inclined to tolerate from him what he would not have accepted from anyone else: deviation in doctrine, as long as it did not touch the foundation. In 1540 he still said this about him: "The little man is pious, and if he has done something wrong, he didn't intend anything bad, but he was preoccupied."

And in the early years Melanchthon felt drawn to Luther and held to him like steel to a magnet. Under Luther's influence, the scholar became a theologian, the humanist became a reformer. At age twenty-four he was in charge of the University when Luther went to Worms in 1521. But the religious confusions that befell Wittenberg in Luther's absence, and the unrest against which Melanchthon stood helpless, and which Luther quickly and easily quelled by the power of his word after he returned—these were a thorn that imbedded itself deeper and deeper in Melanchthon's soul. It wasn't just knowing that he was only number two. This concern troubled him as well: the brutality and senselessness that emerged in the Wittenberg riot and then threatened to break all bounds of civilization and law and would destroy the blossom of knowledge. And at the same time he began to have doubts about whether he, as a theologian, could stay in his position, or if, on the other hand, God was placing before him the decision to dedicate all his energy to education and to halting its demise.

His bond with Luther and theology was so heartfelt that he could hardly have let it go, just like that. But in his most confidential letters, we at times encounter his longing to be allowed to devote himself to learning, soon even complaining, then finally speaking harsh words about the dependence, yes, the servitude and slavery in which Luther held him. But these complaints flow from momentary disagreements rather than expressing a persistent mindset, as shown by the fact that in spite of everything he continued in his position until Luther's death, and only after Luther's death was he entitled to first place.

A man like Melanchthon would have been welcomed with open arms anywhere! What could have kept him from breaking the fetters he speaks of in his letters? Only the certainty that he was agreed with Luther in all essential doctrines, and the conviction that he was indispensable in Wittenberg could have kept him there. Despite all his complaining, he remained steadfast even through the attractive offers from the opposing side. We must therefore not put too much weight on those letters. His sensitive and easily excitable, self-deprecating, and suspicious nature probably saw many things as worse than they actually were.

The worst years were 1536–38. In August 1536, Cordatus began the controversy in which he picked out a point in the doctrine of justification where Melanchthon and Cruciger seemed to differ from Luther in the idea of the necessity of good works. This was a very considerable charge for Melanchthon, for Cordatus was rightly regarded as one of the most loyal among Luther's adherents, and he wasn't alone in his mistrust of Melanchthon. Luther himself was deeply disturbed at first, but didn't let himself get carried away. Even when he worried about the future, during his illness in Smalcald, he soon arrived at the firm conviction that his life's work could be entrusted to no better hands than Melanchthon and Cruciger's after his death. A friendly discussion between the two friends (Luther and Melanchthon) in the spring of 1537 deprived Cordatus of any basis for further attacks, though he was difficult to appease.

But the gap that seemed to open up here between the leader of the Protestants and his most famous co-worker couldn't remain hidden. The Elector viewed Melanchthon with suspicion. Prestigious Catholics regarded this as an opportune time to win him for Rome. And in the summer of 1537 Doctor Jacob Schenk learned from a confidential letter that Melanchthon had stated that receiving the Supper in one kind was permissible under pressure from Catholic authorities, and used it as a weapon for a new attack.

After an initial fit of temper, Luther put the sword back in its sheath, fended off the mistrust of the Elector and his Chancellor, Brück, and didn't let it turn into an inquisition looming over Melanchthon. He stated rather that he wanted to share his heart with him and pray for him.

And the scandal that was brought on Wittenberg by Melanchthon's student Simon Lemnius and his epigram in 1538 left hardly more than a temporary irritation for Luther.

The storm clouds that hung over Wittenberg during these years would not have risen so menacingly had Melanchthon shown himself to be completely open toward Luther. The friendly discussion between the two men had dispelled all misunderstandings in the spring of 1537. A frank discussion between them would certainly have put to rest much earlier the more dangerous of Schenk's attacks. Katie bitterly lamented that that didn't happen. She tried to work it out, and even Cruciger would have gladly mediated a settlement between Luther and Melanchthon. But at that time Melanchthon's wife emphatically opposed these attempts at reconciliation.

If Cruciger, Melanchthon's most trusted friend, had not attested to this fact for us, we would hardly consider it credible. Cochlaeus in his private conversation portrays Mrs. Katherine Melanchthon for us as a woman who found it hard having to be the wife of only a Master and to have to stand behind the Doctor's wife, while Katie Luther, as one born to nobility and as Luther's wife, was the most prominent among the professor's wives, and showed herself to be as proud and high-spirited as a countess. Now Cochlaeus is anything but a good source of information, and we would have to beware of putting our trust in him if he were alone. But other contemporaries reliably attest Katie Luther's pride to us as well. And when Cruciger reports that Melanchthon's wife tried to prevent a meeting between her husband and Luther, that certainly points not to her trying to calm her husband's bad mood, but rather spurring on his sense of offended pride and definite envy of Luther and Katie's priority.

We do not hear Luther speak about Melanchthon's wife even once, either in his letters or in the *Table Talk*, while he enjoys sending greetings to the wives of other friends with some friendly words or a joke. Her husband doesn't include heartfelt greetings from her in his letters either. There is never a thought of her visiting the Black Cloister, while her children were the playmates of Katie's children, and her husband often sat at Luther's table, evening after evening for weeks at a time. It really seems she stood somewhat outside the intimate friendship that connected her house and Katie's through all those years.

The relationship between Melanchthon and Katie gradually developed into a more cordial one. The dislike he had for her in the beginning soon disappeared when he got to know her more and saw what happiness she brought Luther. When she was deathly ill at the end of January 1540, he wrote to a friend: "If you want to pray for our church; then pray that God will also comfort the Herr Doctor and preserve his wife." He asked other friends to pray for Katie's recovery at this time as well. And in June of the same year he himself almost despaired, and out of pain, shame, and regret wanted to die because his and Luther's advice concerning Landgrave Philipp's bigamy had led to such a great scandal. Then Luther wrote these words to him in a long comforting letter: "My Katie also bids you to be brave and happy." How highly Melanchthon must have esteemed Katie if Luther might hope he could lift his dejected friend out of his despondency by referring to her and what hopes she had in him!

"A friend in need is a friend indeed."[1] In mourning for Luther after he passed away, Melanchthon found the purest expression of love, honor, and gratitude. Even he, more than others, had learned that in the often gruff and tough man there beat a heart that was true and without guile. Where Luther was able to help, he never failed to do so. He had forcefully intervened when a blow that human power could still ward off threatened Melanchthon's house. It was the end of 1543. Melanchthon's eighteen-year-old son Philipp secretly got engaged to a young girl from Leipzig named Margarete Kuffner. There was really nothing bad to say against the

---

[1] The German expression is literally: In days of sorrow and sadness genuine friendship is maintained.

girl; she belonged to a respected family, she was a sister-in-law of Melanchthon's friend Paul Eber. But a betrothal between him and Margarete seemed impossible because of young Philipp's immature age. He still didn't know how to do anything and hadn't made a name for himself. However, the engaged couple didn't want to leave each other. In fact, Margarete wrote a touching letter to young Philipp and begged him to remember the oaths with which he had promised her marriage. Melanchthon was deeply distressed. But as a father he was also tender and was not inclined to break off his son's foolish engagement by force. Yes, he surely would have given in, even if it would break his own heart and his wife's.

Then Luther came to their aid. Luther was deeply saddened to see how the University's reputation suffered under similar circumstances. With his powerful personality and the great weight of his authority he stepped in against the secret engagement. He released Melanchthon's son from the oaths he had sworn to the girl. The two young people didn't die of broken hearts either. Margarete Kuffner gave her hand in marriage to a clergyman in 1545, and Philipp Melanchthon the Younger, when he had reached the proper age, married a widow from Torgau in 1550.

Despite the many sorrows, misunderstandings, and disagreements, which were not absent even in the final years, Luther and Melanchthon remained close. Their contemporaries didn't want to divide them, and when succeeding generations mention the name of one, the image of the other immediately comes to mind. They are buried next to each other in the Castle Church, just as their houses stand next to each other as well.

Melanchthon's House

Melanchthon's home is right on *Kollegienstraße*, a little over a hundred paces west of the Black Cloister. The narrow side faces the street, only three windows wide, enclosed by a gable above, which is decorated with round arches. The form it is in now comes from the second half of the 1530s, from the same time when Luther also was making renovations and additions to the Black Cloister. Early on April 11, 1536 about six o'clock, the foundation was laid; on June 16, 1537 it was completed. Here now lived the *Praeceptor*

Germaniae [the Teacher of Germany] with his wife Katharine and their adolescent children Philipp and Magdalena (born 1530, married in 1550 to the physician Caspar Peucer). The eldest daughter Anna was already married to George Sabinus since 1537. A younger son George had died at a young age in 1529.

On the second floor we see Melanchthon's study. This room still has the bed where he died on April 19, 1560. In a room on the third floor a painted coat of arms with inscriptions carved on it commemorates the fact that even this great man had to dedicate a portion of his precious time to a *Bursa*, and just like the Black Cloister they had no lack of guests in this house. "Today at my table eleven languages are spoken," Melanchthon once wrote: "Latin, Greek, Hebrew, German, Hungarian, Slavic, Turkish, Arabic, Modern Greek, Indian, and Spanish." The lecture hall in which Melanchthon used to lecture was in the garden behind the house. There is supposed to have been a path that led from the garden to the little Cloister garden.

Johann Agricola

Next to Melanchthon, Agricola was closest to Luther's heart and home for a long time. Johann Agricola—his German family name was Schneider—came from the city of Luther's birth, Eisleben. For that reason he was often simply called Master Eisleben or Islebius. Perhaps ten years younger than Luther, when he had finished his studies in Leipzig, he came to Wittenberg in 1516. Here, as he himself confesses, he was reborn and become a believer through Luther's teaching and God's grace. Soon he belonged among Luther and Melanchthon's most trusted friends. When he left Wittenberg in 1525, a lively exchange of letters maintained the connection between the friends and their spouses. Katie also often sent greetings to Agricola's wife Elsa. She was ready and willing to take her ailing friend, Elsa, into her own care even though she wasn't feeling well herself at that time. She occasionally supplied her with a servant girl in Wittenberg, and she thanked her for gifts; a dress that came at New Year's in 1527 was almost too precious, but a second shipment of the crabapples[2] that Elsa Agricola had sent would be welcome, for she was extremely fond of crabapples.

Beginning in 1525 Agricola was head of the Latin school in his hometown, Eisleben. One of the oldest Protestant "School Regulations" bears his name. The first popular collection of German proverbs is his work. He was a fiery preacher, a cheerful, amiable associate. Three times, as preacher, he accompanied the old Elector Hans to the Diets: 1526 and 1529 to Speyer, 1530 to Augsburg. Here, at the bottom of a letter from Melanchthon to Katie, he wrote the words: "I, Johann Agricola Eisleben, also mean well, my dear Mrs. Doctor." And from here, via his wife, he also sent her a humorous letter, of which Luther writes:

> I have received your letter to my lady, dear Agricola, and I can easily predict the response. When she reads it, she will burst out laughing and say: 'Oh, what a real rascal that Master Eisleben is!'

Then when the young Elector John Fredrick in Vienna received the investiture of Electoral Saxony in 1535, he had Agricola with him as traveling preacher as well. Little Eisleben was too small a place for the highly gifted and high-aspiring man. He looked for a larger circle of activity, and Luther complied with his wishes and called him to Wittenberg at the end of 1536. Since he didn't find a suitable place to live right away, Luther and Katie took him and his wife Elsa and their nine children into the Black Cloister. In fact, Luther entrusted to him the administration of the church and the university and the care of his house and his own family when he was in Smalcald with Melanchthon and Bugenhagen in 1537.

But in the summer of that same year, their friendship suffered an incurable wound. Agricola began to teach that preaching the Law was unsuitable and unnecessary to produce knowledge of sin and repentance; everything was included in preaching grace. It was impossible for Luther to yield even one step to this Antinomian doctrine. In vain Frau Elsa and Frau Katie tried to intervene. The

---

[2] Kroker's note: The fruit, which was ripe in September, tastes similar to medlars [crabapples].

urgent pleas of the one and the tears of the other were not able to change his mind. He stubbornly insisted that Agricola must simply retract his error. Then he would be ready to be reconciled, for he was not resentful. He said to his friends: "If Agricola came with his little wife and said: 'Herr Doctor, I have been foolish; forgive me!'—then everything would be all right." But it wasn't to happen. The controversy lasted three years, since Agricola came around several times, but always broke away again.

He clearly didn't realize how far he had distanced himself from Luther. Otherwise how could he in good conscience have appealed to the Elector as arbitrator between himself and Luther in March 1540? And he never would have dared to break his word as he did when he secretly ran away in August 1540, despite his promise to stay in Wittenberg. He entered a very prestigious position in Berlin. But if he had hoped to find that Luther would listen to him more as court preacher to Joachim II of Brandenburg, then he didn't know Luther very well. The intervention of the Hohenzollern [prince] had as little weight with Luther in a matter of faith as his own lord's, and even Melanchthon's attempts at mediation had only outward results.

Agricola finally retracted, but Luther could no longer bring himself to believe him and trust him again. One time the Wittenbergers had given the little Master Eisleben the nickname *Grickel* or *Gricklichen*; now *Grickel* and *Jäckel*—Agricola and Schenk—were two lost men for Luther. When Agricola came to Wittenberg in the spring of 1545 with a letter of recommendation from his Elector, Luther showed him the door. Only Frau Elsa and her daughter Magdalena were allowed to visit Katie and him. But after all that had happened, their reunion brought little joy to the Black Cloister.

Luther's confidential statements, however, show how difficult it had been for him to turn his friend away. In 1540 he said now he could sympathize with what Christ must have suffered during Iscariot's betrayal. In his younger years he was reconciled more easily. But experience had taught him that friends who once foundered and yielded on the foundation of doctrine would never again become true friends, though they might seem to return. As a result of such disappointments, Luther later held on to the word of the Apostle Paul: "Reject a divisive man after the first and second admonition."[3] His sudden break with Agricola, however, is further evidence that he did not allow himself to be influenced in his lenient attitude toward Melanchthon out of friendship or the concern of losing this co-worker. Where it concerned the heart of doctrine, there was no leeway for him. What held him and Melanchthon together can only be that they were both convinced that they agreed on all essential doctrines.

Justus Jonas

The friendship between Luther and Justus Jonas, the Castle provost, remained completely untarnished. Born in 1493 in Nordhausen as son of the council master Jonas Koch, he was baptized with the name Jobst (Jodocus, Justus) Koch, but at the University of Erfurt, where he studied law, he called himself Justus Jonas after his father's first name. Under the Erfurt humanists he most definitely became acquainted with Luther, and Luther never forgot that Jonas had found the courage to accompany him to Worms of his own free will in 1521. In that very same year, Jonas went to Wittenberg and here devoted himself entirely to theology. Since then, he stood in the front ranks among the Reformers, less known through his own writings than through his practical work as visitor and organizer and through his numerous, excellent translations of Luther and Melanchthon's Latin writings. He was an excellent writer, an eloquent speaker. If Luther was ever troubled, then his wise Katie secretly had Doctor Jonas called to the table, for no one understood how to cheer up Luther with conversation as well as he.

He is often mentioned among the evening dinner guests, and his interaction with Luther and Katie was tremendously sincere. How often Katie sent him greetings when he was out of town! Half jokingly, half seriously she warns him through her husband not to drink too much of the good wine with his pains from kidney stones, otherwise he would return home "as jagged and rough from the

---

[3] Titus 3:10 (NKJV).

stones on the inside as barrels are when they are emptied," and then in the end they would have to listen to him complain that he had gotten his pains in Wittenberg, while really he had laid the groundwork elsewhere. Luther faithfully delivered even this wordy exchange to his friend, for he fondly remembered getting the same admonitions from "Lord" Katie when he was at the Coburg. And when Luther sent news to Jonas about his wife and his children when he was out of town, surely Katie was the intermediary here too. Jonas thanks her for her friendship through return greetings and gifts and warm interest in the joy and sorrow in her house.

When Katie notified Jonas of the birth of his fifth son, when he was in Augsburg, at the bottom of Melanchthon's letter, to which Agricola also added his greetings, Jonas wrote these words to her: "Dear Godmother! I also wish you, little Hans Luther, and little Magdalena, and Auntie Lena a much happier time. Smooch my dearest little son for me in my name." And during Katie's serious illness, Jonas shared his concern with Prince George of Anhalt on January 24, 1540, when they all were on edge for the life of the "best" lady: "If this letter of mine is dull and less cheerful, but instead somewhat sad, yes, very worried, the reason is the anxious distress in which we are kept." She was critically ill and seemed almost on her deathbed. He wishes the lady recovery by a miracle of God.

And his own wife Katherine, the "provost's wife," was Katie's closest friend of all the Wittenberg professors' wives. The two ladies were, as Luther writes, one heart and one soul. Katherine Jonas was also a noblewoman by birth, from the Falk family; her father Erich Falk was an old Saxon soldier. Jonas had married her in 1522. Their marriage was richly blessed with children, and although death snatched many away, there was still a little flock left. Just as the young Just Jonas was little Hans Luther's playmate and later schoolmate, so Sophie, Elsa, Joachim, and Katherine Jonas were about the same age as Katie's younger children.

For both women it was certainly difficult to part when Jonas was called to Halle in 1541. In the summer of 1542 Katherine was already back to visit Katie. But at Christmastime the shocking news of her death came from Halle unexpectedly. Katie was still grieving over the recent death of her little daughter Magdalena. This new blow almost did her in. And with heartfelt words her husband grieved for the deceased, whom he had truly loved on account of her cheerful and gentle character and her faithfulness and good manners. Her perspective had always been comforting to him, for he had hoped she would be very close to his family after his death.

Katie seems to have been offended that Jonas gave his motherless children a second mother after just a few months. Even Luther asked his friend to wait a while. Then he sent him a wedding gift anyway, and greetings to his young wife, but explicitly only in his name. Katie remained silent.

After the death of his second wife Jonas married yet a third time. After the unfortunate outcome of the Smalcaldic War, he had to leave Halle. He died on October 9, 1555 as Superintendent at Eisfeld in Thuringia.

Johannes Bugenhagen

Also in the closer circle of the oldest and most trusted friends of Luther's house was Johannes Bugenhagen, born 1485 at Wollin in Pomerania, pastor of the City Church of Wittenberg since 1523, later General Superintendent of Electoral Saxony. Like Jonas, he was an excellent organizer. The success of the Reformation in Northern Germany and in Denmark is his work. Often called simply Doctor Pommer or Pomeranus after his homeland, he displayed the best characteristics of Low German stock: energy, tenacity, and loyalty. At Katie's table he often reverted to his Low German dialect and threw many rough words into the conversation, but his short, witty expressions usually hit the nail on the head. Even when Luther suffered emotional afflictions, he often found the right thing to say. Luther used to make his confession to him; he was probably also Katie's father confessor.

Even before his appointment as city parish pastor, he had married a young and, so it seems, poor girl. We know only her first name, Walpurga, and her birthdate, May 1, 1500. During the awful year of pestilence in 1527, she stayed at her husband's side just as bravely as Katie. But when the epidemic snatched away Deacon Rörer's wife in the parsonage, Bugenhagen along with Walpurga and the two little children Michael and Sara went over to Luther and Katie—not out of fear of infection, for the pestilence was also in the Black Cloister—but during these weeks of tribulation, Luther wanted to have his friend closer, as comfort and companion. At the same time as Katie bore little Elisabeth to her husband, Walpurga Bugenhagen gave birth to a little boy Johannes in the Black Cloister. The two children were allotted only a short life. Little Michael also died young. Only the third boy, who was also called Johannes, survived. The only daughter, Sara Bugenhagen, later married the Electoral Saxon Councilman George Krakau.

Bugenhagen was often out of town in the service of the Gospel, and Luther substituted for him in the pastoral office. Bugenhagen had his wife with him on these trips, which took him to Braunschweig and Hamburg in 1528 and 1529, to Lübeck in 1530–32, to Pomerania in 1534 and 1535, and to Denmark from 1537–39. But, on the other hand, in the spring of 1542 when he was in Northern Germany, it seems that Walpurga stayed in the Black Cloister again, although her husband also had his own house in Wittenberg on Neustrasse. Even though it was only a "cottage," it was still big enough that Walpurga could have some livestock. She churned her own butter, and one time when the milk wouldn't come together, which could only be the fault of the devil and his witches, Doctor Pommer sat down on the butter churn and—Luther doesn't hesitate to say what he did. But we may not repeat it.

We really mustn't criticize such stories by our concept of modesty. We always have to keep in mind how crude things were in those times, and how much superstition they had. Devil and demons, witches and warlocks, dryads and water sprites, and ghostly apparitions terrified Catholics as well as Protestants at that time, and most scholars believed that people's fate was written in the stars. Luther was one of the few who put no stock in the vain art of astrology. That was why he had locked horns many times with Melanchthon, who was a trusting and avid astrologer. But in everything else Luther was just as superstitious as his contemporaries, and his Katie certainly no less. So one time at the table she told about a devil that had lived with his wife in the Mulde as in a beautiful room. (That was a memory from her time in the convent.) According to popular belief, not far from the Nimbschen Cloister a dangerous water sprite lived in the Mulde river, which was so deep here at the precipice of Trumpet Rock or Raven Stone that it seemed almost bottomless.

Bugenhagen died in Wittenberg, weary of life, on April 20, 1558, three years after Jonas and two years before Melanchthon, who was the last of the great older generation to die.

Caspar Cruciger

Among the younger generation who were called to continue the work of the Reformation, the most prominent was Caspar Kreuziger, or Cruciger, born in Leipzig, a son of the merchant George Cruciger. He later lived in Wittenberg and was so richly blessed with earthly goods that Jonas once exclaimed: "God be praised that even a pious theologian might be rich!" Born on January 1, 1504, Caspar Cruciger was introduced to the ancient languages early at the university in his hometown, and was soon won for the Reformation as well. He was almost still a boy when he heard the great debate between Luther and Eck in Pleissenburg Castle. Twenty-one years old when he finished his studies in Wittenberg, he was entrusted with the administration of the Latin school in Magdeburg. Beginning in 1528 he taught as professor in Wittenberg. On account of his erudition, peaceableness, and piety, Luther and Melanchthon saw him as the one qualified to be their successor.

Since 1524 he had been married to Elisabeth von Meseritz. Luther himself had performed the ceremony for them. Elisabeth, like Katie, had fled from a convent. She confessed her devout faith in her hymn, "The Only Son from Heaven," which Luther put in his earliest hymnbook, *Gesangbüchlein* (1524). She had a very heartfelt relationship with him and Katie. He used the familiar "you" and called her "dear Elsa." She once brought her friend Katie a piece of gold jewelry from the church fair in Leipzig, and Luther thanked her for it with a gift in return, which was certainly less expensive, but no less well-intended. After her premature death in May 1535, Cruciger entered a second marriage in April 1536 with the Leipzig noblewoman Apollonia Gunterode, a daughter of the

Leipzig councilman Kunz Gunterode. The wedding, however, was celebrated neither in Leipzig nor in Wittenberg, but in the castle in Eilenburg, which the Elector had put at their disposal at Luther's request, for Leipzig was still under the dominion of Duke George, and it would have been much too expensive to hold a wedding feast in Wittenberg. This time, too, Luther himself preached the wedding sermon.

After Duke George's death, Cruciger implemented the Reformation in his hometown, together with the Gotha pastor Friedrich Mekum (Myconius). The people of Leipzig would have liked to keep him as their Superintendent, but, as Luther very sincerely explained to the Elector, Cruciger was indispensable in Wittenberg. Not only did he record Luther's sermons and lectures, which others did as well, he also prepared some of Luther's best writings for publication. Early on, he also took part in important negotiations and decisions, and proved his worth as keeper of minutes at several Diets through his writing skills, presence of mind, and staunch commitment to the Bible.

Cruciger was also a member of the "high council," the "Sanhedrin," with whose assistance Luther undertook a meticulous revision of his translation of the Bible from 1539–41. In the evening hours Melanchthon, Bugenhagen, Jonas, Cruciger, Aurogallus, and Rörer came for the regular negotiations, which then took place under Luther's chairmanship in the Black Cloister. Sometimes, pious scholars from elsewhere were also present: the Hebraist Bernhard Ziegler from Leipzig, Johann Forster (Forstemius) from Augsburg. Luther submitted a text to his friends, and with lively exchange the foreign words would be discussed, their meaning examined, their sense determined, the best rendering in the German language put on paper. Rörer kept the minutes. When the work in Luther's study was finished, the friends stayed for a while for supper at Katie's table, and as the *Table Talk* shows, many more difficult passages were then discussed.

As Cruciger is listed here among the best men of Wittenberg, his name is also found between the names of Melanchthon and Bugenhagen at the bottom of Luther's 1542 will as witness. And after Luther's death the Elector appointed him as guardian for

Katie's children alongside Melanchthon. In the difficult time of the Smalcaldic War, he endeavored to preserve at least a remnant of the University in Wittenberg. His premature death on November 16, 1548 meant a bitter loss for Protestantism.

George Rörer

Lastly, Master George Rörer, with his industriousness and his conscientiousness, was a true German scholar. Born at Deggendorf in 1492, he first came to Wittenberg as an adult and was solemnly ordained there by Luther as the first evangelical clergyman. He was active as deacon in the City Church and at the same time served as Luther's permanent secretary and the book printer Hans Lufft's academic proofreader. Tirelessly he wrote down Luther's sermons. For this work he later found an eager co-worker in the young Andreas Poach from Eilenburg. How many of Luther's words would have been lost without the devoted work of these two men! Rörer was the fastest among the stenographers of his time. He had devised his own shorthand, which wasn't always very easy to read and wasn't always clear either. In his position of trust—Luther often mentioned him only by his first name—he was certainly not without influence, although he refrained from putting himself forward. In jest, and yet not only in jest, Luther once placed him among the men to whom he himself sometimes had to defer. His word was not without weight even in the internal concerns of the Black Cloister. Luther called him and Sieberger and Katie his three Moseses, next to whom he was only a single Aaron. Rörer's most beneficial work began in 1539, when in cooperation with Cruciger he published the first (Wittenberg) collected edition of *Luther's Works*. He was also the most important co-worker on the second (Jena) edition. He died as librarian at Jena on April 24, 1557.

Augustin Schurf

By virtue of his position as house physician, Augustin Schurf was a frequent guest in the Black Cloister when Luther or one of Katie's many wards was ill. During the year of the plague in 1527, he actually seems to have lived with Luther and Katie. His wife Hanna was one of three afflicted with the plague. She lay ill in Luther's house, but recovered again. His brother Jerome Schurf, the great lawyer, on the other hand, was no friend of Katie's in later years. Indeed, it seems she was hostile toward him, and during the quarrel between Luther and Schurf the common talk in Wittenberg was that Katie added fuel to the fires of her husband's anger. Of course, it was probably no secret to her that Schurf had most fiercely disapproved of her husband's marriage. And in the bitter controversy over canon law and the validity of secret engagements, she was certainly on her husband's side, not simply because he was her husband. When even the Elector wanted to prohibit the lawyers in Wittenberg from teaching that the children of married priests should not be entitled to inheritance, how much more would Katie, the married nun, have been infuriated and offended by such teaching, as a wife and mother!

Lucas Cranach

Many other members of the University and many of the citizenry are mentioned occasionally as guests in the Black Cloister. Cranach and his family were true friends of Luther and his household. Cranach was the only one Luther told by letter that he had to be kept in hiding for a while after the Diet of Worms. Also, along with his wife Barbara, Cranach had escorted Katie to the Black Cloister on her wedding day. Katie's little Hans was their godchild. Cranach frequently painted or made woodcuts of Luther and Katie's portraits, and Cranach's sons, Hans and Lucas, and his students were busy working on the illustrations reproduced in Luther's writings. In times of need Luther called on Cranach's help, and Cranach listened to Luther's advice in important matters and shared and sympathized with him on both happy and sad occasions. When the young highly-gifted Hans Cranach was supposed to travel to Italy in 1537 for his artistic training, Luther strongly supported the decision. But when the young man died due to the different climate in Bologna, Luther himself went to the large house on the marketplace to comfort the grieving parents.

Ambrosius Reuter

Also residing along the marketplace were Mrs. Felicitas von Selbitz, who is remembered many times in the *Table Talk* and in Luther's letters, and Ambrosius Reuter, whose house was one of the most famous in Wittenberg. There was a large painting on the gable: on one side Luther, who is knocking off the pope's triple tiara with a huge feather pen, on the other side Melanchthon, who is knocking down the pope with a box of quills with an inkwell hanging on it, and in the middle there is a pig with a golden crown on a silk pillow. The people of Wittenberg preserved this picture, essentially a caricature of the papacy, as a commemoration of the sad incident Reuter had experienced in his youth in Leipzig.

Twenty-three years old, he had come to Leipzig as a student in 1520, and here he got caught up in a controversy with a Catholic cleric over Luther's doctrine. His opponent informed on him, and he was put in prison. But he had some countrymen and friends in the city. When they heard that a cruel inquisition was to be conducted against him, they went out the gate to the city moat and shouted to him in short Latin words that it would be a matter of life and death, and that he should take care of himself and make his confession to God. His life wasn't really in serious danger. And Duke George, who was very heavy-handed otherwise, didn't want a religious murder on his conscience; yes, here he showed unexpected leniency.

Two years later, Reuter's countryman, Sebastian Fröschel from Amberg, even dared to preach evangelically. The duke then had him summoned to Pleissenburg Castle, accompanied by three mayors and the whole council and assembled city servants, and he spoke to him very sternly: Earlier he had been a beautiful little frog [*Fröschel*, a pun on his name], but now he had become a poisonous toad. But in the end the duke was content to banish the young man from the country, and many years later, as deacon in Wittenberg, Fröschel fondly remembered that day when he had been brought to the castle in Leipzig with so much pomp and circumstance.

Reuter would probably have also gotten off lightly. But he thought about escaping. He succeeded at breaking an iron bar out of the window of his prison. Then he took apart the little bed that had been given to him because it was cold winter, made a rope for himself, and was going to let himself down out of the tower into the city moat. But since the rope was still too short, he finally had to jump down, and he badly injured his leg. He limped around in the moat for a good while in the dark of night, in great anxiety and concern about how he might get out of the moat and escape. Then suddenly he saw a pig, and hoping that the animal might run back toward where it had come in, he chased it and followed it until finally it ran to a place where a section of the wall had caved in. And although the opening was narrow, he successfully forced his way through and reached the city undetected. There he remained hidden with one of his friends for several days.

Finally Reuter made his way to Wittenberg. Meanwhile, however, a false report had come to Leipzig that the fleeing Lutheran heretic had been seen in a village inn in Düben. So a wagon and soldiers were quickly dispatched to apprehend him again. They passed him on the road. But since they didn't expect to find him until they got to Düben, they didn't at all suspect that the young man, who was disguised as a poor carpenter, might be the fugitive they were looking for. And when he complained to them that he couldn't get very far because his leg was hurt, they felt sorry for him and took him into the wagon and let him ride along a good part of the way until finally he peacefully parted from them. They went on toward Düben in order to get the fugitive, but Reuter arrived in Wittenberg safe and sound another way.

Here he finished his law studies and in 1523 married a rich widow. When she died, he got married a second time, to one of Luther's relatives, and when she died in 1548, he married yet a third time. From all three marriages he had no less than twenty-three children, of whom twelve survived him. Since 1534, he sat on the city council. He also had a small textile trade. During the Smalcaldic War, he was mayor. After the war he resigned from his post and took over the office of University notary, which, after his death in 1564, went to the younger Philipp Melanchthon. Reuter highly esteemed Katie, not simply as a relative. As a widow she asked the Elector to appoint him as third guardian for her children, while she dismissed as guardian Doctor Major, who is often mentioned among the dinner guests.

Spalatin

But the Wittenberg friends weren't the only frequent guests in the Black Cloister. If Katie had had a guest book, many pages would be filled with the names of friends visiting from out of town. There were princely personages, prominent officials, clerics and scholars, parents who brought their children to the University, travelers who couldn't leave Wittenberg without seeing Luther, or who had come to Wittenberg just for that purpose. Katie's hospitable home was open to all of them. She would have preferred to see Luther's oldest and most trusted friends, Spalatin and Hausmann, even more often than she really could. There was a lively exchange of letters in which Katie often spoke to the friends even through her husband's pen. This correspondence had to bridge the gap that separated those two from Wittenberg.

George Burkhardt, born at Spalt in Franconia in 1482 and thus called Spalatinus, was superintendent of Altenburg, and he also got married soon after Luther did. As Luther jokingly called his Katie *"Kette"* [chain], he did the same with Spalatin's wife, whose name was also Katharine. When Katie held her little Hans in her arms, she also wished for her namesake and her husband to have a little Spalatin. The letters flew back and forth. Nevertheless the people of Altenburg, among who were Brisger and his wife since 1525, complained that Luther wrote too seldom. He read the parts that pertained to them, and at the Coburg he could return Spalatin's rebuke: Messengers came, but with empty hands. "Don't you bring letters?" Luther then asked, but the answer was: "No!" "How are your lords?" "They are well!" Then they surely could have written, Luther thought.

But in the final years, even Katie found that her husband didn't write often enough. The gracious lady of Zölsdorf had many requests of Spalatin ever since 1540. To thank him, she sent her friend a medicinal plant that was supposed to help against kidney stones, and she sent his daughters some books when she had gone to Altenburg to see her husband who had come home sick from

Smalcald and she had enjoyed the hospitality of the Altenburg parsonage. Spalatin, whose name is also at the head of the list of historians of the princely house of Wettin, died before Luther, on January 16, 1545.

Nikolaus Hausmann

As pastor in Zwickau, Nikolaus Hausmann, born at Freiberg in 1479, was likewise too far from Wittenberg to be able to visit often. Luther esteemed this friend especially highly on account of his piety and his honest character. Luther was shocked that the Zwickau council got into intense quarrels with him. Several times he urged him to come to Wittenberg; a new little room was already prepared for him. When he finally arrived, Luther said he wanted to share his poverty with him. Hausmann was active in Wittenberg for a while. Since he had remained unmarried, he was certainly able to be content with his little room. But Katie's little children may have been quite a puzzle to him, the old bachelor. Melanchthon once said to him that it would really be a shame that a man with gray hair didn't know what an experience it was when little children were teething.

Hausmann was better in his position in caring for souls than in caring for children. In the autumn of 1532, the three princes of Anhalt called him to be court preacher at Dessau in order to implement the Reformation in their land. And six years later, the council of Freiberg entrusted to him the administration of the church in his hometown. On October 17, 1538 he left Luther's house. Both of them had tears in their eyes. They knew that they would never see each other after this. Already on November 6, news came from Freiberg that the old man had suffered a stroke in the chancel at his inaugural service. With all efforts to spare him, Luther was prepared for the loss by Katie, Melanchthon, Jonas, and Lauterbach. When the realization of his friend's death sank in, he broke into tears and said: "So God takes away the pious, and afterward the chaff is burned up. He was a dear friend to me!" And he sat in mourning between Melanchthon and Jonas the whole day. And even Camerarius, who was on a visit in Wittenberg, and

Caspar von Köckritz, an old friend of the house, came to comfort him.

Katie's Hospitality

Friends were always welcome to Katie. Having so many guests visit from out of town was often a heavy burden, yet we hardly ever hear a word of complaint from her about it. The mother and homemaker, who was very busy otherwise, took it for granted that her house was like a guesthouse during quiet times, and like a hospital during the years of plague. Sometimes not a single room in the large building was vacant. Even a princely visit had to be declined then. So in the summer and autumn of 1537, the old Elector's wife Elisabeth of Brandenburg, widow of Joachim I, lay physically and emotionally ill for weeks in the Black Cloister, and Katie sat on the princess's bed and kept her calm. Then her daughter, the princess Margarete von Anhalt, wanted to come to Wittenberg with an entourage to visit her sick mother. But there was no more room in the Black Cloister, and everything in the city was full of students and no inn had a vacancy. Luther had to write to the princess and assure her and her husband, Prince Johann, that her noble mother [*Frau Mutter*] was lacking nothing under Katie's care. But he and Katie breathed a sigh of relief when the Elector's wife was finally able to leave their house.

When Katie had become a widow, Chancellor Brück dared to speak before the Elector of the large household about the wasteful way she managed it. We have learned about Luther's income, and we have seen how well Katie understood keeping expenditures lower than revenues, and how she succeeded in gradually bringing them out of the great poverty of the early years to a certain affluence. Now we have also learned what obligations were placed on her by her husband's position. Certainly the household she presided over was large, very large, but it was not her fault. Though from time to time some poor relatives of hers might also sit at the table, their number was insignificant compared to the multitude of those her husband brought into the house.

We don't hear much about how she actually managed to satisfy all these obligations, how often she must have dreaded and worried, how untiringly she must have worked and pitched in herself. But, besides Luther's statements already cited earlier, we do have a weighty testimony from him, that is, what he told Bugenhagen in Gotha in 1537, when he thought he was going to die. He asked his friends Melanchthon, Jonas, and Cruciger to bring his final greetings, and went on to say: "Comfort my Katie! She shall endure the pain, remembering that she has been happy with me for twelve years. She has served me not only as a wife, but also as a maid. God reward her for it!"

9.

LUTHER'S DEATH

> To your wife, Lady Katherine, the best lady, I
> herewith say: 'Farewell.' . . . After I return home, I
> will send her something through the merchants, which
> she should wear to remember me. I love her from my
> heart. She was created to see to your health, so that
> you might serve even longer the Church which was
> born under you, that is, all who hope in Christ.

That's what Capito wrote to Luther after he had been in
Wittenberg in May 1536. And then when he sent a ring to
Neobolus, he designated the simple gold ring as a gift to Katherine
von Bora, the best lady, and as a sign of his affection toward her:
"She is deservedly deemed worthy because she cares for our
mutual teacher with meekness and diligence."

What Capito had keenly experienced on his short visit is also
for us Katie's highest praise: the loving, tireless care with which
she surrounded her husband and nursed him devotedly during his
sick days.

Luther's Illnesses and Katie's Cures

Luther almost had more sick days than healthy ones. When he got
married, they were fewer; and he would have predicted that he'd
have a long life. His firm and tough body, inherited from his
parents, was weakened by the excessive punishments to which he
had subjected himself as a monk, and he threatened to succumb

under the almost superhuman mental exertions in the intense and rough battles. The pains that afflicted him again and again were both physical and emotional at the same time: congestion and dizziness, headaches and ringing in the ears, anxieties and worries, which grew into severe bouts of unconsciousness. And connected with them were the most severe emotional agitations, deep melancholy, mental afflictions,[1] torturous doubt about the justness of his cause, yes, doubts about God's grace. There were the struggles with the devil, which he often mentions in his letters and in the *Table Talk*.

Even before his marriage he was discovered unconscious in his room one time, and in the deep sadness that had followed this attack his friends had refreshed him through music. Then the illness was quiet for a few years. But after he had an attack in January 1527 that almost destroyed his heart, his pains took him by surprise on July 6, worse than before or ever again. Bugenhagen and Jonas, who were around him and Katie during these days, have left us detailed accounts, along with Doctor Schurf. And Luther himself writes to Melanchthon about his condition. For more than a week he had been tossed back and forth in death and hell and was shaking all over his body.

In the comfortable family life that Katie created for him after the early years of poverty, his illness seems to have eased. Still, headaches and dizziness often forced him to lay his pen aside, and his afflictions always returned again. But combined physical and emotional pains never again afflicted him as hard as that severe attack of July 6, 1527.

A new, excruciating pain had come upon him in 1526, pain from kidney stones. This brought him close to death in Smalcald in February 1537. The home remedies that Katie sent from Wittenberg no longer helped, and the physicians of the princes gathered in Smalcald and the famous physician George Sturz, whom the Elector summoned from Erfurt, had tried for days to treat the illness or at least to ease his unbearable pains, but it was in vain. Then Luther wanted to be taken out of Smalcald on February

---

[1] *Anfechtungen.*

25; he didn't want to die in the presence of the monster, the papal nuncio. But Melanchthon superstitiously held him back, for the constellations were not favorable. Not until the next day did the patient leave Smalcald for Gotha with his companions Sturz, Bugenhagen, Spalatin, Myconius, and Schlaginhaufen.

The shaking wagon on the poor roads in the mountains brought him dreadful torments. Yet—was it the shaking that led to a breakthrough, or the thin red wine that he drank in Tambach? Suddenly he got better. Even from Tambach, where they rested that night, he was able to send a letter to his dearest Melanchthon, who had to stay behind in Smalcald. And from Gotha, where he stayed the following days with Myconius, he reported to his Katie:

> I was dead. And I have commended you to God and to my most gracious lord, along with the little children, as though I would never see you all again. He has been very merciful to me for your sake! But I had given notice to my grave.—God has worked a miracle on me this night and He is still doing so through the intercession of pious people. That's what I'm writing to you about, for I think that my most gracious lord commanded the high-bailiff to send you to me, since I was dying at the time, so that you might speak with me or see me. That isn't necessary now, and you may stay there at home, since God has so richly helped me, that I foresee myself happily coming to you.

His letter must have been a real comfort for Katie who feared for his life. But he wasn't able to hold her back. Even before she could get on her way, she sent one of her nieces to care for her husband, and Jonas hurried toward his friend along with the young girl. But in Gotha he suffered another relapse of his illness, a relapse so bad that he again feared for his life and finally ordered all those around him to leave, except Bugenhagen. Bugenhagen faithfully recorded the words Luther spoke to him in the still of the night (February 28–March 1). His account is in fact designated as Luther's first will. But it is not his actual last will and testament.

Not until some days later could Luther be brought from Gotha past Erfurt to Weimar, where Melanchthon met with him. The trip then continued to Altenburg. In Spalatin's house Katie greeted her husband who, by God's grace, had been given to her anew, and on March 14 they were back in Wittenberg. His recovery progressed quickly. After just fourteen days he was able to preach again. But the pains from the stone always flared up again, as they usually do, and the white grains of amber that Duke Albrecht of Prussia sent as a remedy really weren't able to help at all.

Numerous other illnesses weakened him as well. He was spared the severe plague-like illness to which he fearlessly exposed himself, but he was repeatedly troubled by fever and rheumatism. In 1538 he suffered a lot from dysentery. Dizzy spells kept returning. In 1541 an extremely painful earache came as well. An open sore on his leg, which had appeared already in 1532, gave him lots of difficulties. The doctors later kept the wound open artificially, since they hoped this would keep the blood from rushing to his head. So Katie had to worry about him and take care of him again and again. She was tireless in her care and limitless in home remedies. As her son, Paul Luther the physician, later testified, she not only helped with female disorders but also with other advice and treatment. She even prepared the thistle drink[2] that helped her husband in his illness in January 1527, although the doctors, as Luther himself wrote, didn't want to know anything about it.

It was not uncommon, by the way, for women to do a little doctoring. It didn't even bother princesses to prepare handmade medicines. They didn't use the most appetizing ingredients for this. Luther also wrote to Katie from Smalcald: "Your skill doesn't help me, even with the dung."

Where had Katie learned the skill? One possible way was from old Auntie Lena, who lived in the Black Cloister until her death and who had once been head of the infirmary in the Nimbschen Cloister in her younger years.

---

[2] Common Modern English name: Blessed Thistle. Also called: *Cnicus benedictus* or *Centaurea benedicta*.

Katie's Health

Katie herself enjoyed good health. Of course, we often hear of little pains, but we rarely hear that she was really sick. One time she was struck with unconsciousness; another time she was so weakened by fever that her husband lamented: "Dear Katie, please don't die on me!" She had just gotten over a severe and lengthy illness in the first month of 1540, when she was deathly ill as a result of a miscarriage. On January 18 she was still alert and healthy so that Luther could tell the Elector that he would come to Eisenach if his presence were needed there. On January 22, however, her condition was almost hopeless, and although they were constantly caring for her, she had given up on her life and just kept repeating the words of Psalm 31: "In You, O Lord, I put my trust; let me never be ashamed." With this she was quiet and comforted. Had it not been for the children, Luther later said he wouldn't have prayed the Lord's Prayer for Katie any more, but would have commended her soul to Christ. For the sake of the children he continued his fervent prayers to God to let him keep her. On January 24 she was like a breathing corpse, and despite all tonics that were poured into her, she kept falling back into unconsciousness, a sad picture.

But the very faithful care that watched over her every breath and every movement succeeded in keeping her alive. Slowly the illness subsided. They had believed she was out of danger on February 9, but three days later they once again feared for her life. Then the recovery began and continued. Food and drink tasted good to her again. As her husband wrote on February 26, she even got out of bed and was trying to take her first steps, but it was more like crawling, as she helped herself around by grabbing onto tables and chairs. She first had to learn to walk again. But soon she was happily recovered and regained her strength. And on April 8, Luther was able to write to Melanchthon: "My Katie is completely recovered."

A few weeks later he bought her the Zölsdorf property. The portrait medallion that she had made for her dear Zölsdorf that same year, 1540, shows no trace of the severe illness she had overcome. Her face is plump and full; her facial expression is uncommonly lively and energetic. For the forty-year-old woman, her life's sun was high in the sky again, but for her husband the sun was setting.

Luther's Final Years

Many things came together to upset and embitter Luther in the final years of his life. How often, under the burdens of age, we hear him complain that he is tired, worn out, not worth anything any more! How often he longs to leave this sinful world for a better one! The moral conditions in Wittenberg were better than at other German universities, but he was frustrated when he saw immodesty becoming more and more brazen. He doubted the world really could be improved, for greed and usury, tyranny, discord, disloyalty, wickedness, and dishonesty raged everywhere—among the nobility, in the court, in the city halls, in the city, and in the country. And beyond this, people despised the Divine Word and were ungrateful as never before. Agricola's defection and the disagreement with Schurf was a harsh blow. In earlier years he had certainly endured greater adversities unshaken, but now his intellectual powers were weakened.

Irritated and embittered, he wanted to leave Wittenberg forever at the beginning of 1544, and it took the pleading petitions, yes, tears from Bugenhagen and other influential men from the church, the University, and the city to stop him. In the summer of the next year, in the company of Cruciger, along with his eldest son Hans and his lodger Ferdinand von Maugis, he traveled to Zeitz to see Amsdorf. But on the way, especially in Leipzig, where he rested at the home of the rich councilman Heinz Scherl, he heard terrible things through the grapevine that had been kept secret from him in Wittenberg. On July 28 he therefore wrote to Katie from Zeitz:

> Grace and peace! Dear Katie, Hans will surely tell you everything about how our trip has gone. In fact, I'm not sure yet whether he should stay with me. Dr. Caspar Cruciger and Ferdinand would say so. Ernst von Schönfeld has hosted us well at Löbnitz, Heinz Scherle at Leipzig even better. I would really like to

arrange it so that I wouldn't have to return to Wittenberg. My heart has grown cold, so that I no longer enjoy being there.

And I wish you would sell the garden and acreage, house and farmyard, so that I could return the large house to my most gracious lord. And if it were best for you to settle at Zölsdorf because I'm still alive and could help you pay to improve the little place, for I hope my most gracious lord would have my salary continue for at least a year during my last days. After my death the four elements at Wittenberg will probably not put up with you. So it would be better to do whatever there is to do while I'm alive.

Let Dr. Pommer and Master Philipp know this (as you will), and have Dr. Pommer herewith bless Wittenberg on my behalf. For I can no longer endure [people's] anger and apathy. With this I commend you to God, Amen. Tuesday, Knoblochstag [Garlic Day], 1545. Martinus Luther.

Katie would have hurried to share this letter with both friends. Already on August 1 the University reported this to the Elector, and that very same day Melanchthon, Bugenhagen, and Major on behalf of the University, and on behalf of the city Mayor Gregor Matthes and the printer Hans Lufft, who was city judge at that time, were sent as delegates to Luther. But the Elector sent Dr. Ratzeberger with a reassuring letter on August 5. Their combined efforts and promises succeeded in bringing Luther home, after he had spent a few more days in Leipzig—this time with Camerarius—and in Torgau with the Elector. He was back in Wittenberg on August 16, 1545.

He hoped he could go to his final rest soon and without a difficult struggle with death. In the winter of 1542 and 1543 when he was tormented once by his severe headache, he said to his wife: "Katie, if I am not better tomorrow, then I want Hans brought home from Torgau, for I would really like him to be here at my end." Katie had tried to quiet him: "Look, my lord, don't be concerned about that!" But he had replied: "No, Katie, this is no illusion. I won't die so suddenly. First I will lie down and become ill. But I will not lie there for long."

He was spared a long illness. But his Katie was not allowed to be with him to close his eyes. That last blessed little hour that he had often longed for didn't come upon him in Wittenberg, but in Eisleben, the city where he had been born and baptized.

The Counts of Mansfeld, in whose territory Eisleben lay, had once been rich and powerful, as powerful as the lords of a grand territory. Their wealth came from mining where silver-bearing copper had been found. Through the inheritance being divided and through poor management, however, the old dynasty of the Counts had been split into several lines and was deep in debt. Conflicts had arisen over dividing up the territory, the maintenance of churches and schools, and the production of the silver mines. These conflicts again and again awaited an arbitrator with the complicated and convoluted rights and claims of the various lines. Then Duke Albrecht turned to Luther, and at the same time to the Elector, asking that Luther be allowed to take over the office of arbitrator. The Elector consented, but reluctantly.

After Luther's death he wrote to the Mansfelders in rather harsh words, that he really would have wanted to see blessed Martin spared from these matters as an old, frail man. Chancellor Brück even spoke about the Mansfeld "dirty dealings." Luther himself called one of the many disputed points of conflict a real porcupine, yes, pricklier than a porcupine. But despite his weakness he was ready faithfully to perform this last service that his lords required of him.

At the beginning of October 1545 he was in Mansfeld for the first time with Melanchthon and Jonas. But since the counts had to render military service to the Elector against the Duke of Braunschweig Heinz von Wolfenbüttel, the trip was unsuccessful.

On Saint Martin's Day, back in Wittenberg, he once again had his most trusted friends with him: Melanchthon, Bugenhagen, Cruciger, Major, and Eber. When they were leaving after an enjoyable meal, he spoke serious words to them:

While I'm alive, there will be no danger, God willing, and good peace will remain in Germany. But when I am dead, pray then too, for there will be a great need of prayer. Our children will even have to take the spear in their hands.

And he pointed young Paul Eber to the portrait of the Apostle Paul, whose name he bore.

A week later, on November 17, he gave his last lecture and finished his exposition of Genesis with the words: "I can do no more! I am weak. Pray for me that God grant me a good, blessed final hour."

During the days of the Christmas celebration, he was with Melanchthon a second time at the Castle Mansfeld. To his companion, he dreaded to think about going out into the country in the cold winter days; his sickness also forced him to break off the negotiations.

Luther's Last Days

So, on January 23, 1546, Luther went to his homeland for a third time, this time to Eisleben. Melanchthon could not accompany him on account of his illness. His three sons, however, followed him as his entourage, along with their teacher Rudtfeld and his assistant Aurifaber. In Halle, where they were held up for three days by high water and ice floes, Jonas joined them.

At the border they were met by more than a hundred riders and escorted to Eisleben with honor. Meanwhile, however, Luther caught a cold, and before they arrived in Eisleben he had already become so weak during fits of vertigo and constriction that they feared for his life. Yet he recovered once again. He took part in the proceedings, and held out even though the tiresome matter so grieved him that on February 7 it was touch-and-go, and he would have gotten up and left. Only concern for his country and his homeland held him back. But he got the satisfaction and joy of his participation leading to agreement.

A sense of foreboding concerning his death, which he had already expressed in Wittenberg, also filled him in Eisleben. But in his letters to Katie he doesn't talk about it. The letters are cheerful and confident, affectionate, playful. He assured his dear wife again and again what good food and drink he had here, and how fine they treated him so that he would never forget them. He tells her that her sons are visiting Uncle [*Oheim*] Jacob Luther in Mansfeld. He tells her about the progress of the negotiations, and that the young lords and ladies of Mansfeld are again in agreement and happily riding sleighs with their silly little bells. Just four days before his death he sent her some trout that he had received as a gift from the countess. Only his requests and admonitions that Katie not worry about him show us how afraid Katie was for him.

Of course, it was only with a heavy heart that she had let him go. And her worry had become overpowering when the news of his first illness had arrived and the pills, aquavit, and other remedies were ordered for him. This gave her sleepless nights. She even added her home remedies to the package and wrote many devout and concerned letters, as a well-educated, holy, and conscientious lady, as her husband jokingly called her in those days. Sometimes seriously admonishing, sometimes lovingly teasing, he dismissed her concerns and tells her: "You, just pray, and let God worry! That is: Cast your care on the Lord who cares for you."

Yet in the end, even he became concerned. The wound on his legs that had been artificially kept open had almost completely closed. On February 14 he therefore asked Melanchthon by letter, even though he was already on his way home, to send a courier to him with the caustic that he used to use in Wittenberg; Katie would know where it was in his room. But to Katie he wrote on the same day: "Dear Katie, we hope to return home this week, God willing. God has shown us great grace here." The counts had been reconciled in his presence.

Luther's two younger sons, Martin and Paul, had returned to Eisleben from Mansfeld. Along with them Jonas and the Mansfeld court preacher Michael Cölius, Aurifaber, and Rudtfelt were with Luther when he suffered from severe constrictions again in the evening hours of February 17. They used warm compresses on him, and Duke Albrecht himself, who had been summoned by Aurifaber, prepared the medicine for him: wine into which he grated some horn of unicorn (narwhal tooth). The attack seemed to pass. He slept peacefully for several hours. But an hour after midnight he woke up again. The constrictions pressed even harder around his heart. He got weaker. Again they used warm compresses on him, and the countess and both physicians, who had been quickly summoned, smeared a poultice on him with the recuperative liquids Katie had sent, but his fleeting life was to be kept no more. Between two and three o'clock in the early hours of February 18, a Thursday, he passed away. His last coherent words were: "Father, into Your hands I commend my spirit. You have redeemed me, faithful God." And when asked if he would die steadfast in Christ and the doctrine, which he had preached, he answered with a clearly audible "Yes."

Katie Learns of Luther's Death

At four in the morning, Jonas wrote a detailed account for the Elector of his great friend's last days and his death. The letter was copied many times in the following days and then also disseminated in print. An express courier brought the letter to Torgau, where the Elector was at that time. Jonas sent a second express courier to Wittenberg. The Elector immediately wrote twice to Chancellor Brück, and he received the first message in Wittenberg on February 19, at six o'clock in the morning. He immediately summoned Melanchthon, Bugenhagen, and Cruciger. They already knew what had happened; a quarter-hour earlier the second messenger from Eisleben had met them. At Brück's request they proceeded to the Black Cloister to prepare Katie gently for the sad news. But she already sensed what brought the three friends to her when they came so troubled and at such an early hour. Melanchthon reported to the Chancellor:

> It is easy to see that the poor woman is deeply shocked and greatly troubled, but especially on account of the three sons whom the sainted Doctor had in Eisleben, not knowing how they might react to their father's death.

Those are the only words we hear from a contemporary about her pain.

She was so deeply brokenhearted, that she—the tirelessly busy lady—disbanded her group of lodgers. But she soon overcame her depression, for in her piety and her sorrow she had, besides the comfort she found in her pious God-given faith, something else that kept her standing: the sense of pride at having been the wife of such a man. This pride still speaks to us as well from her letter of April 2 in which she thanked her sister-in-law Christiana von Bora, Florian's mother, who was also widowed, for her sympathy:

> Kind, dear sister! I can easily believe that you have heartfelt sympathy for my poor children and me. For who would not easily be troubled and saddened over such a precious man as my dear husband was? He served not just one city or a single country, but the entire world. For that reason I really am so sad that I can't tell anyone how full of sorrow my heart is. And I don't know what I'm thinking and how I'm feeling. I can't eat or drink, nor even sleep. And if I had had a princedom or empire and lost it, I wouldn't have been as sad as now when our dear Lord God has taken this dear and precious man from me, and not just from me, but from the whole world. If I think about it, then I can't speak nor even have someone write because of the pain and crying (God surely knows that).[3]

And as Melanchthon and Eber later report, she lamented particularly that her husband had died so far away from her, and that she hadn't been able to take care of him and show him her love. She was allowed to follow him only on the last and most difficult walk, the procession to the grave.

---

[3] Kroker's note: Katie did not write this letter in her own hand, but dictated it to someone else.

Luther's Funeral Procession

The Counts of Mansfeld wanted his body kept in his homeland. But the Elector decided that it should be laid to rest in the Castle Church in Wittenberg. After the body was mourned and wept over by many in the house where he died, rather than the chancel of St. Andrew's Church, in the morning hours of February 18, it was laid in a pewter coffin that had been quickly cast. And for that day, his body remained in the house where he died. On February 19 at two o'clock in the afternoon, amidst Christian hymns, it was brought into St. Andrew's Church and lay in state in the chancel. Jonas preached the funeral sermon. That night ten citizens of Eisleben held the funeral vigil. On February 20 Cölius preached in the morning, and at one in the afternoon the funeral procession headed toward Halle, led by the Count and Countess of Mansfeld and a large crowd of people, who followed to the outermost city gate with weeping and pious hymn singing, while the closest relatives, along with the three sons of the deceased, and their companions traveled on. Count Hans and Hans Hoyer with some forty riders accompanied the long procession, which was met in the villages on the way with the tolling of bells. In Halle they were met by the clergy and the town council, the whole school, many citizens, women and children, amidst such loud weeping and wailing that Jonas and Cölius, who were last in the procession, heard it in their little carriage. And the crowd in the alleys and in the marketplace was so large that the procession often came to a standstill and arrived too late at the Church of Our Lady for another service to be held. In the sacristy the citizens of Halle held the funeral vigil. On February 21 at six o'clock in the morning, the procession left Halle again as the bells tolled. At the border of Electoral Saxony and in Bitterfeld, the Elector's representatives; the city captain of Wittenberg, Erasmus Spiegel; and the leaders of Düben and Brehna, were already waiting with their retinues. But that day they only got as far as Kemberg.

Their arrival had been expected in Wittenberg on February 21. Melanchthon didn't receive news of the delay until noon. In a short Latin flyer he notified the University that the body would arrive the next morning about nine o'clock. So, on February 22, a Monday, a day dawned such as Wittenberg had never seen before. Already in the early morning hours the professors and students, the council and the citizenry streamed out in droves behind the Black Cloister, in the courtyard where a little carriage stood ready for the widow and her closest friends. The people stretched out to the Elster Gate. And in the streets thronged townsfolk and country people who had hurried into the city.

About nine o'clock the smaller bells announced that the procession with the mortal remains of the immortal man was approaching. The clergy and the teachers arranged themselves in front with the students. Following them on horseback were the Electoral representatives and the two Counts of Mansfeld with their retinues, some sixty riders. A four-horse wagon carried the coffin. Then Katie rode behind it in her carriage with her little daughter Margarete and some matrons. The three sons, Johannes, Martin, and Paul, walked behind them, next to them their Uncle [*Oheim*] Jacob Luther and their cousins George and Cyriakus Kaufmann from Mansfeld and other relatives. Augustin Schurf followed as rector of the University, accompanied by the young princes, counts, and free lords, who were studying in Wittenberg.

Then came the oldest and most trusted friends of the deceased: Brück, Melanchthon, Jonas, Bugenhagen, Cruciger, Jerome Schurf, and behind them came the other professors and masters, the mayors and councilmen, followed by the infinitely long train of students and citizens, men, women, and children, all with loud weeping and wailing, amidst the tolling of bells and the singing of Christian hymns. They entered the city through the Elster Gate and went past the Black Cloister, along *Kollegienstrasse*, across the marketplace and Castle Street down to the Castle Church. Here Bugenhagen preached the funeral sermon, Melanchthon gave the Latin memorial speech. Then the younger University teachers lifted the coffin and lowered it into the grave in front of the pulpit.

The day before the funeral Katie had received a letter from the Elector himself, in which he expressed his sympathy and assured her and her orphaned children of his gracious generosity. They needed it.

Luther's Will

In his first serious illness in July 1527, Luther couldn't think about a will yet. At that time he had asked his Katie to entrust herself to God's gracious will, and then fearing he would die, he had his dearest little Hans brought to his bedside. And when the little one smiled at him, he said:

> Oh you good little child! Now, I commend my dearest Katie and you to my dearest faithful God. You have nothing. But God who is the father of the orphan and the defender of the widow will certainly protect you and take care of you.

And he spoke with Katie about the silver tankards, gifts from rich lords, which were the only real valuables in their household, adding: "You know we have nothing else." But Katie suppressed her pain and her sorrow. She was proudly aware that her husband, who was suffering right in front of her, belonged not only to her but also to the world, and that she still needed him. She comforted him with full and firm confidence in God's grace:

> My dearest Lord Doctor, if it is God's will, then I know that you should be with our Lord God rather than with me. This isn't just about me and my child, but also many pious Christian people who still need you. Don't worry on my account! I entrust you to His divine will. God will certainly keep you.

Ten years later, in February 1537, Luther had been laid up, mortally ill again, in Smalcald. Elector John Fredrick now came to his bedside and promised to take care of his wife and children as though they were his own. The prince was sincere and still young, and his word was pure as gold. But if the prince should pass away before his time, would his servants honor what their lord had promised? Would his survivors be mindful of what had been bequeathed to Luther? People are uncivilized; the world is ungrateful. Luther knew that only too well. He feared that even after his death a Pharaoh could still arise "which knew not

Joseph."[4] Luther was haunted by a conversation Jerome Schurf had with Katie about the Black Cloister and Elector Hans (who had presented a valuable piece of land to Luther as a gift). Schurf asked, "Does the house belong to you yet?" When Katie said "No," he sincerely advised her: "Take it! And when someone offers you a pig, then hold open the sack! If Christ has been forgotten, then Luther will certainly be forgotten as well."

But not only would the ingratitude of the world become apparent, but jealousy and hostility also would raise their head and stretch their claws against his widow and the minor children. Indeed, as long as he sheltered his family with his powerful form, no one dared do anything against them publicly. It didn't take long, in the city and in the court, soon here and soon there, before there was whispering and murmuring about Katie's pride and her bossiness, about her large and wasteful management of the household, about the influence she was supposed to have had on her husband, that she asserted herself, not always with a peaceful attitude! The defenseless widow could sense the grudge held by some. Luther realized that after his death she would be a troubled and miserable woman, and already in her young and healthy and happy days, he had her memorize the Psalm 31, in which the psalmist entreats the Lord to stop the false tongues that spoke stubbornly, proudly, and mockingly against the righteous.

After the difficult days in Smalcald, he seems to have thought seriously about making a will. If he wanted his Katie to be secure in all circumstances, then he had to put down his last will in the form of a written testament. The old strict Saxon law was still in effect in Electoral Saxony at that time. This said that a widow was promised only the "morning gift"[5] and the so-called *Gerade*.[6] The *Sachsenspiegel*[7] explicitly lists all the items in household effects that are to be counted under the *Gerade*. In 1504 the Wittenberg

---

[4] Exodus 1:8 (KJV).

[5] *Morgengabe:* a gift from husband to wife after the wedding night.

[6] In Medieval German law, a widow was entitled to certain items from the household: food, some furniture, clothing, jewelry, including things that would be passed on to female relatives at her death. The specifics varied by region.

[7] The *Sachsenspiegel* (Saxon Mirror) was a German law code from the 1200s.

council gave its citizens even less discretion. Luther had heard the quip about the law that summarized everything in a few words: "After the death of her husband a wife should be given a chair and a spinning wheel."

This sentence seems to have tormented Luther even after he had once again recovered. A few months after his return from Smalcald, he spoke sharply about this in the circle of lodgers: Human law must not be interpreted according to the letter, but rather according to the sense. Now, many women have worked in their house for thirty–forty years; but if, as widows, they are to keep only a chair and a spinning wheel, is that worth a *Groschen*? One has to pay servants better than that; yes, one would give that much to some unknown beggar at the door! Therefore one must interpret the law according to its sense: chair, that would be house and yard; and spinning wheel would be livelihood. This is what the law means to say, and yet in Wittenberg and in other places one deals with the poor women according to the letter and kicks them out like the dogs.

Luther's interpretation was too broad. The *Sachsenspiegel* leaves no doubt about what should go to the widow and what should not. House and yard belonged not to the widow, but to the heirs, who might be the children or, if there were no children, the man's nearest blood-relatives. But even the *Sachsenspiegel* in fact made it possible for the man to assure his wife a definite income if he should die first. Under certain formal conditions, including especially the consent of the feudal lord and the appointment of a guardian, he could assign to her the legal right to some of his property for her lifetime, and the heirs could not contest such a written will.

So Luther had to be explicit in designating a portion of his property as an inheritance for his Katie. But he put it off year after year. He didn't really want anything to do with lawyers, and he didn't want to appoint a guardian for Katie; she would be the best guardian of her children herself. When Melanchthon some years later wrote out his own will according to all the terms of law, Luther certainly agreed with his friend's decision, but he added:

> I don't know how to make a will. My books are right
> here which I leave to my children; may they see that
> they are not cleverer than their forebears were. You,
> Katie, I designate as heiress of everything. You bore
> the children, you nursed them; you will not manage
> their affairs to their disadvantage. I am opposed to
> guardians; they seldom do well.

And finally on January 6, 1542, while threatened by repeated bouts
of illness, he wrote down his own will. He neither sought the
prince's consent nor did he designate a guardian for Katie, but he
trusted that his handwriting and his seal would merit far more trust
than a notary.

The specifications of the will, which should prove valid for
Katie and their children, clearly listed the inheritance: First the
little Zölsdorf property, secondly Brisger's (Bruno Brauer's)
cottage as residence, thirdly the tankards and jewels whose value
Luther estimated at about 1,000 *Gulden*. On the other hand, she
would take on the debt, which was reckoned at about 450 *Gulden*,
if he did not succeed in paying it during his lifetime. The bequest
was to be his thanks because she acted as a true and pious wife,
forever dear, worthy, and beautiful. His wish was that his widow
not be put in the hands of the children, but rather the children be
entrusted to their mother to honor her and to be subject to her. And
if Katie should marry again after his death, then he trusts that she
would act as a mother toward the children and faithfully share
everything with them. He asked the Elector graciously to protect
the will, and he asked his friends to be witness for his dear Katie
against vile gossip.

At the bottom of the will Melanchthon, Cruciger, and
Bugenhagen each in their own hand testified that everything that
was there was Luther's handwriting and his last will.

In this will, Luther had assigned to his Katie only a portion of
his property as inheritance. But two years later, on February 1,
1544, he once again considered the detailed decisions about his
property and had them recorded in the city record book by the
printer, Hans Lufft, who was city judge at that time: In case he
preceded her in death, Katie should keep as her own property

everything that he listed as his own in the city limits, and she should have the authority to use it for her own enjoyment, profit, and pleasure without any objection and hindrance by her children: first of all, Bruno Brauer's [Brisger's] cottage; secondly, Klaus Bildenhauer's garden; thirdly, the garden at Specke Street; and fourthly and fifthly, the acreage[8] and the garden at Oak Pond. By Katie's authorization the loyal Wolfgang Sieberger would take over the legal matters of the property left by Luther.

In this way Luther carried out his intention, and indeed, above all, designated his Katie as heiress. But concerning the most valuable part of what he owned (the Black Cloister) he had determined nothing, probably because he occupied this property as a gift of his lord and he could not dispose of it without the knowledge of his lord. Everything else he directed to his Katie as heiress by his will and by entering it in the city record book. And the designations in the record book were not contestable.

The will, on the other hand, was not legally binding in this form. But the Elector, as lord of the land, could grant it legal force. From the beginning he was on Katie's side. When Chancellor Brück communicated with him from Wittenberg on February 19, 1546 that there was no ready money in Luther's house, that already fourteen days ago Katie had to borrow 20 *Taler* from Melanchthon, and that the gruff butchers and fishermen threatened to besiege the widow, immediately he sent 100 *Gulden* to Melanchthon instead of the 14 *Taler* requested by Brück, and he empowered him to deduct his expenses from it and to give the rest to the widow. He didn't even think about withholding his princely confirmation from Luther's will.

At the same time, he wasn't allowed to bend the law. Now he just had to make good what Luther had stubbornly failed to do; the widow and the children were not allowed to remain without a guardian. The confirmation of the will on April 11, 1546 therefore went through long, drawn-out proceedings, in which Katie pleaded for her wishes and her rights as a mother, while Chancellor Brück

---

[8] Hide of land.

opposed her and even Melanchthon and Cruciger at first would rather have abandoned her.

The chancellor was guided by his official position, but also by his aversion toward Katie. As a loyal servant of his lord, in his first *Opinion* of March 13, 1546 providing for the survivors so that pious people had to regard the Elector as praiseworthy, he advised that above all the Lady—that is, Katie—had no cause to think ill of the Prince. At the same time, however, in his aversion toward Katie, he intended to take from her any influence on the management of the property and the rearing of the children.

His aversion stemmed, as we know, from an earlier time. It had increased more in the last winter. On behalf of the Elector, Luther had prepared a document against Duke Heinz von Wolfenbüttel. Brück, for political reasons, wanted to see a passage in it toned down or left out. So he sent one of his officers to the Black Cloister. Unfortunately, however, Katie was present at this conversation and called to her husband: "Oh, dear sir, they don't read anything at court! That does it! They certainly know what you're like!" And Luther became angry and cranky and said he didn't want to do anything too quickly. Brück reported this to the Elector on December 18, 1545, and carefully added that Luther had let himself be persuaded against the court in other things. The Wachsdorf property might be behind it again, and it was the "rib," that is, Frau Katie, who goaded her good and pious husband on.

Melanchthon and Brück had their particular thoughts with Luther's decision to leave Wittenberg forever,. And when Luther then didn't take into his own hands the proposal for an arrangement that would remove the worst abuses in weddings and baptisms but declared that he was simply unwilling to be mocked about this at court, and when things didn't get better so that he still wanted to leave, then Brück likewise believed that something might have riled up the *Herr Doktor*. He didn't exactly mention Katie by name, but from the context it was clear that he had her in mind.

At any rate, in his aversion toward Katie and in his wish to sever her influence, he now became unfair toward her. He cast suspicion on her with the Elector. He was all too willing to believe the gossip that was going around Wittenberg. He brought up criticisms that she didn't deserve. As we have seen, he was poorly informed concerning the management and the real value of Zölsdorf. He should not have blamed Katie, but Luther himself for the large and wasteful management of the household. His concern for the poor lame Wolf was out of place. Should we blindly follow him then in his other statements? He even dared to make assertions about raising the children that immediately proved to be untrue! Even less should he have implied that he twice came upon the rumor that Katie might get married again. This question Luther himself had addressed in his will. At that time people weren't as tactful in these things as we seem to be now, at least outwardly. This wasn't particularly malice on Brück's part. But numerous other remarks from him are hateful indeed, and from the proposals that he submitted to the Elector, there is much more intercession for the children than for Luther's widow.

It was comparatively easy to arrange the guardianship. Katie's own wish was to see this matter settled quickly, for shortly after her husband's death, the Münster heirs again offered the Wachsdorf property near Wittenberg for sale to her. Because of this, in the second week of March she directed a petition to the Elector and asked him to help her obtain the property and to appoint a guardian for her. At the same time she stated frankly—or "blunt and short," as the chancellor called her petition—that there was no provision of money or grain there, that she and her children therefore would be dependent on the intervention and support of the prince.

Katie entrusted this written request to Melanchthon, asking him to present it to the chancellor for examination. On March 9, toward evening, Melanchthon, Bugenhagen, and Cruciger were with the chancellor on another matter, and Melanchthon took the opportunity to fulfill Katie's request. The chancellor himself read the request aloud. Its content seems to have surprised Bugenhagen. "Then they heard," he exclaimed, "who really had an eye on the Wachsdorf property! Before, they had assumed it was the Doctor who really wanted to have it; but now they realized who had been pushing for it." And there was all kinds of talk among them, and the three friends were, as Brück writes, completely unanimous in the view that, if the widow acquired the property, it would be to her own and her children's detriment; she would begin building on it just like at Zölsdorf, which amounted to more than 1,600 *Gulden*, and yet wasn't even worth 600 *Gulden*. But if she were to build and live out in Wachsdorf, then her sons would also move out into the country and abandon their studies, so that they would only learn to be country squires and to catch birds. Besides, the property was worthless and in poor condition; because of the water, no cellar could be built; and if the Elbe overflowed its banks even a little, most of the fields would be flooded. Finally, Melanchthon called a halt to the pros and cons. He asked to have the request forwarded to the Elector and to discuss it no further. Katie wouldn't take advice and be persuaded. As always, she wanted to deal according to her own judgment.

When the chancellor reported to the Elector on March 13, there had already been conversation in connection with the guardianship. Brück himself mentioned Melanchthon and Cruciger as the best guardians, because they had been the most trusted friends of the deceased, and they could advance his sons in their studies more effectively than others. But both of them refused right away, as Brück writes, because they feared that Katie would not listen to them, and they would often have to take harsh words from her.

Katie herself wanted the city captain Erasmus Spiegel and her brother Hans von Bora as her guardians, and as guardians for her children their uncle [*Oheim*] Jacob Luther in Mansfeld, the Wittenberg mayor Ambrosius Reuter, and Melanchthon. Melanchthon wanted to be replaced by Doctor Major, but Katie didn't want him to be guardian. So Melanchthon settled for referring them to the Electoral physician Doctor Ratzeberger as an old friend of Luther's house.

The chancellor, therefore, wrote a new *Opinion* to the Elector. He advised against appointing Melanchthon as guardian, for he would be less suited to offer resistance to Frau Katie if necessary. But if the Elector still couldn't be persuaded, then it would be best to appoint Melanchthon and Cruciger as secondary guardians so that the two of them might remain unburdened with the business of the guardianship, but would be obliged to encourage the three sons to the fear of God and to learning, virtue, and discipline. The chancellor also eased the thought that the Elector had on account of his physician. If decisions could first be made so that the estate would be arranged, the children cared for, and the questions about whether Wachsdorf should be purchased or not, then the guardians who lived out of town would no longer need to make frequent trips to Wittenberg. On March 24, in two documents, the Elector confirmed Erasmus Spiegel and Hans von Bora as Katie's guardians; Doctor Ratzeberger, Jacob Luther, and Ambrosius Reuter as guardians for the children; and Melanchthon and Cruciger as secondary guardians.

Luther's Estate

The next task awaiting them in settling the estate would be made easier since the Elector confirmed Luther's will. The estate comprised the following pieces:

1. The Black Cloister. Luther and Katie had valued it at 6,000 *Gulden*, much too high. And for a long time no buyer was found. The University did not take over the property from the heirs until 1564, for 3,700 *Gulden*.

2. The Gardens. Brück speaks only of one garden of about thirty–forty acres and values it at not less than 400 *Gulden*. But there were three or even four gardens, as we know, and they had been worth more than 1,000 *Gulden*. The garden at Oak Pond and the two acreages, it seems, were sold soon after Luther's death. The heirs valued the other two gardens, at Sow Market and at Specke Street, at 500 *Gulden* when the inheritance was divided on April 5, 1554.

3. Books and Household Effects. As long as Katie was alive, both remained undivided. After her death the four children took over the estate in this way: all linens and the feather beds to daughter Margarete, the books went to the three sons, and the rest—pewter, brass, copper, furniture—were divided in equal parts.

The real value of these three entries might be considered a very substantial 5,000 *Gulden*. Then came Katie's inheritance:

1. The Zölsdorf Property. The chancellor and the three friends valued it at less than 600 *Gulden*; it was sold in 1553 for 956 *Gulden*.

2. Brisger's (Bruno Brauer's) Little House. It was sold in 1557 for 300 *Taler*, which is not quite 350 *Gulden*.

3. The Gold and Silver Items. If we value them at 1,000 *Gulden* following Luther's estimate, then this inheritance had a value of 2,300 *Gulden*. The whole estate was therefore worth almost 8,000 *Gulden*.

Besides this, the children could now expect the payment of 1,000 *Gulden,* which the Elector had arranged for by their father in the event of his death, and after that five percent interest added annually. The provision was issued only to the children, as the chancellor expressly emphasized. Katie, therefore, had no share of it.

Finally, there was the prospect of another fund of 2,000 *Gulden* for the heirs. At the shocking impact of Luther's death, the Counts of Mansfeld had promised to grant this sum to the widow and the children. But the promise, which was drawn up on May 8, 1546, postponed the payment of 2,000 *Gulden*, to which interest of five percent should be added annually, until the beginning of 1548 in the Leipzig New Year's Market. And with the indebtedness of the Mansfelders, there was a real question whether this deadline would be kept. In fact, only half was paid out at Katie's death, the other 1,000 *Gulden* still remained.

If Katie could have decided for herself to sell the Black Cloister, and could have found a buyer for it, then acquiring Wachsdorf would have been easier. It was not Luther's intention for his widow to keep the large house. The chancellor likewise figured that she would sell it. But she told Melanchthon at their very first conversation that she wanted to keep it. She didn't want to sell Zölsdorf either. Furthermore, she wanted to keep the Boos on lease, even if Wachsdorf came up.

The chancellor had earlier been against the acquisition of Wachsdorf. This wasn't the first time he thought like this. He didn't think there was much good about the property. But when he saw that it would be hard to persuade his lord, the Elector, to deny the widow her first big request, as a clever diplomat he resigned himself to guiding the matter in such a way that he hoped Katie would soon reconsider on her own. He advised the Elector to add another 1,000 *Gulden* to the 1,000 *Gulden* the children were promised, but only for the children. Then each child would get 500 *Gulden*. The Elector should withhold the daughter's portion, but the 1,500 *Gulden* of the three sons could be laid down for Wachsdorf if the guardians would confirm the purchase of the property. Therefore, according to Brück's proposal, the property would be bought, not for Katie, but for the three sons. The Münster heirs, however, wanted 2,000 *Gulden* for Wachsdorf. Who should pay the last 500 *Gulden*? Brück indicated the Mansfelders! Obviously he wanted to scare Katie off. He thought she had enough to do taking care of everything and having to be in charge anyway; she would want to remain the noble lady. If Wachsdorf were bought, not for her, but for the children, then she would soon forget the property. She wouldn't want to be burdened with the work this "box of bricks" would impose on her if she got no benefit from it. How mistaken the chancellor was in judging Katie's intentions and her motherly concern! She immediately agreed that Wachsdorf be bought for her sons.

The chancellor now brought forth a new consideration, which he had touched on already in his first *Opinion*: Wachsdorf was not worth the 2,000 *Gulden* it would cost, for it would hardly bring in five percent a year at such a price. Oaks would then have to be cut down for two, three, four years; and it would require manpower equal to that of half a horse. Melanchthon and Bugenhagen supported him and likewise tried to persuade Katie that the property would be of no benefit to the children. But she insisted on it. She wanted to have it. She hoped to enjoy it a great deal, and even stated that she had no plans for any particular buildings there. And she got her way, although in the end the Münsters demanded 2,200 *Gulden* for the property.

On May 16 the guardians wrote to the Elector that they could no longer oppose the widow, otherwise it would appear that they would hinder her welfare and forget the Herr Doctor's good deeds. Since nothing could be expected from the Mansfelders now, they asked the Elector to put up the daughter's portion for Wachsdorf as well, thus 2,000 *Gulden* in all. The widowed lady was to be humored for the sake of the Herr Doctor; they stepped aside!

The experts whom the Elector sent to Wachsdorf found the purchase price somewhat too high, but the Elector finally let himself be swayed from that point of view, since the guardians had also agreed to intercede for Katie. He gave the 2,000 *Gulden*. Of the remaining 200 *Gulden*, the guardians gathered half, and for the last 100 *Gulden* Melanchthon wrote to Nikolaus von Amsdorf on May 13 and asked him, a wealthy man, to donate this sum to Luther's children, or to loan it to him, Melanchthon. On Pentecost Monday (June 14) the Wachsdorf property was transferred to Luther's heirs.

Indeed, most difficult for Katie was the fight for the children. The Elector had already declared himself ready to take Hans, the eldest, to the court and the chancellery. Brück's plan, however, was also to separate the two younger sons, Martin and Paul, from their mother and to leave her only the daughter. He had already presented the detailed proposals to the Elector in his *Opinion* of March 13. With this he intended to break up Katie's splendid household. If she didn't have to be concerned about her sons, then she wouldn't have to keep young people in the house to help raise them. Now each of the three youngsters would have his own tutor and student mentor! And the rest of the domestics would be superfluous then, since one maid would suffice for the young daughter. The daughter Margarete then would have 30 *Gulden* annually, rather 40 *Gulden* if the Elector would graciously add another 10 *Gulden*, but the mother would have the large house for the time being. If she wanted to keep it and have boarders with her, then she could rent out the rooms that would bring her some profit. In addition, she would have the brewing rights, the gardens and acreage, and the Zölsdorf property. She and her daughter would have the interest from the Mansfeld bequest. Perhaps the Elector would give them two *Wispel*[9] of grain annually for some years to come; perhaps they would even be allowed some cords of wood. So it would be much easier for the widow to manage the household.

To achieve his plan, he presented it to the Elector as though the rearing of the sons would be in poor hands with their mother. The

---

[9] *Wispel*: an old measurement, varying from about 24 to 70 bushels.

eldest was already inclined to enter the Electoral chancellery, but Katie would entice him away. One might say she had alleged that Hans was a foolish (simple, not clever) fellow, that they would mock him and make fun of him in the chancellery. Even according to Melanchthon's judgment, Hans would not be suited for studies, for he was too old and he lacked the basics. The two younger sons would become country squires and fops with their mother. It would be best to separate the three from their mother and even from each other, and to take the eldest into the chancellery, but to have the two younger ones, each by himself, board with a scholar whom they would come to honor and respect.

The chancellor thought that it would be difficult to get Katie to accept these proposals. He writes: "The result will be conflict between the lady and the guardians on both counts!" But Katie was also a diplomat. She said that she would be pleased with this, and while the guardianship and the acquisition of Wachsdorf was being negotiated through an exchange of letters, she saved her strength for the decision. She came close in two letters of the Elector of April 14. In those letters, Melanchthon and Cruciger received instructions to arrange for raising the children according to the chancellor's proposals, and Spiegel and Reuter would be directed to cut down expenses in managing the Black Cloister and dismiss the unnecessary domestics. Did the "conflict" start now? We hear nothing about it. We don't have any other information until four weeks later, on May 16. On that day Cruciger, Melanchthon, and Reuter direct a long petition to the Elector. But it is no longer the chancellor who is behind them, but Katie herself.

As the guardians report, they had spoken with Hans Luther and suggested to him that he was now old enough to decide for himself whether he wanted to continue in his studies or not. They advised him to enter the Electoral chancellery, for he would do well there in their opinion. After a lot of discussion he gave them his answer in writing. This statement accompanied the correspondence of the guardians. In it Hans asks the Elector to let him study another year at the University, since that would have been his father's wish.

Concerning the two younger sons, Martin and Paul, the guardians report that they had asked for tutor Ambrosius

Rudtfeld—the chancellor had written about several tutors! In examinations it had been shown that Martin had indeed studied, but Paul would have been behind by several weeks. He was capable in music, but not so competent in grammar. The mother herself, however, replied that she didn't doubt that the Elector had kind intentions toward her and she humbly thanked him, but she asked the Elector graciously to consider that her youngest boy was often weak and might be better off with his mother. With the University teachers, whose homes were already overflowing with young people, her boys' health might be endangered, and they might also fall into bad company among the various young people from out of town more easily than if they stayed with her, for they would not be allowed to leave the house without her permission. Of course, the guardians didn't dare ask the Elector outright to rescind his first directive, but this wish can be discerned well enough from their report. They also emphasize Paul's poor health. They give Rudtfeld the honorable testimony that he is a scholarly, faithful fellow. They offer that they themselves will watch over Martin's studies.

In his decision on May 21, the Elector also allowed the sons to stay with their mother, yet the guardians should see to it that "the sainted doctor's sons all three be diligently instructed to continue in virtue, discipline, and doctrine and that they would not be allowed too much idle wandering either together or individually."

So in every important matter Katie had gotten her wishes, against the chancellor's designs. The struggle had not been easy. In many points it had been hard fought, without our hearing about it. Melanchthon, who was spared the actual business of the guardianship, complained three times in these weeks with almost the same words: "We are really being pestered!" At any rate, the guardians had a difficult position between Katie's strong will and the chancellor's opposition. Her victory was determined when they finally got on Katie's side; for the Elector, in loyal memory of Luther's service and merit, only wanted what was best for the widow. She owed thanks to him more than the others, but most of all she had herself to thank.

10.

IN POVERTY

With Luther's death, the sun faded from Katie's life. The portrayal of her is shadowy for us too. The accounts we have of the last years of her life are meager, and what they tell us is almost all about hardship and sorrow.

She was probably able to look to the future with hope, after she got over her first despondency. In house and farmyard she remained the lady of the house, and increased her little kingdom even more by acquiring Wachsdorf. When it became known that she wanted to take in boarders again, a new group of lodgers was quickly formed. Summer semester in Wittenberg began on May 1. On May 30 the young Austrian nobleman Augustin Römer von Waidhofen died in the Black Cloister. At that time Katie already had a *Bursa* again. Melanchthon and Cruciger had already seen to it that the spacious rooms of her house didn't stand empty.

The friends also remembered to retain the support of her husband's noble patrons. Of his own initiative, in March 1546, Duke Albrecht of Prussia interceded with the Elector for Luther's widow; it wasn't necessary. On April 16, Jonas asked King Christian III of Denmark to be a most gracious lord to the widow and the children, and on June 7 the king declared his benevolence in gracious words. Meanwhile on June 5, Bugenhagen, on behalf of himself and Melanchthon, asked the king even more assertively to grant Luther's widow the honorarium of the 50 *Taler* that Luther would have expected that year. On October 14 the king ordered the payment of the money. But before the messenger could get to

Wittenberg, the University was completely closed and Katie herself in poverty.

The Smalcaldic War

With a dark outlook on the future, Luther had already seen the threatening clouds gathering in the south. It was like the sultriness over Germany before the rising thunderstorms while the matter of unity was being discussed in vain once more in Regensburg. At the same time, with the news of Luther's death, the rumor had penetrated the easternmost regions that Emperor Charles V was preparing for war. And it was reported in Königsberg with fearful foreboding, that the old Emperor Fredrick II Hohenstaufen, who had been buried three hundred years earlier, had been seen in the Empire. Duke Albrecht of Prussia, therefore, wrote to the Electoral treasurer Hans von Ponickau on March 24, and asked him for information about what was up with this devilish ghost.

The Smalcaldic League of the Protestants, however, appeared to have grown in the face of all dangers. Elector John Fredrick of Saxony and Count Philipp of Hesse; the Low German cities (the champion of which was proud Magdeburg); the High German imperial cities of Strassburg, Frankfurt, Ulm, Augsburg, and Nürnberg; and the people of Württemberg and the Palatinate were strong enough to set up an impenetrable barrier against the ill-prepared Emperor. Wouldn't the Swiss Confederation also have to take up arms if it was a matter of faith? Would the King of England abandon the German Protestants? Could the King of France allow Charles V to be dominant by a victory in Germany? When the Emperor declared war in Regensburg on June 16, the Protestants confidently took up the war. By human calculations the victory had to be theirs. Melanchthon was convinced of this as well. But, at the same time, he read the stars, and they told a different story.

No help came from abroad, and the German Protestants were lacking any one man who would lead them forth to victory. The Elector was sluggish and slow to act. The Count no longer showed the determination with which he had threatened the Catholic princes in Augsburg in 1530: "Make peace! That's what we want. If you don't, and I have to perish, then I will take at least one or two of you with me!" In the summer of 1546, the armies stood across from each other along the Danube for weeks—on the one side the Protestants with their German soldiers, strong but indecisive and unable to force the decision—on the other side the Emperor with his southern[1] advisors and his Italians and Spaniards, in the minority, but firmly determined to avoid any attack of the opponents until he was strong enough to lead the decisive attack himself.

The decision wasn't made at the Danube, but at the Elbe near Wittenberg. Duke Moritz of Saxony, son of Heinrich the Pious, because of his high-strung ambition couldn't expect much from his fellow believers, but he could expect everything from the Emperor. The Electoral hat, which his cousin John Fredrick wore, was a reward of victory valuable enough to entice the Protestant Duke into the Catholic camp. In league with the Emperor and his brother King Ferdinand, Moritz sent his Count a letter of resignation on October 27 and marched into his land. He found almost no opposition at all. The Elector was still camped on the Danube with his army; his eldest son had to be content with holding Wittenberg and Gotha.

Wittenberg was the main stronghold. Through fortification work in recent years, it had become almost invincible for the art of war of that era, and the citizens felt safe hidden behind the high ramparts; no one left the city. But the University had to be a heavy burden during a siege. Bad feelings between the motley student body and the soldiers showed up even before the enemy approached. For that reason, the Elector had thought about moving the University in the summer. The University closed on its own in early November, even before the rector had arranged its suspension on November 6. Only a few students stayed behind, and on November 9 when the message came that Duke Moritz had taken Zwickau and was moving toward Wittenberg with his armies, a wild flight began among the professors. In the cold of winter, old men, women, and little children went out into the country, and thick snow covered the wagons and the passengers.

---

[1] Southern Europeans, in general.

Katie Flees to Magdeburg

Katie probably also left the city that day. With her children she went to Magdeburg, where the University hoped to find a refuge during the war. Old Wolf Sieberger seems to have stayed behind as guardian of the Black Cloister.

Cruciger and Eber stayed in Wittenberg. Also, the church and school workers persisted together, with Bugenhagen at the forefront. After peace returned, he wrote a history of the time in *The True Story of How It Went for Us in the City of Wittenberg.* But even he had sent his children away and brought them to safety in Zerbst. Melanchthon delayed a few more days. But on November 13, he was in Dessau, on November 15 in Zerbst, where he stayed with his family, for the council at Magdeburg took on quite a number of refugees, but they would not permit public lectures, even though Melanchthon himself traveled to Magdeburg several times on this matter.

Meanwhile, on November 16 the people of Wittenberg burned the outskirts of the city, including their summerhouses and gardens. Many of the poorer people who only had their little houses in the outskirts became poor as beggars, and some well-to-do citizens suffered great loss, but the leaders did not dare allow the enemy to settle in close to the ramparts. Ahead of the light cavalry sent by king Ferdinand of Hungary to assist the duke, were the infantry and forces of the Meissen cavalry, already approaching Wittenberg. These included the light cavalry or hussars, as the frightened people called them, as well Croatian, Wallachian, and Polish border people, a wild people, such as had not lived in central Germany since the raids of the Huns. The fear that preceded them was even greater than their skill as warriors.

Had Moritz hoped he could take Wittenberg with a surprise attack? After he had stormed the city in vain on November 18, he didn't repeat the attack. He was not prepared for a regular siege. But his army stayed in the area for weeks, until finally, during Christmas, the Elector advanced from Southern Germany in quick marches. On December 21 he was in Fulda, on December 24 in Langensalza. On December 25 and 26 Duke Moritz withdrew his troops from Wittenberg and threw his best infantry mostly against the threatened city of Leipzig. On January 1, 1547 the Elector was in Halle, where he let his army rest for several days, and on January 6 they were near Leipzig, but this city withstood bombardment for three weeks.

With the departure of the duke's men, the roads to Wittenberg were clear again. Katie might have been able to return home now. Bugenhagen's family came back to Wittenberg soon after Christmas. Melanchthon's wife was back in Wittenberg for New Year, Melanchthon himself on January 13, yet he stayed only a few days and then went back to his family in Zerbst. He thought that the worst was yet to come, and this fear kept Katie in Magdeburg also. We hear nothing else about her stay in Magdeburg. Where did she live? How did she support her children and the servants who had accompanied her? Was she in deep poverty? We don't know.

She was not completely without support at this time. It seems that the 50 *Taler* Christian III of Denmark had promised was indeed held back in Hamburg on account of the war. Because of this, Bugenhagen wrote to the king again on November 15, 1546. But on January 10, 1547 Melanchthon had 150 *Taler* in hand in Zerbst, a third for himself, another for Bugenhagen, and the other third for Katie. And hardly three weeks later, another 200 *Taler* came from the king, or rather 196 *Taler* because the messenger, the old Silesian from Wittenberg, had spent 4 *Taler* on the way. This time, besides Melanchthon, Bugenhagen, and Katie, Jonas was also remembered with 50 *Taler*.

But a very gracious letter from the king was included for Katie. The words with which she thanked her princely patron from Magdeburg on February 9, 1547 came from her heart: The king's letter and his donation had been a great comfort to her in her misery and poverty. The fact that she immediately adds her thanks, with a new request, not for herself but for Doctor Major, testifies to her compassion and her selflessness. Her husband, now deceased, had loved Dr. Major like a son for over twenty years, and now Dr. Major was in poverty with her in Magdeburg with his ten living children. At her request, he also received 50 *Taler* paid by the king at Easter.

In the meantime, the war had spread farther to the south. On January 27 the Elector had to lift the siege from Leipzig, but in the following weeks he retaliated against his cousin on the field to the same extent that the latter had attacked him in the rear. Up to the Ore Mountains, the Electoral forces made inroads through the land. Only a few fortified cities remained for the Duke, such as Freiberg and Dresden.

Katie Returns to Wittenberg

During these weeks when the Elector's star was shining brightly again, Katie left Magdeburg and returned to Wittenberg with her children.

But while the Elector was satisfied in gaining easy victories over his cousin, the Emperor himself was the deciding factor. On March 21 he broke camp from Nördlingen. Slowly he led his army to the north, tormented by attacks of gout that forced him to travel in a sedan and to rest again in Nürnberg for several days. On April 5 he was in Eger; shortly before this, King Ferdinand and Duke Moritz had joined him. On April 18 he was in Gnandstein, the castle of the lords of Einsiedel. From there he went east beyond Rochlitz, Colditz, and Leisnig toward the Elbe.

Across the river the Elector was near Mühlberg. The Emperor's assault, which had been delayed all winter and now came on him with great force, surprised him. When the enemy cavalry came across the river on April 24, he beat a retreat, but it was already too late. Toward evening he had to face the pursuers on the Lochau Heath. After a short battle his soldiers fled, he himself was taken into the Emperor's custody covered with blood.

The first refugees approached Wittenberg soon after midnight. Thought to be enemies by those in the city, they were not allowed into the city until daybreak. The refugees brought the first news of the defeat to the citizens and to the Elector's wife Sibylle, who was in the castle with her two younger sons. For a long time afterwards the desperate cry of the princess' lament for her husband under the noise of gunfire, rang in Bugenhagen's ears. There was great confusion in the city. The gates were kept shut; no wagons were allowed to leave. Finally, when one day after another passed without the Emperor coming, calm restored and free passage was given to those who wanted to flee.

Katie Flees Again

Walpurga Bugenhagen and Katie, along with their children, were also among the families who fled from Wittenberg for the second time at the end of April.

Melanchthon had gone from Zerbst to Magdeburg. All of a sudden Katie was standing there in front of him with tears in her eyes and asking him to find her a place of refuge. She thought about going to Denmark. Their king supported her and had promised his favor, and Melanchthon approved her decision. He actually accompanied her to Braunschweig with her family. Major also followed them with his large family. The council in Halmstedt received them hospitably. Likewise they were well received by the council at Braunschweig and found satisfactory accommodations in the city. As he wrote from Braunschweig on May 4 and 5, Melanchthon boarded Luther and Major's families with the evangelical abbot, while he himself was going to stay with the Superintendent Nikolaus Medler until he found a small house for his family.

In the days that followed, he and Major traveled on with Katie. Major wanted to accompany her to Denmark; Melanchthon wanted to go along at least to Lüneburg. But already in Gifhorn, Duke Franz von Lüneburg advised them not to travel farther, because the country was full of soldiers and the trip would not be without danger. So they returned to Braunschweig, as Melanchthon reports on May 9. Katie stayed, while Melanchthon later brought his family to Nordhausen to his friend, the mayor, Michael Meienburg. From Nordhausen he wrote to Major on May 28 and asked if Luther's widow still intended to go to Denmark. News had come from Halle that the refugees could safely return to Wittenberg. If that was true, then Katie would rather return to Wittenberg with the hope that she would be able to manage her farms again.

The news was indeed true. The Emperor had besieged Wittenberg since May 5 without hazarding an attack on it. He achieved his goal more by negotiations than by force. To save his life, the unfortunate Elector had to turn the fortified city over to the victor on May 23. Thuringia was allocated to his sons; he himself as a prisoner had to accompany the Emperor who held him in custody for years, and he was no longer Elector. Electoral Saxony was turned over to his cousin Moritz. The new lord of the land assured the people of Wittenberg of his sympathetic concern, and he endeavored to keep for the University the great men who had established its reputation. Most of them stayed in the city, because they felt more closely tied to it than to the princely house of the Ernestines. The gray-haired Lucas Cranach, however, willingly followed his lord to prison.

Katie Again Returns to Wittenberg

After the last imperial forces had withdrawn on June 6, Elector Moritz accepted the homage of the citizenry. On June 8, as rector of the University, Cruciger sent a written invitation to the professors who had fled to resume their teaching in Wittenberg. A week later, on June 14, old faithful Wolf Sieberger died. And on June 28, Katie received a letter in Braunschweig in which Bugenhagen and Reuter asked her to return home. He reported that in Wittenberg everything was safe now; her properites and the house had remained intact. This letter, which at the same time brought the news of Wolf's death, made up Katie's mind to return home.

When the two friends assured her that her properites and the house were intact, they meant only the Black Cloister and the household furnishings. Whatever was outside the city wall was certainly destroyed. When the people of Wittenberg burned down the outskirts of their city and chopped down the fruit trees in their gardens, they surely didn't spare Katie's garden at the Sow Market. And how it must have looked farther out in the country! A Pomeranian nobleman, who had driven toward Wittenberg with the Emperor, reports:

> The villages around Wittenberg were desolate, the people had fled from all farmyards, all cattle were driven away, nothing was left in the farmyards. In the

fields one could see the bodies of farmers or a dying farmhand lying here and there, mangled by dogs. The southern troops, who had come with the Emperor, had lived almost as badly as the Hussars. They had also plundered and desecrated. But the Spanish were bloodthirsty, and despite the Emperor's prohibition against torching and burning, they had a devilish delight in burning down the plundered farmyards even down to the pigsty.

In order to keep the people in the territory, Elector Moritz had to promise his new subjects that he would let them get lumber for rebuilding their farmyards, and give or lend grain to those who were completely impoverished.

Wachsdorf and the Boos on the way to Wittenberg, Zölsdorf on the road between Leipzig and Altenburg, went back and forth between friends and enemies several times. Bugenhagen expressly states that these properites had suffered massive damage from the war, and even Katie herself laments about her poor destroyed and devastated properites. The damage to the barns and stables was probably not the worst thing. As we know, Katie raised cattle, especially in Zölsdorf and at the Boos, which had good pasture growth, and Wachsdorf, according to the description of Chancellor Brück, was better suited for tilling. Had the cattle been saved at least? It doesn't seem so. Katie was impoverished by the war. In 1552 she still calls herself poor, "a poor woman and now abandoned by everyone." Melanchthon and Bugenhagen already called her a poor woman in 1548, 1549, and 1550, and Bugenhagen adds: "She would not be poor if she knew how to take care of her properity, but she doesn't."

The loss she suffered in her cattle herds was difficult to compensate. This required cash. Katie had to take on new debts, yet she protected herself from overburdening her properties. At her death there was, first of all, a debt of 400 *Gulden*; the Leipzig lawyer Master Franz Kran, who was in service to Elector Moritz, had probably advanced her this sum at Melanchthon's request. In addition, several tankards were pawned. All told, her debts amounted to nearly 1,000 *Gulden*. She had possibly already had to get rid of a tankard or two during the war, but the majority of her debt didn't come until the final years of her life, and were brought on by the destruction of her properties.

The income from the Black Cloister was barely sufficient for daily life. The University of Wittenberg reassembled, and Katie's table had not lost its old drawing power. From two cases of death reported from the Black Cloister in September 1548 and November 1550, we may draw the conclusion that her group of lodgers had numerous members in the final years of her life.

Johann Stromer from Auerbach was with her for almost five years at that time. He was a nephew of the famous Leipzig physician Heinrich Stromer, who usually was simply called Doctor Auerbach, after his birthplace. His house in Leipzig—made famous by the Faust saga—even now bears the name *Auerbach's Hof*. In this house the young thirteen-year-old Johann Stromer had stood before Luther in 1539, and the few words with which the great man had offered him his drinking tankard remained unforgettable to him, and at the same time they were a prophetic wish for a long life journey, rich with honor. Beginning in 1548, after his enlistment with Duke Moritz in the Smalcaldic War, he was again studying in Wittenberg, first theology, then medicine, and finally law. He died at age eighty-two as professor at Jena on October 11, 1607.

Even the two larger halls behind the living rooms in the Black Cloister did not stand empty. In the summer semester of 1551 Bartholomäus Lasan used them for his lectures on Herodotus.

By her industriousness Katie would have gradually put her properties in better order again and would have been able to recover from her losses, if new difficulties directly on her properties hadn't been put in her way by malicious neighbors so that even in the year she died she had complained to the King of Denmark that her friends had done her more harm than her enemies ever did.

Already in 1548 she brought a lawsuit before the court of the Earl of Brandenburg. Melanchthon, therefore, wrote to the Provost George Buchholzer in Berlin on February 20 and asked him to take the case and also to get Chancellor Johann Weinleb to participate. If the Elector of Brandenburg had been in the country—Joachim II was at the Diet at Augsburg at that time, where the so-called Interim was being patched together—then he surely would have gladly helped Luther's children in their need. Luther had offered spiritual food, and it would only be fair for the pious princes to offer physical food to his children. What this lawsuit was all about doesn't really come out in Melanchthon's words.

In the summer of 1548, a new lawsuit began before the Electoral officer in Leipzig. The lord of the manor at Kieritzsch laid claim to Zölsdorf. Melanchthon reports him to be a contentious person. A friendly settlement was not possible, because his demand was much too high, as Melanchthon writes to Camerarius on August 31. Hans von Bora, Katie's brother and guardian, was likewise against a settlement, and as previous owner of Zölsdorf he surely knew the situation. Katie now wanted to transfer her representation to one of the most capable Leipzig attorneys, the Electoral advisor Doctor Johann Stramburger. Melanchthon really doubted whether the very busy man would find time for the poor widow, but he asked Camerarius to speak with Stramburger about it, and he actually took on Katie's case. Her case was thus in the best hands. Nevertheless the trial took a long time. In January 1550 Katie still had to appear before the official in Leipzig herself, and at her request Melanchthon had intended to accompany her, but then was held up by urgent matters. Camerarius, who lived in the large garden of the University, now had the opportunity to repay Luther's widow for her earlier hospitality, and in the end Stramburger seems to have brought the trial to a good conclusion. The gift Melanchthon mentions on April 30, 1550 was probably Katie's thanks to her lawyer.

But she would not enjoy peace for long. The siege of Magdeburg brought new adversity and a new lawsuit, which began in November 1550 and continued into midsummer of the next year, and then Elector Moritz led his army against the Emperor. It was a heavy burden for any territory at that time when troops marched through and when they had to house them, even when they were friendly troops. "The widow of our Father Luther complains bitterly," Bugenhagen wrote to Christian III on January 11, 1552. "It is obvious that she, along with her neighbors, has suffered a lot of damage on her farms this year." When there were excessive tarriffs, which made the people of the territory feel oppressed, or when the crude soldiers directed their destruction against them, Katie and her neighbors had to make their complaint to the Electoral court, and indeed against Hans Löser, the son of the old hereditary marshal, who had been Paul Luther's godfather.

Besides this, Katie also had the painful experience that the very people who had freely and generously offered free service while her husband was alive, now didn't remember the deceased in any way at all. The ingratitude she had to endure was so great and was such common knowledge that Melanchthon and Eber didn't dare to pass over it quietly in the public record when they announced Katie's death to the University. They wrote:

> When the war broke out, she wandered around in poverty with her orphaned children, amid very heavy burdens and great dangers. And besides the disregard and neglect, which were common toward widows, she also felt the ingratitude of many of those from whom she had hoped for kindnesses on account of her husband's tremendous public service for the church, but she was scandalously disappointed.

It seems she never turned to the new lord of the land despite her need. She would hardly have expected anything from him. Moritz was one of the princes who enjoyed the outward benefits of the Reformation without sincerely embracing it.

Only the King of Denmark helped her again and again. The letters[2] that Melanchthon, Bugenhagen, and Katie herself wrote to him, asking for his help and thanking him for it, kept his generous hand open. In fact, year after year Katie received the 50 *Taler* Christian III had once promised her husband. After her death, her eldest son thanked the king for paying this annual stipend to his sainted mother "up to the present time."

---

[2] Dates of the letters: Melanchthon (September 3, 1548), Bugenhagen (July 17 and September 6, 1549; June 18, 1550; and January 11 and March 22, 1552), and Katie herself (October 6, 1550 and January 8, 1552).

Katie's Concern for Hans

Another prince who had been Luther's patron, Duke Albrecht of Prussia, supported the survivors, but not by sending money. In 1549 he volunteered to take care of the oldest son until he had finished his studies. Hans Luther was still staying with his mother. According to a later account he is supposed to have served as an ensign in the Smalcaldic War, and he would have been old enough for military service, and strong enough. Many students at that time took up the spear rather than the pen. But when Hans went to East Prussia in the spring of 1549, this was—as Katie writes—his first trip away and the first time he left home, and his mother could hardly have chosen these words if he had already been an ensign on the field in 1547. It seems rather that, along with his mother and siblings, he fled and then returned to Wittenberg. Here he now turned to law; according to Melanchthon's source he was also suited for this discipline.

In the spring of 1549 George Sabinus, who was professor in Königsberg and who was highly regarded by Duke Albrecht of Prussia, was visiting Melanchthon, his father-in-law, in Wittenberg. He also spoke with Katie about the Duke's gracious attitude and the offer to bear the cost of her oldest son's studies, and at Melanchthon's advice the widow decided to send her Hans to the University of Königsberg in distant East Prussia. On May 29 she wrote a long letter, which Hans was supposed to deliver to the Duke, thanking the Duke most humbly for his gracious support and sympathy for her poor, bereft children. And she asked him to receive her Hans in his grace and protection, and to bear with him patiently if he didn't know how to act at first, because it was the first time he left home and he was still inexperienced.

Jonas had already written a letter of recommendation to the Duke for the young Luther on May 24, and Melanchthon presented a glowing, indeed almost too glowing, testimony for him on May 25. He calls him, not only blameless, determined, truth-loving and disciplined, skilled and persistent in physical efforts, but he also praises his spirit and his eloquence. But he doesn't talk about his diligence.

Hans didn't completely fulfill the hopes with which his mother had let him go. For almost two years he studied in Königsberg. For a lawyer who later wanted to move up into higher offices, the best recommendation at that time was to attend one of the famous Italian or French universities. So again on April 24, 1551, Katie turned to the Duke and asked him to send her son Johann (Hans) to France or Italy to complete his studies, and to give her request a favorable reply. In her weakness she had many things to discuss with her son, which would be important for him and his brothers and his sister to take note of, so she wished to see him in Wittenberg for a while beforehand, for after the Duke's decision, he would either return to Königsberg or go abroad.

The Duke's reply on July 12, 1551 was a bitter disappointment to the boy's mother. The Duke could no longer be silent about her request. His gracious intent was not being realized in her son as he had really hoped. Her son had not done his studies properly; he had also participated in some dealings that would have been better left undone. The Duke added, however, that he was still sympathetic toward her and her son even now, especially for the sake of her dear husband now asleep in God. If her son would be content in Königsberg, then he would still continue to support him, but he could not agree to send him to Italy or France.

Three days after the Duke had written this, on July 15, 1551, the University of Königsberg issued a beautiful testimony for Johann Luther; so the dealings that the Duke mentions must not have been anything really bad. With this testimony Johann returned home in order to comply with his mother's wish. She was ill, as she herself had written, and in the premonition of an impending death she longed to see him one more time.

11.

FROM WITTENBERG TO TORGAU

Those were gloomy years for Katie, since after the death of her husband everyone strangely positioned themselves against her and nobody wanted to attend to her. The poverty she lived in, the indifference she faced, and the hostility she was exposed to bent her pride and broke her health. But she would not go to her final rest in her dear Wittenberg.

The summer of 1552 once again brought an outbreak of the plague over the city. Already at the beginning of June, the Council at Torgau had offered the University a place of refuge in their city. In early July the professors had to release their students. Some went home; others followed their teachers to Torgau, where lectures were taken up again in the Franciscan Cloister on July 17.

Katie's Death

Katie stayed in Wittenberg into September. Only when the Black Cloister itself was visited by the plague did she leave and go to Torgau, for the sake of her children. But on the way the horses were frightened and threatened to drag the wagon off the road. More for the sake of the children than for herself, Katie jumped, but hit the ground hard and fell into the ditch, which was full of cold water. The shock, difficult fall, and chill brought on paralysis.

For over three months she lay sick in bed in Torgau and slowly faded away. God's Word comforted her and sustained her in her suffering. In fervent prayers she wished for a gentle death. Frequently she entrusted both the church and her children to God and prayed that He would preserve the pure doctrine, which He had restored in recent times through the voice of her husband, and keep it unadulterated for posterity.[1] On December 20, she was released from her suffering, by death.

On December 21, Paul Eber, as Vice-Rector of the University, invited the students to the funeral, which took place the same day. The author of the long document in Latin was most likely Melanchthon. In commemoration of the heavy sorrow that the deceased must have borne in the final years of her life, ahead of his reflection he put the words that the Greek tragedian Euripides in his *Orestes* had Electra, the king's daughter, say as she stepped onto the stage:

> No evil is so horrible for language to describe,
> No fate or God-imposed adversity,
> Which does not bring its burdens on mortals.

Socrates was once so powerfully moved by these words in the theatre in Athens, that he shouted out loud for the actor to repeat them. And who has not come to know that there are disasters, more diverse and sadder than we can imagine? But we Christians, in every tribulation, find comfort in faith in God and our Lord Jesus Christ and in the hope of eternal life. Luther's widow also turned to this hope in her great suffering.

Melanchthon briefly describes Katie's sorrow over the death of her husband, her poverty, and her abandonment, the accident that put her on her sickbed, and he describes the God-given patience with which she had endured her long illness. In closing he asks the students to show her the final honor of high esteem for her excellent piety, sharing the sorrow of her orphaned children, remembering the merits of her husband, which are never sufficiently praised.

At three o'clock in the afternoon the students gathered in front of the house where she died. They lined up from the Franciscan

---

[1] Kroker's note: Quite recently it is reported that Katie on her deathbed said: "I will keep clinging to my Lord Christ like burrs on cloth." This report actually first comes from the year 1850 and is based on a strange misunderstanding.

Cloister into the next street, which led to the castle; that was the house that now bears the number 457 on Luther Street.[2]

Katie found her final resting place in the nearby parish church (St. Mary's Church). Here the gravestone, which the four children erected for their mother, stands in the chancel even now. The inscription reads: "ANNO 1552.20 December: Here in Torgau Dr. Martin Luther's blessed bereaved widow Katharina von Borau fell asleep, blest in God."

The stonework is done by hand and doesn't indicate much more than that the deceased still had a full figure and a plump face even in the final years of her life. Over her left shoulder is the von Bora coat of arms, over her right shoulder Luther's coat of arms; both of them, along with the gravestone, were repainted in 1617 and 1730. The unusual headcloth that the deceased is wearing is probably not a widow's dress or burial dress, as had been assumed, for Katie is wearing the same headcloth on the medallion in the Kieritzsch Church. Much less is it a peasant's costume, for the benevolent, rich Lady Apollonia von Wiedebach is wearing a headcloth just like it in her image in the Leipzig Museum.

With this headcloth, the medallion of Katie in the church at Kieritzsch is shown to be genuine. How could a later artist have come to give Frau Doctor Luther such an unusual headcovering for this memorial! And from what source would he also know that precisely in 1540—this year is in the inscription—Luther had bought Zölsdorf? Besides, both medallions, Luther and Katie's, are testified already in 1750, by the pastor at Kieritzsch at that time, as a "precious artifact from antiquity." This likeness of Katie is important indeed, for, in its resolute facial expression, it is the only thing we have left of the *fax domestica*, the houshold torch, of which Cruciger speaks.

Katie's Portraits

Among the oil paintings we have of Katie, the one reproduced on our cover is one of the most valuable. It is the counterpart to

---

[2] The house where Katie died is now a memorial in her honor. The current address is Katharinenstraße 11 in Torgau.

Luther's portrait in chapter three of our book. Both paintings are, in fact, by Cranach's own hand, even if not from the time when his skills were not at their peak. They come from the year 1526. They are distinct by their preservation ahead of several other very similar portraits of Luther and Katie from 1525 and 1526; they are also the most impressive.

Several portraits from 1528 and 1529 likewise had earlier been traced back to Cranach himself, but are clearly the work of apprentices. They are only interesting in that they show Katie's face somewhat fuller than the painting from 1526. Both spouses tended toward stoutness. For this reason, a famous oil painting in the City History Museum in Leipzig, also copied in copper engravings, should be removed from the list of portraits of Katie. The elderly, rather gaunt matron that stands before us in this Leipzig portrait really bears no resemblance to Katie, and is probably her friend Walpurga Bugenhagen.

The woodcuts of Katie from that time perhaps go back to Cranach's drawings, but are not to be compared in significance with the Cranach portraits from 1526 and the Kieritzsch medallion from 1540. The numerous copper engravings and woodcuts from later time generally have no independent value.

While collectors and wishful thinking have connected Luther and Katie with many artifacts that were never in their house, negligence and unawareness have let many genuine pieces go to ruin. Even as late as 1846, a descendant of Luther in the female line must have grieved that his stepmother, after the death of his father, had burned as wastepaper valuable "autographs and other mementos" that came from Luther and Katie's properity and had been entrusted from one generation to the next!

Fate of Luther and Katie's Children

Luther and Katie's assets were, as we know, divided among the four children on April 5, 1554 at the settling of the estate.

The oldest son, Johann (John, Hans) Luther, was already active at the chancellery in Weimar at this time. The old, hard-tested Duke John Fredrick was released from custody by Emperor Charles V in the summer of 1552 and on September 26 returned to Weimar amid the jubilation of his loyal people. The duke died on March 3, 1554, hardly two weeks after the death of his wife Sibylle. Johann Luther probably had the old duke to thank for his appointment to Weimar. At the end of 1554, he already had the title of advisor of the chancellery. When the Grumbach matter led to war, in spring of 1566 Duke John Fredrick the Mediator released him to East Prussia, where his sister Margarete had married. After that, it seems he served at the electoral court of Brandenburg for a while. On a second trip to East Prussia, Johann Luther died at Königsberg on October 27, 1575. Since 1553, the same year he had held his appointment to Weimar, he was married to Elisabeth Cruciger, a daughter of the deceased Professor Caspar Cruciger. There was only one daughter from this marriage; she was later married, but her marriage remained childless, and so this branch of the family, even in the female line, already died out with the second generation.

The second son, Martin Luther, studied theology, but never entered the ministry. He died in Wittenberg at a young age on March 3, 1565. His marriage with Anna Heilinger, a daughter of Wittenberg mayor Thomas Heilinger, was not blessed with children.

The youngest son, Paul Luther, the doctor, married Anna von Warbeck, the daughter of the electoral vice-chancellor and advisor Veit von Warbeck, at Torgau on February 5, 1553, just a few weeks after his mother's death. If the date of the marriage has been passed on to us correctly, Katie would have gotten to know her future daughter-in-law. After Paul Luther had been trained as Doctor of Medicine in Wittenberg in 1557, he taught for a while at the newly established University of Jena, but soon went to the court of the three Ernestine dukes as personal physician. During the siege of Grimmenstein in 1567 he remained in Gotha at the side of Duke John Fredrick. After his lord was captured he served Elector Joachim II of Brandenburg who kept him as his personal physician and highly-esteemed advisor. Just a week before his death the gray-haired prince was a guest at Paul Luther's house on December 28, 1570 and in one drink emptied the whole large silver tankard that Luther had once received as a gift from the Swedish King Gustav

Wasa. On January 3, 1571 the Elector died at Köpenick. In the same year Paul Luther was called to Dresden by the Saxon Elector August to be personal physician. In the end, he also served his successor Christian I. But in 1590 he left the Calvinist-minded Dresden court and returned to orthodox Leipzig. He died there on March 8, 1593. Six children came from his marriage. The oldest son, Johann Ernst Luther, continued the line; his great-grandson Martin Gottlob Luther, born at Wurzen on July 5, 1707, was the last male descendant of Luther and Katie. But several families still thriving trace their family tree on the female side back to Paul Luther.

Already in 1554 the young rich East Prussian nobleman George von Kunheim, heir to Mühlhausen and Knauten, sought the hand of the only daughter, Margarete Luther. Orphaned at a young age, he had been raised under the supervision of his lord, Duke Albrecht. Beginning in 1550 he had studied in Wittenberg, where he had room and board with Melanchthon's friend Eber. He was still a minor when he got engaged to Margarete on his own initiative, and his sponsors, who did not approve of his choice of bride, prevailed upon Duke Albrecht to order the young lord von Kunheim home immediately. Then with tears in his eyes Melanchthon wrote to the prince on December 18, 1554, and his intercession appears to have decided the situation in favor of the two young people. On August 5, 1555 a very festive wedding was held in Wittenberg in the presence of many counts and noblemen and the professors. After a very happy marriage, Margarete died in 1570 at age thirty-six, at Mühlhausen between Elbing and Königsberg. Of her nine children, three outlived her, and in the progeny of her oldest daughter, Margarete von Kunheim, this branch of the family has also continued on the female side to the present.

12.

VOICES OF CONTEMPORARIES AND OPINIONS OF LATER GENERATIONS

Katharine von Bora has become immortal as Luther's Katie. Those who loved her and hated her because she was Luther's wife have presented us with a picture of her life.

Where there is light, there are also shadows. Shouldn't we expect failings alongside the great virtues Katie had?

Her virtues are clear and obvious to everyone who will simply look, and we may limit ourselves here to pointing them out briefly. The foundations of her character were her tireless industry, her efficiency, and her frugality. Through these good qualities she gradually elevated her household. The accusation of greed does not hold up when we see the gentleness and hospitality she exercised at her husband's side; she was frugal, not greedy.

She stands before us blameless as a homemaker; likewise, as wife and mother. Passion and love did not bring Luther and Katie together, but from their marriage a true love developed that was rooted in mutual respect and in understanding each another. True love overcame everything that tends to come between man and woman. A statement he made in December 1535 illustrates how much confidence Luther placed in his Katie: "The Epistle to the Galatians is my Epistle to which I have entrusted myself; it is my Katie von Bora."

Out of her motherly love came great concern, a trait that added something new to her overall character. Out of love for her family she was easily inclined toward cares and worry, but hardship found her ever brave and fearless. Her husband spoke often enough about the self-sacrifice with which she took care of her husband and her children.

In her motherly love was she sometimes lenient toward her children? Her husband complained that many things were kept secret from him in his house, and Chancellor Brück pointed out to him the danger that his widow could give her sons too much free rein. The two oldest did not advance to higher positions, even later. But can we blame their mother for this? Martin was sickly and Johann not well gifted; there was a lack of talent, not a lack of nurture. And Paul, the youngest, who grew from boy to young man all during the time when Katie was a widow, was the most capable. Katie's motherly love was huge and capable of any sacrifice. She risked her own life on her last journey to Torgau in order to save her children.

In her love for her husband she also found the power to suppress a bad characteristic, at least toward him. She was proud and assertive, as is often the case with someone of an energetic nature. And being Luther's wife certainly didn't make her more modest and humble toward others. A little note that Luther once wrote—unfortunately, we don't know when or to whom—reads: "My Ketha has kindly admonished that you should by no means marry a peasant wench, for they are rude and proud, don't respect their men, and can neither cook nor make wine." *Haec Ketha, 4. hora*, Luther added in Latin, which means: Katie had spoken these winged words at four o'clock. As we know, Luther himself considered his Katie haughty before he married her. But he soon saw that she was more submissive and obedient to him than he had expected. Toward others, indeed, she remained proud. The lodger who recorded Luther's statement about her pride added: *sic est*, "so it is." She submitted only to one lord, her dear husband. She humbled herself before him even to serving as a maid, as he himself testifies.

But how is her desire for power to be reconciled with her humility? The answer to this question lies in the relationship between her and her husband. We have now gotten to know Katie as a faithful spouse, loving mother, and dutiful household manager. Was she perhaps even more to her husband?

It is regrettable that she is quoted so seldom in the *Table Talk*—the lodgers kept themselves only to Luther's words in their records—and that her correspondence is lost, even the few business letters, letters of requests and thanks. The single letter to her sister-in-law Christina von Bora resounds with a deep tone and lets us imagine what we have lost since we can no longer read the numerous letters she wrote to her husband, and later to her oldest son Hans. At the same time, we are robbed of the chance to gain a more definite representation of her spirit and her temperament.

Undoubtedly she was a bright woman, or as she is called by her contemporaries, a clever, intelligent lady. She had a lively spirit and a jovial disposition. She was also a refined lady, without being an educated woman. Her earlier biographer, Albrecht Thoma, has rightly shown this. She could find her way through the Bible as well as her *Small Catechism*. She said that she would prefer to let someone else do the writing, but the little correspondence we have from her hand is not at all awkward; rather it shows skillful and characteristic flourish. She understood Latin well enough to follow a simple conversation, and she could interject some Latin words herself. The letters her husband directed to her, however, are completely in German. In one he inserted a couple Latin sentences, which were intended less for her than for Bugenhagen. And one time when he sent a longer Latin letter, he asked her to have Bugenhagen or Peter Weller read it, that is, to translate it for her. It was certainly easier to take part in conversations as they were held at Luther's table, with German and Latin mixed together, than to understand a whole long document of theological content. She found the Greek language dreadful. Her husband wasted his time in vain trying to get her to memorize in Greek the passage: "The just shall live by faith." She just replied: "Dear God, who could repeat that!" She even pronounced the Greek word "Catechism" in her own way, but it would be wrong to blame her "*Kattegissema*" on a defect in character; then one would have to direct the same reproach against Luther himself, for he, too, occasionally writes *Porse* instead of *Bursa*.[1]

Katie was well-versed in the Bible and pious, but she had no tendency toward theology. More than once through teasing paradoxes her husband brought her to the point of being irritated and embarrassed. One time in 1532 he said that it could still happen that a man could take more than one wife. "The devil believes that!" Katie shouted in horror, and when he tried to justify his statement, she retorted with a passage from the Apostle Paul, but the *Herr Doktor* picked this passage apart and joked with her until she declared: "Before I would allow that, I would rather go back to the cloister and abandon you and all the children." That same year he once said: "The devil chokes us all; Satan choked God's Son," then she cut him short: "Oh, no, dear Herr Doctor, I don't believe that!"

Another time he put to her the question whether she believed that she was holy. Astonished, she answered: "How can I be holy? I am still a great sinner." Lauterbach's wife made a finer distinction by replying: "I am holy since I believe, but a sinner since I am human." Luther was looking for the answer: "I believe in my holiness since I am baptized and a Christian and I believe in the Sacrament of Baptism." Neither of the two women found this correct answer. Likewise, Katie missed the mark when in 1540 she said of Doctor Schenk: "I wouldn't want to give my daughter to Doctor Cuckoo, for he doesn't preach the Gospel clearly." Luther had to correct her: "Not at all! The Gospel he preaches correctly, but the Law he preaches falsely."

Luther was certainly not influenced by Katie in his theology, and he was only teasing when he called her his "deeply-learned" lady. She was even less serious in giving her advice for filling pastoral vacancies. To be sure, Luther wrote to her on July 2, 1540:

> I have asked Doctor Pommer, the pastor, as well as the Count of Schwarzburg for a pastor for Greussen. Then you too as a wise lady and 'doctoress' might give advice to help, along with Master George Major

---

[1] Compare the related English words: burse and purse.

and Master Ambrosius, as to which of the three I have indicated to Pommer would be ready. It is not a bad parish, yet you are clever and would make it better.

Doesn't this perspective open up an amazing picture here? Katie has a seat and a voice among the Wittenberg theologians! But the picture disappears again just as quickly. Aside from that, we don't really know where the joking stops and the seriousness begins with these words. It is not about finding the most diligent or the most worthy among the three men Luther had suggested—all three were certainly worthy—but it was about persuading one of them to accept the call.

With her lofty gift of speech Katie also had a great persuasive skill. Luther himself even said to her: "You persuade me to do whatever you want!" And contemporaries who were very close to him, such as Cordatus, Cruciger, and Agricola, tell us unanimously that she had a power over him like no one else.

But what did her influence really consist of, and in what areas did it assert itself?

From the beginning Luther had entrusted the whole household to Katie. In this kingdom of hers she had almost unrestricted rule, and he was fine with that, to the extent that he never tired of teasing her about her rule and presenting himself to his friends as the poor, oppressed husband. Just a week after their wedding, he had invented the nickname "my Lord Catherine" [*mein Herr Catherin*] for her, and with ever-new pleasure from that time on, he varied the theme: *mea Ketha—meus Ketha*.[2] He wrote a joking letter to Mansfeld Chancellor Müller on March 18, 1535 and signs: "*Doktor Martinus, Doktor Luther, Doktor Hans*," and it comes out in a note in the margin, "*Doktor Luther*" was Katie and "*Doktor Hans*" was his little nine-year-old son, Caspar Müller's godchild. So Katie was "Doctor Luther"—but without detriment to his authority.

It would certainly be strange if someone would take all these expressions of Luther's differently than they are intended, in jest. Luther really wasn't carved from the wood that docile husbands are

---

[2] Luther here makes a wordplay on the German word "*Kette*," which means "chain." He also varies between feminine form "*mea*" and the masculine "*meus*."

made of. And when he spoke seriously about his Katie, his words sound completely different; then he praises her eagerness and willingness to serve. The bustling gracefulness with which she ruled and governed in the house, and her modesty and wisdom, were also highly praised by Capito and Jerome Weller, who was a lodger of hers for many years. Weller writes:

> I remember that Luther often said he counted himself fortunate that God had given him such a docile, modest, and wise wife. She brilliantly understood how to tend and maintain his health, she knew skillfully how to adapt to his personality and gently to put up with his failings and unpleasant traits.

Luther knew his failings. If Katie had her pride and her strong will, then he had his stubbornness; he called his head *stubbornissimus* [*sinnigissimum*, stubbornest]. An incident Lauterbach recorded might demonstrate how much he was like that, even in little things. Already in the summer of 1538, Luther had spoken about the unskillfulness of German workers: "Little work, much pay," should be their motto. In Italy there would be tailors more skillful, so he didn't want to have any more new pants made: "I have patched this pair of pants four times myself. I will patch them again before I have new ones made." But he doesn't seem to have used durable material like one of his Leipzig opponents, the miserly Doctor Jerome Dungersheim von Ochsenfurt, who secured the seat of his pants with parchment and shoe wire. The next year, Katie one day found a piece of cloth cut out of the trousers of one of her boys, and when she looked into who had done the terrible damage, it came out that the Herr Doctor had sewn this patch onto his own pants with his very own hand. He excused himself by saying that Fredrick the Wise and Elector Hans would have patched their pants as well, but he couldn't prove that they would have cut up the little prince's pants. Katie's mood would not have been very peaceful that day.

In such a large household they couldn't avoid little disagreements. Yet we hear about it very seldom, and that is even more remarkable, since Luther and Katie by nature certainly didn't wait until they were all alone for a criticism or a little curtain lecture.[3] Impatient and without controlling his mood in front of his lodgers, he once complained that he had to be patient even with Katie von Bora—that the tailor, shoemaker, bookbinder, and his wife made him wait again and again. Another time he lamented that if he were free to marry again, he would carve an obedient wife out of a stone, for he had doubts about obedience in all women. Just one time is it reported to us that she had a minor quarrel with him, and that he then said to Veit Dietrich that if he could withstand *her* anger, then he could withstand anyone's anger. As usual, her pleas and tears would have quickly softened his mood. And even if it turned into a little storm, they both knew that in a real marriage such things only touched the surface and didn't go deep. Luther says about a married couple living harmoniously: "If they both grumble and mumble at the same time, that must do no harm! Things don't always go in a straight line in marriage; if some incident happens, it is to be expected."

The relationship between the two spouses in the Black Cloister was such that it is a model for every Christian household. Indeed, the lady may have felt like "lord" in her kingdom, yet only insofar as in the midst of it all stood the man to whom her work and her concern and duty were directed.

Now, several contemporaries report, however, that Katie's influence on her husband went beyond her domain. Concerning the disagreement that caused a divide between Luther and lawyers in the last years of his life, it was almost common talk in Wittenberg that the Herr Doctor was acting at the inspiration and instigation of his wife. This rumor was shown to be unfounded gossip, and Luther himself spoke out about it very sharply: perhaps in matters of the household or the table (the "boarding house") he let himself be led by his wife, but in the matters of conscience and Scripture he knew no other teacher and doctor than the Holy Spirit.

There can be no talk, then, about Luther letting himself be guided by his wife in theological questions. But the facts before us from the first year of his marriage are that he occasionally let

---

[3] A curtain lecture is a wife's private scolding of her husband.

himself be influenced in such questions—he himself testifies that he wrote his decisive treatise against Erasmus only at her request. Also, from the last year of his marriage, Chancellor Brück testifies that he gave a harsh answer to Chancellor's Brück's official because of some words from his wife.

In the face of these facts it is impossible to speak about unfounded gossip. Rather, they will force us to look even more closely at the weighty testimony of Agricola and Cruciger.

Agricola, after fleeing Wittenberg, inscribed recollections of his life in his own hand in an old Hebrew book. In it he also recalls the Antinomian controversy and states that Luther didn't even want to read his letters of defense: "Then his wife Ketha, regent in heaven and on earth, Juno, the wife and sister of Jupiter, who guided the man wherever she wanted, once spoke a good word about me. Jonas did the same also." And only then did Luther read his letters. The frustration with which Agricola had fled from Wittenberg at that time still rings in these words.

But with calm words Cruciger writes to his friend Veit Dietrich in Nürnberg on February 15, 1544, during the quarrel between Luther and the lawyers: "You know that many think he has a torch in his house that inflames him."

So these men believed it was true that Katie actually had a huge influence on Luther. And yet—might Luther himself dismiss any suspicion of influence on him by his wife? Without a doubt. He thought only about the doctrine for which he stood and the questions of theological controversy in which he fought against his adversaries. Katie seldom stepped forward either to calm him or stir him up out of objective motivations. She was led, rather, by her personal involvement and by her feelings. In the blunt candor with which he spoke of his friends and enemies, and in the honor with which she viewed him, it was inevitable that his friends became her friends and his enemies her enemies as well. His greatness was her greatest pride. But since, in this world, people and things cannot be separated from each other, her influence occasionally extended beyond the person and to the thing.

In the first months of their marriage, when she insisted that her husband could not leave Erasmus unanswered, she had been pushed into the forefront by Camerarius, as we know. Camerarius was driven by objective reasons. The diatribe that Erasmus had published was the Humanists' declaration of war on the Reformer. And with the prominence of both men, the battle had to be taken up and fought until there was an honorable accord or one of the combatants was defeated. Katie maybe had little understanding of such deliberations, but she understood that the opponents could easily see her husband's stubborn silence as conceding defeat—a concern which Luther himself shared otherwise—and she didn't stop assailing him with urgent pleas until, after he had indignantly procrastinated almost a year, he finally overcame his reluctance and wrote his reply in a few weeks.

If she was dealing with her husband in love here, in other cases she let herself be governed by friendship. As she interceded with Melanchthon for one of her lodgers, Master Sachse, she herself pleaded Melanchthon's case with her husband and tried to arrange a friendly discussion to settle their disagreement.

Although Agricola was happy for her intercession, he had to learn for himself that her influence had its limits, so that he instead found an impassable barrier in her husband's even stronger will and steadfastness to his convictions. Despite her tears, Luther remained irreconcilable toward Agricola.

On the whole, when she disagreed with him, she was really only able to work on him when a mood or a rage overtook her. In that case, to be sure, she had great power over him. Indeed, she wasn't an apathetic or simple kind of person who completely came undone in the little cares of daily life or hadn't participated in her husband's life's work and his battles. She was clever, lively, and articulate, and she hated his opponents. One time she wished for something almighty to strike down everything that stood against him. Surely she also stood at his side in the disagreement between him and the lawyers. Obviously she was not the creator of this disagreement herself, but she stirred up his wrath. As her conflict with the officer of the Chancellor showed, just a few words from her were enough to cause her husband's anger to erupt out in the open.

Many times, her influence might have had an effect without us hearing about it. In chapter five, we got to know two extremely vehement letters of Luther's, the one to Quartermaster Fredrick von der Grune on account of the impending fortification work at the Black Cloister, the other to Spalatin on account of a real or supposed injury Katie had suffered from the Altenburg tax collector. The excessive vehemence of language is otherwise completely unmatched in Luther, and in a second letter to Spalatin he apologizes for it: He said he didn't put much weight on such matters, but he had gotten married! Wouldn't Katie have been the torch here too?

With his irritable temperament and her energetic character, her influence might have been more often detrimental rather than beneficial. This hurt them both. This is how it came to be said that he let himself be influenced by his wife, even in purely practical matters—a suspicion, which, according to everything we know, is definitely to be dismissed—and from this suspicion, antagonism toward her grew. Chancellor Brück's aversion was probably rooted chiefly in his belief—rightly or wrongly—that Katie's opposition had stood in his way more than once.

So we will also have to concede that Katie sometimes had a strong influence on Luther. But we may still point out that she did not act out of lust for power, but out of love for her husband or out of friendship for his co-workers or out of enmity toward his opponents. We would only be able to speak of her lust for power if she had persuaded him to do something against his will, but, as far as we know, that was never the case. Whenever she actually was able to compel him the way she did against Erasmus or against Brück's officer, then his opinion met her halfway, and for him her effort to sway him meant that he concurred rather than that he was persuaded.

The position Luther held towered over everything. That was the only reason that contemporaries criticized his wife for things they would have found understandable and just fine in any other woman. Or isn't it a woman's proper right to share her husband's concerns and occasionally to express her opinion, whether asked or not? A man characteristically retains the decision for himself. In this, Luther also did not let his Katie control him, as his hesistancy toward Agricola shows.

But finally, from his letters we learn how far he let her in on the church and political questions that occupied him. After all, the first letter he wrote to her, from Marburg on October 4, 1529, contains almost exclusively information of theological content. And even in later years, besides all kinds of instructions and greetings, he sent her theological and political news as well, sometimes quite detailed, sometimes only in little hints. He knew that she was not completely engrossed in running her house. She also brought an open heart and a certain understanding to the things that moved him.

He expected a good wife to be a kind, charming, and entertaining life companion to her husband. Katie was that for him, and he loved her for it. "I love my Katie," he said in 1532. "Yes, I love her more than I love myself, that is certainly true; that is, I would rather die myself than have her and the children die." He knew that she was not without faults, just as he knew that he had his faults, but he said that he wouldn't give up his Katie for either France or Venice, for God had given her to him, as he also was given to her. She was a faithful wife, and her virtues were much greater than her shortcomings.

Such was the judgment of the great man who stood beside her in this world, and we do well to content ourselves with his judgment.

We don't want to hold her up as a saint or indeed as an angel. She was a woman with strong emotions, and she knew how to love and how to hate. But we also don't want to let our picture of her be disfigured and to fault her and blame her where her own husband excuses her faults and praises her virtues.

For him she was the right woman, and he became the complete Luther only after he married her. The mighty Doctor Martinus, whose spirit lives in us, would have needed no Katherine von Bora to become the personality of world history that he is. But the dear Herr Doctor, in whose faithful German spirit we rejoice, is unthinkable without his Katie.

Appendix

Gnad vnd Fride yn Christo zuvor, gestrenger, ernuester, lieber herr geuatter!

Euch ist wol wissentlich, wie Euer gnaden vngeferlich fur dreyen Jaren gebeten, daß myr das gut Booß myt seynen zugehorungen vmb eynen gewonlichen zynß zu meyner teglichen hawßhaltung wie eynem andern mochte gelassen werden, als denn auch meyn lieber herr bey doctor Brug dieselbige zeyt deshalben hat angeregt; ist aber dasselbig mal vorblieben, daß ichs mecht bekommen, vylleicht das doselbst nicht loß ist gewesen von seynem herrn, der es vmb den zynß hat ynnen gehabt.

Ich byn aber vnterricht, wie der kruger von Brato, welcher es dyße zeyt ynnengehabt, soll iczund solch gut loßgeschrieben haben; wo solchs also were, ist meine freuntliche bytte an Euch als meynen lieben geuattern, wollt myr zw solchem gut fodderlich sein. Vmb denselbigen zynß, ßo eyn ander gybt, wyll ichs von herczen gerne annnehmen vnd die zynße deglich an zwen orth vberychen. Bitte gancz freuntlich, Euer gnaden wolde myr Ewer gemueth wyderschreyben vnd das beste rathen yn dysem Fall vnd anczeygen, wo ich etwas hyrin vnbyllichs begert, vnd woldet denen nicht stad geben myt yrem argkwone, alß ßolde ich solchs gut fur mich odder meyne kinder erblich begeren, welche gedancken yn meyn hercz nie kommen synd. Hoffe zu gott, er werde meynen kindern, ßo sie leben vnd sich fromlich vnd ehrlich halten wurden, wol erbe beschern; bytte alleyne, daß das myrs ein jar odder zwey vmb eynen zimlichen geburlichen zynß mochte gelassen werden, damit ich mien haußhaltung vnd Vyhe deste bekemer erhalten mochte, weyl man alles allhier vfs tewerst kewfen muß vnd myr solcher ort, der nahe gelegen, ßehr nuczlich seyn mochte.

Ich habe meynen lieben herrn iczt yn dyßer sachen nicht wollen beschweren, an Euch zuschreyben, der sunst vyl zu schaffen; ist auch on noth, daß Euer gnaden solchs meyn antragen ferrer an ymandes odder an meinen gnädigsten herrn wolde gelangen lassen, ßunder ßo Ir solche myne bytte fur byllich erkennet, daß Irs myt dem schosßer zw Seyda bestellen wolt, daß myr solch gut vmb eynen geburlichen zynß wie eynem andern mochte eingethan werden.

Domyt seyet gott bepholen.

Gegeben zu Wyttembergk
Montag nach Jubliate ym 1539 jhare
Catherina Lutherynn

TIMETABLE

1483	November 10: Martin Luther is born in Eisleben
1499	January 29: Katherine von Bora is born at Lippendorf
1504 (or 1505)	Katie at the Convent School at Brehna
1508 (or 1509)	Katie in the Convent at Nimbschen
1515	October 8: Katie's consecration as nun in Nimbschen
1517	October 31: Luther's Ninety-five Theses
	April 4–5: Katie's escape from the Nimbschen Convent
	—until 1525: Katie's stay in Master Reichenbach's (and in Cranach's) house in Wittenberg; Baumgärtner and Doctor Glatz
1525	Spring: The Peasant Revolt
	May 5: Elector Fredrick the Wise dies; John the Steadfast
	June 13: Luther and Katie's Wedding
	June 27: The Wedding Celebration
1526	June 7: Johann (Hans) Luther is born
	July 6: Luther's first severe illness
	Late autumn: Plague in Wittenberg
	December 10: Elisabeth Luther is born
1528	August 3: Elisabeth Luther dies
1529	May 4: Magdalena Luther is born

1530	April–October: Luther at the Coburg
1531	November 9: Martin Luther Jr. is born
	? Acquisition of the little garden at the Oak Pond (*Eichenpfuhl*)
1532	February 4: Transfer of the Black Cloister to Luther and Katie and their heirs
	April 19: Acquisition of the garden at the Hog Market
	August 16: Elector John the Steadfast dies; John Fredrick the Magnanimous
1533	January 28: Paul Luther is born
1534	December 17: Margarete Luther is born
1535	Summer: Plague in Wittenberg
	—until 1540: Remodelling and new construction at the Black Cloister
1537	February: Luther's second severe illness in Smalcald
1539	? Lease of the Boos property
	Autumn: Plague in Wittenberg
1540	January—February: Katie's severe illness
	May: Acquisition of the Zölsdorf property
1541	Acquisition of Brisger's little house
1542	January 6: Luther's will
	September 20: Magdalena Luther dies
1544	Acquisition of the hop garden at the Specke and the garden at Elsholze
1546	February 18: Luther dies at Eisleben

February 22: Burial in Wittenberg

March–June: Execution of the Estate; Acquisition of the Wachsdorf property

Summer: The Smalcaldic War breaks out

November: Katie's first flight from Wittenberg; Stay in Magdeburg

1547   March?: Katie's return to Wittenberg

April 24: Battle at the Lochauer Heath

Katie's second flight from Wittenberg; Stay in Braunschweig

Beginning of July: Katie's second return to Wittenberg

1548   —1552: War losses and lawsuit

1552   Summer: Plague in Wittenberg

September: Katie injured on the trip to Torgau

December 20: Katie dies in Torgau

December 21: Burial in the parish church at Torgau

Peer Reviewed

Concordia Publishing House

Similar to the peer review or "refereed" process used to publish professional and academic journals, the Peer Review process is designed to assist authors to publish book manuscripts through Concordia Publishing House. The Peer Review process is well-suited for smaller projects and some specialty topics.

We aim to provide quality resources for congregations. Our books are faithful to the Holy Scriptures and the Lutheran Confessions, promoting the rich theological heritage of the historic, creedal Church. Concordia Publishing House (CPH) is the publishing arm of The Lutheran Church—Missouri Synod. We develop, produce, and distribute resources that support pastoral and congregational ministry.

**For more information, visit:
cph.org/PeerReview**